India's Blue Pulse: Preparing For A Maritime Future

India's Blue Pulse: Preparing For A Maritime Future

Editor

S.Utham Kumar Jamdhagni

Vij Books India Pvt Ltd

New Delhi (India)

Published by

Vij Books India Pvt Ltd
(Publishers, Distributors & Importers)
2/19, Ansari Road
Delhi – 110 002
Phone: 91-11-43596460
Mobile: 98110 94883
e-mail: contact@vijpublishing.com
www.vijbooks.in

ISBN: 978-93-95675-35-2 (Hardback)
ISBN: 978-93-95675-34-5 (Paperback)
ISBN: 978-93-95675-36-9 (ebook)

Contents

Chapter 1

Introduction

Roman philosopher Seneca once said *"If one does not know to which port one is sailing, no wind is favourable."* Seneca could have meant this in the literal sense, or used it as a form of figurative speech, with a specific event in mind. In the absence of expressed context, and for the purposes of this book, we will assume that it was the latter - merely metaphorical. Ignorance, neglect or indifference can prove fatal to any adventure, especially those maritime. This statement lends itself not just to those who physically undertake the journey but to all those involved in enabling it. It is an apposite warning for any modern maritime power - India, in our case.

India's position as a hub for East-West maritime exchange has long been recognized. Her geographical primacy in the region continues to underscore this significance. With increasing maritime reliance, and the Indian Ocean Region's predominance as a security-sensitive area, India needs to carefully evaluate its use of the region for economic and defence functions. Simply put, it has to ascertain '*which wind is favorable*'. Doing this, is not as simple a task. India's placement in all things maritime is such that it requires her to weigh challenges, with plausible actions and their repercussions, strategically.

In order to truly represent the above-mentioned strategic thought, it is imperative that perspectives from the diverse mix of stakeholders are assessed. This includes those who are entrusted with the responsibility of ensuring the nation's security i.e., the Indian Army, Navy, Air Force and the Coast Guard. It also includes those who are not, and yet are interested in the bigger security picture i.e., academics, both professors and students, alike.

This book is a much-needed compilation of these perspectives, ranging from theoretical, legal approaches to pragmatic ones. It offers a panoramic view albeit not exhaustive, of the approaches of India's forces towards understanding the littoral expanse, along with a glimpse into their preparedness and policy outlook in protecting Indian interests.

Each chapter in this book, although inherently different in terms of subject matter, have a common denominator. They deal with strengths and gaps in the respective topic and future trends in that regard in India's maritime security. The conceptual requirements to develop doctrinal or strategic thinking, and toponymic analysis of constructs like the Indo-Pacific have also been included. The skeletal structure of the book is dictated accordingly.

The first and second substantive chapters, contributed by academics, presents the theoretical underpinning for India's maritime security. They suggest that more attention needs to be paid to reinforce existing strategic thought towards a maritime realm in keeping with the goal of comprehensive theory building to make optimal the latent potential of India as a wholesome maritime power. The contributors are confident that the focus on non-traditional threats is justified, and technology adoption and policy changes will equip the Indian Navy in facing the future as well.

The third chapter portrays the Coast Guard's perspective, with the author highlighting the complexities involved in securing maritime interests, the rationale for supporting the creation of a Coast Guard organisation in India and the multiple new and emergent issues that form the maritime threat matrix. The author elaborates on the Indian-context-specific difficulty in the creation of maritime domain awareness. He further describes the means of capacity building, coordination, legislation and deterrence that India has already undertaken to address this lacuna. He is certain that sustained, concerted efforts of a holistic nature can help India skillfully tackle maritime security.

The fourth chapter delves deep into the role of the Air Force as a force multiplier in dealing with maritime security. Bringing out the advantages of air power, the author, emphasizes that the dividend that "jointness" can reap will help ensure maritime security. Mapping out the myriad threats, their sources and modus operandi, he spells out the edge that can be derived from an effective air power.

The fifth chapter deals with the concerns surrounding the latest developments in maritime security management - the appointment of the National Maritime Security Coordinator (NMSC). It traces the history of the path to the establishment of this post, re-iterating that it has been a long-drawn process. The contributor argues in favour of the NMSC and the prospective challenges the coordinator could face. He suggests that a uniform and structured bureaucratic system could strengthen India's abilities in this regard.

The sixth chapter sheds some light on another vital link in India's holistic maritime well-being, discussing Merchant Marine. In this chapter, the author points to the part played by Merchant Marine in India's plans to become a Blue Economy and views the government's attempts at legislation, as a step in the right direction.

The following chapters, seven and eight, contend that a closer look at the impact of privatisation of armed security aboard commercial ships and its legality, are warranted. This is particularly important given the projected increase in India's share of the global shipping trade. The contributors, thus sound caution in tackling the issue owing to expected repercussions.

Turning to unique issues, the ninth chapter focusses on the possibility of bioterrorism and the vulnerability of India due to its geographical location and global policy stance. The author posits a conflict between humanitarian crises and medical invasions, indicating how maritime domain awareness could go a long way in equipping India to face an uncertain and potentially disastrous future.

Issue-based discussions buttressed by theoretical constructs, in the next four chapters, undertake an assessment of China through a post-colonial lens, evaluate the significance of the Colombo port, the security dilemma in the Indo-Pacific and the Act East Policy, respectively. Finally, the fifteenth chapter highlights the problem of human smuggling in Tamil Nadu (Indian State) as a case study. These chapters flag emerging issues Indian maritime forces have to grapple with, that directly affect the preparedness levels, effectiveness and net result on maritime security of the region in general and India in particular.

In sum, the book offers a board brush of India's current strengths as a net maritime security provider while recognising the real and present dangers to its effectiveness. It proposes methods to maintain a regular 'blue pulse' in the years to come.

Chapter 2

Towards Indian Maritime Strategic Thought*

Dr. C. S. Anuradha

India's tryst with Strategic Culture

Before we embark on a discussion for the paucity and consequently, the need for a robust maritime strategic thought for India we must venture to lay out the basic understanding of strategic culture, its relation to the Indian context and its present status. Jack Snyder defines strategic culture as,

> *"A sum total of ideas, conditioned emotional responses and patterns of habitual behaviour that members of a strategic national security community have acquired through instruction or imitation,"*[1]

while Ken Booth refers to it as a

> *"nation's traditions, values, attitudes, patterns of behaviour, habits, symbols and achievements and particular ways of adapting to the environment and solving problems with respect to the threat or use of force."*[2]

For the Indian situation the latter description is apt. The ancient traditions of valour, courage and the existence of warrior classes, together with wave upon wave of foreign invaders, who reached the country through northern land routes in the Middle Ages and the presence of European powers

* This is an abridged and updated version of the section on "Theoretical orientation Imperative" in the author's monograph *India's Maritime Power: Precedence and Prospect. Lecture Series 6, UGC Centre for Maritime Studies, Pondicherry University, February 2019 pp16-22*

first for trade but later as colonisers, have all involved the use of force or attempts to use it in the least.

There are a few other perspectives that gain relevance in this context. Kerry Longhurst, for instance, describes strategic culture as

> *"a distinctive body of beliefs, attitudes and practices regarding the use of force, which are held by a collective and arise gradually over time, through a unique protracted historical process."*[3]

Alastair Johnston, on the other hand, opines that it is

> *"an integrated system of symbols (for example argumentation structures, languages, analogies, metaphors) which acts to establish pervasive and long-standing strategic preferences by formulation of the concepts of the role and efficacy of military force in interstate political affairs, and by clothing these conceptions with such an aura of factuality that the strategic preferences seem uniquely realistic and efficacious"*[4].

In the words of Edward Mead Earle,

> *"strategy is the art of controlling and utilizing the resources of a nation—or a coalition of nations—including its armed forces, to the end that its vital interests shall be effectively promoted and secured against enemies, actual, potential, or merely presumed."*[5]

Thus, the sources of strategic culture seem to include:

- Historical and civilisational perspectives of a country
- Geography and natural resources
- Political structure and institutions
- Myths and symbols that have helped nation-building and identity development
- Effects of technology
- Transnational norms and conventions

Indian strategic culture or orientation toward the use of force has long been a matter of debate. Some analysts and writers cite the earlier lack of Indianness and absence of a solitary political unit and the lopsided focus on land frontiers to be the reason for this paucity. George Tanham, in his RAND report "*Indian Strategic Thought: An Interpretative Essay*", posits that the "lack of political unity throughout most of its history" [6] has meant a lackadaisical attitude towards national defence planning. He also underlines the Hindu concept of time where life ("an eternal present") contributes to the neglect of planning.

For India, the precedence of civilisation over nationhood has pervaded her sense of eternity or primordial presence. The timelessness of Indian thought reflects in her strategic thinking too. Further, because India sees herself as ancient and ageless; Tanham opines that there was an automatic assumption of a pre-existent status rather than something that needs to be earned. K. Subrahmanyam, one of the doyens of India's strategic community, concurred with this line of thinking when he declared that the Indian government "*has had no strategic culture and has never thought and planned ahead and never offensively*"[7] and indulges in normative thinking.

Interestingly, pre-independent India comprised many nations and the territory was divided into several principalities, and only the nationalistic fervour that won independence unified the political entity called India. In ancient India, there were very few kingdoms or Empires controlling vast parts of the Indian mainland offering any sense of 'oneness'. The myths and symbols of nation-building had to rely on strong and successful emperors of yore to view India as a 'unified entity' long before the Western idea of uniting various provinces arose in the late nineteenth century. While projecting ancient India as essentially non-expansionist and proof of India's pacifist intentions, India now had to deal with colonisation and external ambitions of territorial conquest. The Nationalist movement had to invoke common cultural traditions to 'unite India'. However, others derive historical examples to assert that India did have a history of strategic thought. Post-independence, though there was awareness that India was a maritime nation, not much was achieved in policy pronouncements. Political leaders like Nehru emphasised the importance of the sea when he remarked that "*India, therefore, has to play an important role in the ocean surrounding her,*" and that "*we should be strong enough to resist the control of any other power*"[8]. Balancing continental challenges vis-a-vis the emerging maritime scenario was found wanting and to some extent, continues. This lacuna ought to be filled to make maritime security "*a vital element of national progress and international engagement*".[9]

Rodney Jones characterises India as 'omniscient patrician'[10] compared to theocratic, mercantilist, frontier expansionist or imperial bureaucratic state forms. Kanti Bajpai, Amitabh Matoo and Varun Sahni have contested the claims of a lack of Indian strategic culture by highlighting the interplay of several factors in the Indian condition. In fact, Kanti Bajpai speaks of three strands of Nehruvianism, Hyperrealism and Neo-liberalism[11]. Sumit Ganguly acknowledges that the existence of strategic thought in India is "implicit and inchoate".[12] Others, like the Russian author Leonid Shavin wish to derive lessons from the Indian experience for other states.[13] The *Nonalignment 2.0*, a report published by an independent group of analysts and policy makers highlights the "*critical need for a strategic consensus and for a unified approach to India's international engagements*"[14]. The recommendation considers that "*China will remain a significant foreign policy and security challenge for India ... as it impinges directly on India's geopolitical space*"[15] Perhaps it is one of the very instances where the country that poses concern is explicitly named. They suggest no strong power alliances in keeping with the report's title, however, they make a convincing case for the development of capability. The report suggests the setting up of a Maritime Commission. This would address the problem of involvement of a "multiplicity of agencies"[16] that deal with the maritime area. Well-defined texts or other literature from the past are hard to find in this regard. Despite this, Post-Cold War, India has realised the vital need for a comprehensive approach to the threat of or the actual use of force. But this alone will not suffice.

Musings Maritime

Whatever the verdict on the presence or absence of Indian strategic culture may be, it is evident that the evolution of maritime strategic thought has been slow and is in dire need of added momentum. K.M.Panikkar's works sought more robust attention to maritime strategic thought. Akin to the historical analysis attempted by A T Mahan in his exposition on sea power, Panikkar also made the connection. India's *omphaloskepsis* towards land meant an unbalanced emphasis on the defence of the land frontier and gross neglect of surrounding ocean waters. Panikkar traced the ancient maritime prowess of Indian kingdoms. He pointed out that the waning dominance of India over the sea was a prime catalyst in the success of western colonial powers in subjugating this vast land. He termed India's landward orientation as "sea blindness" which he urged should be overcome so that India assumes her rightful status in the world .

As pointed out by multiple scholars, history provides a valuable lesson that when the control of the sea weakened, imperialist powers wrested first economic and later, political advantage over the entire territory of India. The resultant colonisation has shaped the country's destiny. The observation is pointed out by Panikkar in his works warning India that "an exclusively land policy of defence" will be "nothing short of blindness".[17] It should also influence our current and future attitude to maritime power.[18] However not much has been achieved in this area until recently. It is pertinent to examine the Post-Cold War attempts at conceiving a maritime doctrine for India. The first document was in 2004, which urged that India "must have a maritime vision"[19] to fulfill her maritime destiny. It was also seen "as the apex doctrine of maritime power and a comprehensive guide".[20] It emphasized the significance of maritime strength as this could not only safeguard national interests, and also help economic growth and development. There is also an acknowledgement that India's geographic reality provides her with an opportunity "to greatly influence the movement/security of shipping along the SLOCs in the IOR"[21] which India requires to shore up its maritime power. The 2004 Indian Maritime Document pointed out the "relative isolation from common awareness" of the maritime environment that permeates India's national life. The esoteric nature of maritime strategy, or rather the characteristic of the Navy's operations "to which the public is never a spectator," is highlighted as a principal issue affecting the evolution of an Indian maritime strategic thought.

Strategy relook

The strategy document '*Freedom to Use the Seas: India's Maritime Military Strategy*' which came later in 2007, was a wider approach to maritime strategy. According to this, the Indian Navy "needs to project power; catalyse partnerships; build trust and create interoperability; and when required use convincing power to achieve national aims."[22] Furthering the 2004 document's idea of the prevalence of a continental mindset, the Indian Navy here talks of the "spread of maritime consciousness through a vigorous campaign."[23] Apart from the aim of maintaining peace and tranquillity the Navy has expanded its scope to meet the expectations of our friends when needed. The gradual widening of the tasks before the Navy mirror the expansion of India's interests and area of influence and the intent to safeguard these interests. However, there are some caveats. In one review of the 2007 document, it is found that despite the movement toward "pro-maritime orientation" there is still a reluctance to deal with contentious topics like Chinese influence in the IOR head-on. Thus, there is a crying need for "a comprehensive strategy to articulate India's broader political and strategic considerations in the development of its maritime power". [24]

The 2009 updation moved from the general "commonalities of maritime thought" to specific concepts and developments applicable to India. 2009 was thus an organic growth of the base documents in 2004 and 2007. The revised text mentions the need for a "balanced fleet" with "adequate reach and combat power"[25]. The *Ensuring Secure Seas* document of 2015 highlights the increasing complexity and unpredictability of India's maritime security environment with the inclusion of a profusion of non-traditional threats. As the Navy is now bestowed with additional responsibility "for overall maritime security including coastal and offshore security",[26] the building up of a robust maritime strategic thought is pertinent. The 2015 maritime strategy version can be seen as a signal, projecting "a robust posture"[27] to friends and foes alike. This text recognises the role "the Navy can play in strengthening and enhancing maritime security in the region".

Present status

The updated version in Ensuring Secure Seas of 2015 and the Nonalignment 2.0 together exhibit a continuous reassessment of India's interests, capabilities and goals. The progression has also seen an expansion in the "arc of influence" that now encompasses the whole swathe of the Indian Ocean from its western to eastern shores. It is now termed the "arc of interest". The reflection is a transformation from an inward-looking state to one that nurses ambition to extend its reach far and wide. It also keeps with the growing economic might of India making it the sixth-largest world economy[28]. The concomitant issues of energy security and sea-lane safety that would sustain the driving factors of development have forced India to place freedom of navigation as an area of concern. The attuning of military modernization together with a greater thrust for indigenous development and production through the "Make in India" programme augurs well for a country that has set its sight for the assumption of a higher global power status.[29]

A definite pattern of expansion of interests and capabilities can be discerned from a close examination of the chronological progression of the various Maritime doctrines and maritime strategy documents. A thorough analysis of the Maritime doctrines published till date brings out some pertinent facts. As spelt out in the doctrines, the Indian Navy's vision documents and operational goals reflect the growing recognition that maritime power is part of India's destiny if not its principal driver. However, a well-defined strategic thought that factors in the overarching rationale and employment of all available national resources is still in the making. The recent impetus in policy planning and implementation that aims to affix a robust infrastructure mechanism is a step in the right direction. This will achieve the twin aims of developing and using essential tools for maritime prowess in both commercial and purely naval fields. The upgradation of India's naval capacity by significantly augmenting weapon systems and platforms to counter the changing geo strategic environment is also underway.

Infrastructure development by way of port-related expansion and much needed improvement in existing facilities will cater to future needs of the higher carrying capacity of ships that are essential to match the much-expected economic growth. Extensive modifications in defence production modalities and requirements indicate the vital need for greater self-reliance. In areas where foreign collaboration is imperative, a relative reduction on external reliance through local production efforts could be attempted. The Sagarmala project is expected to ramp up India's port capacity and the Make in India programme that encourages Indian manufacturers producing ships and naval weaponry complements this approach. Apart from these elements that would form the basis of maritime strategic thought, the creation of "a naval tradition in the public"[30] underscoring that the maritime dimension is intrinsic to Indian national life would truly propel India to become a global maritime power.

Toponymy traction

The acceptance of the "Indo-Pacific" into the international security lexicon and as a major area of present focus in terms of strategic value it adds to world affairs together with the future potential it nurses as a hub of activity also makes a case for a robust maritime strategic thinking architecture for a member country like India.

While economically, the larger Indo-Pacific region comprising various significant sub-regions is intrinsic to the prosperity of individual countries, the area's strategic import cannot be lost. To sustain the current pace of economic growth and progress, India must take into cognizance the primacy of the safety of sea lanes and concomitant challenges through non-traditional challenges like piracy, terrorism, illegal trafficking of all kinds and unsustainable fishing. Ongoing territorial disputes among neighbours in the maritime realm are also of special concern. Global issues like climate change further emphasise the countries' stakes in maritime security. A maritime approach to ideas and philosophies that aim at safeguarding a nation's assets and furthering its interests is thus the need of the hour for India. The newly-announced I2U2 (India, Israel, UAE and USA) is a laudable attempt at shoring up regional cooperation in maritime security besides other areas of interest.[31]

Conclusion

This chapter demonstrates the intermittency of attempts at theorizing rationale for strengthening maritime power and implementing a clear maritime strategy. In doing so, it places emphasis on the imminent need for synergy between the series of maritime doctrine pronouncements and a comprehensive theory building on reason and manner of use of force and all other resources to make optimal the latent potential of India as a wholesome maritime power. India's pursuit of a much improved and resilient maritime strategic thought must continue to occupy centre stage for academia, soldier-scholars and policy makers. This would mean a calibrated updation of maritime strategy incorporating a world vision to widen and deepen India's roles and responsibilities. This would result in a composite framework with strategic, economic, political and all other ramifications of maritime power and more importantly afford a direction into the requirement and use of the navy and all other tangible and ideational resources. Aiding in realising India's responsibility as a net security provider to its neighborhood, such strategic thought would additionally contemplate enhancing its military might and other maritime capabilities. In effect, India would be able to protect its interests while simultaneously ensuring order and stability in the maritime commons. Serving as a lynchpin that drives a sustained, effective and meaningful discourse, the recent policy pronouncements could propel India from being a benign potential power to one that is assertive, cooperative and willing to don the mantle of a true global power adequately reflecting its size, potential capability and world vision.

Chapter 3

Stately Sentinel of the Seas: Indian Navy and Maritime Security

Dr. S. Utham Kumar Jamadhagni

Indian Prime Minister Modi in the *Swavalamban* seminar organized by the Naval Innovation and Indigenisation Organisation (NIIO) said that in the 100th year of independence the aim of the Indian Navy must be to reach "unprecedented heights".[32] It is truly reflective of the aspirations for India's prime maritime force – the Indian Navy.

The vision for a robust Navy in the future is built on recognising the challenging geostrategic milieu that India finds itself in, in today's world. In the words of the Naval Chief Admiral R Hari Kumar, "*We are in a contested present and looking at an uncertain future.*"[33] The chief added that maritime security could be ensured only through co-operation, collaboration, interaction and interoperability. The Naval arm of the nation's fighting forces enjoys a distinct edge over the other two land and air forces. In addition to its mandate as a war fighting unit, roles of policing and diplomacy have been placed on the men in white.

After factoring in the significance of the Indo-Pacific region in India's strategic calculus it is imperative that the Indian Navy be equipped both figuratively i.e., in the doctrinal aspect and in the literal sense of actual hardware to counter the worrying rise of Chinese influence in the region and its projected consequences. As the potential future "center for a growing geopolitical contest"[34], the Indo-Pacific and the Indian Ocean Region assume added importance in India's naval preparedness. China has already resorted to various mechanisms from setting up strategic military bases to predatory economics in order to advance its regional interests. In this context, the naval modernisation programmes require much needed boost and sustenance.

In an effort to understand the role of the Indian Navy in ensuring India's maritime security this chapter will aim to spell out the importance of the primal geographical location India enjoys in the Indian Ocean region. It would also highlight the doctrinal mandate of the Indian Navy which is already being operationalised. The contribution to the maritime security discourse indicates the points of concern in the Indian Navy's policy, programmes and implementation.

Indian Ocean matrix

The Indian Ocean, the only all-weather navigable ocean holds forty per cent of offshore oil reserves, 65 per cent of strategic minerals like uranium, and 31 per cent of gas, comprising thirty per cent of the total world population. Strategic choke points to the Red Sea, Persian Gulf and Malacca Straits along the oil routes are vital. The Indian Ocean has remained the mainstay of Indian naval ambitions. The publication of India's new *Maritime Doctrine* is quite explicit on the central status of the Indian Ocean in India's strategic thought and on India's determination to constitute the most important influence in the region[35].

India, located in the middle of the Indian Ocean, provides the geographic and strategic imperative of a greater role in shaping and being shaped by this namesake water body. India has a long coastline with an Exclusive Economic Zone of 2.02 million sq. km. Out of its more than 1 billion population, nearly 20 percent live in the coastal areas. Many highly populated and industrialised cities like Bombay, Madras, Calcutta, Cochin, and Visakhapatnam are located along/near the coastal areas. There are 11 major ports and several minor ports handling shipping to various degrees of intensity. The coastline of the mainland spans nine States and two Union Territories.[36] There are two groups of the Islands viz. Andaman and Nicobar Islands in the Bay of Bengal, Andaman Sea and Lakshadweep Islands in the Arabian Sea, both of which have been identified as part of the Global 200 ecoregions (Marine Ecoregions) by the World Wide Fund for Nature (WWF). A long coastline, trade route and persisting security issues call for a comprehensive India Ocean strategy.

As a maritime nation India has derived enormously from this stretch of water both culturally and economically. India once reigned over this region and its cultural influence continues today.[37] Now in this modern age, Indian trade flourishes on its waters (97 percent by volume). About half the world's oil and other energy sources cross the Indian Ocean. However, it is not just abundant in economic potential but is the stage for the world's major problems. Interstate territorial disputes, global climate change, illegal fishing, habitat destruction, pollution, drug smuggling, congested sea lanes, unlawful migration and piracy are prevalent in the region.

Doctrinal diktat

The Indian Navy has time and again articulated its goals and objectives through a series of Maritime doctrine documents that gives a glimpse of the role and responsibility the sea-going force envisions itself in the much changing global dynamics. Ever since the first one in 2004 the Indian Navy expanded both its area of focus and the manner of response to emerging challenges of both conventional and non-traditional nature. In fact, the 2007 version titled "Freedom to use the seas: India's Maritime Military Strategy" acknowledges the need for power projection, propelling partnerships, building trust and "use convincing power" if needed.

In the 2009 edition the Indian Navy explicitly aimed for a "balanced fleet" incorporating "adequate reach and combat power".[38] Setting its sights on the widening region of the arc of influence to the arc of interest, the 2015 Ensuring Secure seas document asserts the Indian Navy's willingness to "strengthening and enhancing maritime security in the region". These attempts are concomitant with the growing status of India at the global power table and the assumption of responsibility of "net security provider," especially in the IOR.

26/11 aftermath

The terror attack on November 26, 2008 by terrorists who landed on Mumbai's coast using *dinghies* marked a watershed in India's approach to maritime security. There was a major revamping of marine related security infrastructure. This included command and control decisions, equipment modernization and purchase, and the creation of new institutions and mechanisms that could continually man India's vast coastline.

The Indian Navy has now been given the overall responsibility of maritime security. Joint operation centres have been established in Mumbai, Visakhapatnam, Kochi and Port Blair and would be under the Navy's control[39]. The opening of the Indian Ocean Region's Information Fusion Centre (IFC-IOR) helmed by the Indian Navy aims at information exchange on commercial shipping on a real-time basis with regional maritime nations. This will be accomplished "by building a common coherent maritime situation picture and acting as a maritime information hub for the region".[40] India has also incidentally agreed to be part of the Trans Regional Maritime Network which also aims at maritime commercial information exchange with 30 countries spearheaded by Italy.

Organisational changes and new operational mechanisms have also been introduced. For example, the 'Sagar Prahari Bal' or specialized marine unit of 1000 personnel with special interceptor crafts to protect naval vessels has been formed by the Navy. The task of the SPB is to maintain security at all major and minor ports in India and carry out round the clock patrolling and is also part of search and rescue operations in times of emergency. The Indian Navy has chalked out a three-tier aerial surveillance grid for IOR that would employ long-range, medium-range reconnaissance aircraft, and unmanned aerial vehicles.[41]

The augmentation of "India's international stature necessitates a wide ranging cooperation that will secure its long-term interests both military and non military".[42] The Indian Navy has furthered this goal through bilateral and multilateral cooperation efforts.

SAGAR

The Indian Prime Minister has also unveiled the concept of Security And Growth for All or SAGAR in 2015 that aims at "*fostering increasing cooperation in our region, use of our capabilities for the benefit of all in our common maritime home and assisting our maritime neighbours and island states in building their maritime security capabilities*".[43]

Joint exercises are a principal means of updating preparedness and reviewing standard operating procedures to strengthen maritime security. These are held among the three services within the country and with other Navies and Coast Guards internationally. The Indian Navy conducts a variety of military exercises at the bilateral level like SIMBEX with Singapore, IN-INDO CORPAT with Indonesia; regional level like the MILAN a biennial exercise of Asia-Pacific littoral countries' navies hosted by the Indian Navy and pan regional level like the Malabar involving the US, Japan and Australia.[44]

Considering the amorphous nature of existing threats, the uniformed services dedicated to guarding our seas and shores work in close cooperation with state police, coastal police, fisheries department, customs port, immigration, Central Industrial Security Force, Marine Enforcement and IB. The best illustration in such a coordination effort is the annually conducted *Sagar Kavach* (meaning Shield of the Sea) to check coastal security mechanisms and validate standard operating procedures.[45] It is conducted in various regions all along the Indian mainland coastline by simulated security contingencies that seek to gauge response and detect any shortcomings in performances. Interestingly, India also deepens its triad architecture by developing and commissioning nuclear submarines. Under the Advanced Technology Vessel (ATV) project, India has to date built three submarines *INS Arihant*, *INS Arighat* and the yet to be named S-4.[46] The development of anti submarine capability by India is another shot in the arm for shoring up counter capabilities.

Achilles Heel

The naval preparedness roster sorely lags in defence equipment availability, manufacture and procurement. Despite naval modernization plans, budgeting issues, project plan delays, cost overruns and drastic changes in buying off-the-shelf and indigenous manufacturing models have impacted naval arsenal capability. Although the Navy's budget is touted to be more extensive every year, the capital outlay that caters to purchase of equipment has in fact, declined from 10.41 per cent in 2014-15 to 7.58 per cent in 2019-20. It is only in the current budget 2022-23 that a whopping 45 percent increase [47] has been announced to help buy new platforms and equipment.

While earlier, India's target was a 200 ships strong navy, the above mentioned problems have pared it down to a modest 170 ships by 2027[48]. Attempting to fit existing platforms with battle-ready fighter aircrafts has been facing hardships. The recently inducted *INS Vikrant* aircraft carrier is still on the lookout for French or American jets to be procured through Inter Governmental Agreement (IGA).[49]

Production propellant

The base of any effective fighting force is its ammunition namely weapon systems, platform and delivery vehicles. This skeleton must be ramped up if Indian Navy assumes the 'net security provider role' in the Indo-Pacific region. While earlier India's defence hardware was predominantly import-dependent, much progress has been achieved in self-reliance too.

The development of the defence manufacturing ecosystem in the country itself has become the mantra for all recent government plans and overhauls. The 15-year Indian Navy Indigenisation Plan (INIP)2015-30 was drawn up in 2014 to "enable indigenous development of equipment and systems".[50] In yet another novel effort, the setting up of the NIIO in 2020 allows for a flexible and accessible interface for academia and industry with Indian Navy capability development apparatus. This would further speed up the research-to-induction path avoiding project delays due to combative incompatibility or product-demand mismatch.

The Make in India initiative is a step in the right direction to encourage Indian enterprises to take up manufacturing military hardware. It has also reaped some dividends. The newly launched stealth frigate *Dunagiri* has 29 original equipment manufacturers and MSMEs as contributors.[51] In the future, 88 percent of the Navy's investment of nearly Rs 1,75,000 crores will be through them. In fact, from being one of the largest arms importers in the world, India is now seeking to notch up its export potential in this field. "In January, India signed a $374.96 million deal with the Philippines, its single biggest defence export order for the supply of three batteries of shore-based anti-ship variant of the Brahmos supersonic cruise missile."[52] International collaboration like the proposed joint India-Brazil maintenance of diesel-electric attack submarines enlist cross border assistance in the cause of defence equipment management as well.

Spokes in the wheel

China's foray into the region is an area of continued concern and the Indian Navy is cognizant of its role in countering this challenge.[53] China has already acquired "port facilities in countries around India including Myanmar, Bangladesh, Sri Lanka and Pakistan ostensibly to secure its energy sea lanes and this has extended to many other Indian Ocean littorals spanning the shores of Africa to India's neighbourhood and beyond. While the 'string of pearls' theory attempts to explain the "virtual encirclement of India"[54] by establishing bases, the Indian Navy is wary of it.[55] The PLAN has embarked on a naval modernization plan that aims to make itself a blue water capable one. It has already added a slew of new arsenal in the way of aircraft carriers, nuclear submarines, and surface ships.

SLOCs

The security of Sea Lanes of Communication is of primary importance to a state and it needs to address the gaps that are present in the protection of SLOCs.[56] As a nation that believes in the prerequisite of free and open seas for navigation to ensure the utility of the global common called the seas, SLOC safety is an inherent need. For India, SLOCs are vital to its maritime-based economy, energy imports, and the requirement to safeguard it from disruption from non-state actors. The Indian Navy is ideally placed to "ensure safety of the lifelines of India's growth and propel the country to greater prosperity".[57]

Piracy

One of the most persistent menaces is the threat of piracy in the Indian Ocean region. With maritime trade set to grow by leaps and bounds, the vulnerability of mercantile cargo to pirate attacks is high. The nature of the crime of piracy has also transformed. Not only are piracy attacks highly sophisticated and precise but there also seems to be clear nexus between various maritime crimes where one often fuels or sustains the other. [58] Pirate gangs are often helping drug syndicates and arms smugglers and even funding them.

Narcotic Nemesis

The recent series of hauls of large quantities of heroin[59] and other narcotics from some of India's western coast ports is worrisome. Commercial containers have been detected to carry this contraband.[60] Small boats from neighbouring Pakistan have also been apprehended for the same.[61] Arms smuggling has also been witnessed in these routes off India's island territories. [62]

Humans as Cargo

Incidents of illegal trafficking have also been reported from India's coast. [63] Overuse of natural resources is the bane of human existence. The world's oceans are especially vulnerable to the over-exploitation of fish. With fishing grounds around countries drying up, fishing vessels of many countries venture into the high seas to net fish illegally from coasts or fishing areas of other countries. Chinese fishing vessels, the largest fleet in the world leaving behind the depleted South and East China seas, are scoping for fish further and further away from China's shores. The IFC-IOR recorded more than 200 such incidents in just the first half of last year around the IOR. [64] There are even suggestions of QUAD announcing "a synergy of surveillance centres in Singapore, India, and the Pacific to create a tracking system for monitoring IUUF by China".[65]

Indian fishing boats too, are often apprehended by the Sri Lankan Navy for crossing the IMBL.[66] Indian fishing vessels have been found to have ventured as far as the Persian Gulf. [67] Proper identification of local and foreign fishing vessels and continuous surveillance of suspected transgressors are carried out by the Indian Navy.

Conclusion

Assuming the role of a net security provider for the Indian Ocean region, requires both conceptual and on-the-ground strengths. While the maritime doctrines are periodically updated India's mandate has to train renewed focus on emerging scenarios and pursuant challenges. Recognising the connection between vulnerabilities and the application of technologies, the Indian Navy is poised to offer increased protection and anticipate future courses. The policy measure to augment India's production capabilities of defence equipment is a step in the right direction. The impetus given to indigenous development of naval arsenal, including ships, must be sustained to obtain maximum benefit. However, this must be balanced against immediate requirements. Off-the-shelf purchases could help offset operational difficulties using ageing weapon systems and other equipment.

Continued vigilance over adjacent waters and concerted and appropriate response to emerging problems must remain the mainstay of Indian Navy's approach to maritime security. Strengthening radar surveillance networks and intensifying high technology usage by satellites and artificial intelligence processes could raise the Indian Navy's operational efficiency. Maintaining a close watch on maritime activities in the South Asian neighbourhood and improving cooperative mechanisms in various areas of maritime security at bilateral and multilateral levels must also form part its modus operandi. The frequency of Chinese ships moving in India's vicinity and the development and ostensible use of port and other naval related facilities in the Indian Ocean region must be factored into the Indian Navy's area of operation. Joint naval and coast guard exercises with other maritime powers like Japan, Australia and the United States along with smaller countries, will help India play an active role in the security architecture of the maritime realm.

Ensuring the safety of India's shores through the prevention of maritime crimes and prompt punitive action during interdiction and surveillance could further indicate the navy's actual power in serving India's maritime interests.

Thus, to ensure a positive and progressive maritime future, the Indian Navy's ambition of ably securing and safeguarding the maritime milieu requires the support of a consistent national will.

Chapter 4

Indian Coast Guard: The Bulwark of Maritime Security

DIG B. Ranjan

Introduction

India is a maritime state that has large stakes in the maritime zones and protection of these zones for the growth and development of the nation are paramount. The use of sea routes by terrorists for the attack on Mumbai highlighted the vulnerability of our coastline. Actions to obviate an episode of a similar nature in future are in motion, carried out the security forces, in particular, the Indian Coast Guard and Indian Navy to have foolproof maritime security mechanisms backed by the Government and the involvement of the various stakeholders who are beneficiaries of the maritime environment. The environment necessitates seamless co-ordination amongst multiple agencies across all levels to achieve optimal domain awareness and render the appropriate response to any security threat or incident.

The Indian Ocean is considered the third largest water body, and it washes the shores of 38 countries. India, as a peninsula, shares its maritime borders with seven countries and is strategically located in the centre of the Indian Ocean, on the east-west corridor of oil shipment and trade. We have a total of 34 rigs[68] and numerous extraction and exploratory wells in our EEZ. Around 723 Dhows and 2.4 lacs fishing boats are registered and countless numbers of small traditional boats operate in Indian waters. The analysis of the marine traffic and import data reveals an astonishing one lakh vessels pass through Indian waters, among which around 20,400 ships visit Indian ports annually. The sea lanes of communications and the ocean being one physical entity, the ill effects of maritime economic activities will not be restricted to the man-made boundaries and Indian being in the centre of these activities is highly susceptible to bear the brunt of it.

This chapter will dwell upon the maritime security perspectives, especially Coastal Security from the Coast Guard's point of view. It will include the progress of enhanced capacity building and coordinated approach toward required deterrence.

The United Nations Convention on the Law of The Sea (UNCLOS)

Post World War II, control of offshore natural resources on the high seas, development of seabed mining technology, protection of the marine environment and lastly, independence of formerly colonized regions led to the need for a uniform regime to guard the interests and uniform distribution of ocean wealth. The UNCLOS was guided by three principles, freedom, sovereignty and the common heritage of the mankind[69]. UN conferences on the law of the sea were held to move toward the universal acceptance of the laws pertaining to oceans and distribution of its wealth, and extending its benefits to the landlocked countries.

Among these conferences held, UNCLOS III was successful in bringing the nations together for the formulation of the law of the sea and was characterized by its universality of the participants including governments, public and private bodies, NGOs and so forth, long-duration for almost 15 years including the preparatory work which commenced in the year 1967 and the enormity of the task it had in hand[70]. The convention is characterized by four main features being comprehensiveness of issues covered by the convention, determination of the maximum breadth of the territorial sea, the establishment of compulsory procedures of the dispute settlement and finally the establishment of three new institutions, namely the International Seabed Authority, the International Tribunal for the Law of the Sea and the Commission on the Limits of the Continental Shelf.

In preparation for acceding to the UNCLOS III, India enacted The Territorial waters, Continental shelf, Exclusive Economic Zone and other maritime zones act, 1976, which is in the nature of an umbrella legislation. India has claimed full sovereignty over the territorial waters and sovereign rights for exploration, exploitation, conservation and management of all natural resources, living and non-living in our EEZ.

The Coast Guard

Post accession to the UNCLOS, the world order reoriented and made attempts at the peaceful use of the sea as characterised in the document. However, this peaceful use encapsulated sovereignty as a factor, which brought about the security aspect. This security aspect could only be exercised within the legal framework of the new world order. It gave rise to the need for a statutory constabulary force at sea exercising jurisdiction over crimes committed within the territorial waters, known as a coastal state, flag state or port state under UNCLOS. The changing world reduced the chances of a state-on-state warfare situation. State-on-state warfare was replaced by engagements of opposing groups of non-state actors, embodying a threat to maritime security and the protection of international shipping/ commerce. The presence of piracy and other crimes at sea required a law to maintain good order at sea. Thus, the need for an organisation like the Coast Guard arose.

Generally, humans have been land-based creatures. We have created many organizations for the smooth functioning of society on land. Each organization has been given specific task. Organizations like Police, fire services, hospitals, ambulances, Municipal corporations, administration and inspecting agencies, immigration, fisheries customs, border control etc. Each performs specific tasks on land. However, at sea, the Coast Guard or an agency performing functions similar to that of the Coast Guard, have been given the duties of performing all tasks performed by different agencies on land.

The Coast Guard is an organization recognised internationally and ready to shoulder maritime responsibilities, which are performed and shared by different agencies in one-fourth of the world. The mandate of the Coast Guard also includes support to the Navy during wars and acts as a force multiplier during war-like situations[71].

Origin

The maritime security challenges faced by India in the pre-1990s were the lack of Maritime Domain Awareness (MDA), smuggling, poaching, exploration and scientific research by technologically advanced nations in Indian waters, unregulated fishing and shipping, identification of the vessel in terms of foe or friend, illegal emigration and lastly to monitor, regulate and enforcement of its sovereign rights in EEZ in consonance with the UNCLOS III. The Government of India appointed a committee to set up a separate constabulary marine force in September 1974 primarily for enforcement of maritime laws, the safety of life and property at sea and to perform non-military roles. The Indian Coast Guard (ICG) was formed as an interim organisation in 1977 and was formally constituted on 19th August 1978 with the enactment of the Coast Guard Act.

Besides the duties and functions provided in the Act, the ICG supports other ministries, as provided by the legislation enacted by the Government of India. The support roles undertaken are

(a) Enforcement of anti-poaching measures, monitoring and surveillance of Deep Sea Fishing vessels.

(b) Search and Rescue for merchant ships.

(c) Marine Oil pollution response measures.

(d) Lead Intelligence Agency (LIA) for coastal and sea borders.

(e) Protection of sensitive marine flora & endangered marine species

With the passage of time, the Coast Guard has been entrusted with additional responsibilities as the nodal agency and the Director General Indian Coast Guard has been designated as:

(a) Chairman National Maritime Search and Rescue Board

(b) Chairman National Oil Spill Disaster Committee

(c) Chairman Offshore Security Co-ordination Committee

(d) Indian Governor to Regional Cooperation Agreement on Combating Piracy and Armed Robbery against ships in Asia

The Cabinet Committee on Security, post 26/11(2008), in February 2009 assigned additional responsibilities and

(a) Designated ICG as the authority responsible for Coastal security in territorial waters including areas to be patrolled by Marine Police.

(b) The DGICG has been designated as Commander Coastal Command and is responsible for overall coordination between central and state agencies in all matters related to Coastal security.

Indian Maritime Environment

India has the world's fifth largest coastline of approximately 7517 kms long with a total of about 1208[72] islands in two distinct groups to the east and west of the mainland being Andaman & Nicobar Islands and Lakshadweep islands and four union territories which are clearly at the vanguard of development with both trade and infrastructure growing exponentially. Three of the four metros are on the coast, as is India's financial nerve centre. The coastline also harbours a host of ports, industrial units, military installations, oil refineries and some nuclear power plants. Similarly, there is growing offshore development with associated investment and infrastructure. All of the above mentioned are susceptible to sabotage and disruption.

India's globally admired economy is highly dependent on ocean trade, with over 95 percent of India's trade by volume, and 70 percent by value is done through maritime transport being sea borne[73]. The maritime trade and shipping is booming, and ports of all sizes and ownerships, are being created. There are 12 major ports and 200 notified minor and intermediate ports in India. All have a central role to play in our economic growth, and all are vulnerable to a variety of threats.

The Indian fishing industry is the sixth largest in the world. It has the largest number of fishing boats which approximate around 2.4 Lakhs. There are 7 major fishing harbours, 75 minor fishing harbours and 1,537 landing centres functioning to cater to the needs of over four million fisher folk[74]. Fishing, like agriculture is a tradition in India rather than an industry and hence, trying to regulate or control its activities faces the community's wrath and political consequences. This unregulated fishing activity is what exposed the nation to the 26/11 incident. This is a great national asset and needs protection. India's maritime interests in this vast expanse of water includes oil, offshore oil installations, non-conventional energy potential, and the living and non-living resources of the sea, including fish and the mineral wealth on the seabed.

Threat Matrix

India's long coastline presents a variety of security challenges and in order to counter them, it is important to analyse the kind of activities that can disturb the peace of the nation. The Secretary General, UN has submitted a report at 63rd General Assembly session on developments and issues relating to ocean affairs and the law of the sea addressing some specific threats to maritime security[75].

(a) Piracy and armed robbery against ships have widespread ramifications and affects the owners, ship operators, sea-farers, producers, consumers and increase insurance and security costs[76]. In the last 5 years, there have been 50 attacks[77] on anchored vessels in Indian waters involving petty thefts. However, vulnerability of using ships to block a channel or collide with another asset of bigger value, seeking place of refuge by a vessel with intent to enter and destroy the harbour and ceasing entry to port/harbour cannot be ruled out.

(b) Terrorist acts involving shipping, offshore installations and other maritime interests in the maritime zone could have widespread effects. Such acts also include providing logistical support to anti-national elements by sea route, utilizing fishing boats for embarkation and disembarkation, floating warehouses/collection of intelligence, attacking and sinking vessels to disrupt trade routes. The dilemma of establishing appropriate security measures for fixed and floating platforms, and offshore drilling units with delineated responsibility among the stakeholders and security organisations in the maritime zone further aggravates the risk factor.

(c) Illicit trafficking in arms and weapons of mass destruction including the landing of arms and explosives at isolated spots on the coast.

(d) Illicit traffic in narcotic drugs and psychotropic substances by sea poses a serious threat. It has been reported that approximately 70 percent of the total quantity of drugs seized is confiscated either during or after transportation by sea[78]. In the last 40 years, there have been 133 vessels interdicted by Coast Guard related to drug trafficking amounting to around Rs 5000 crore.

(e) Smuggling and trafficking of persons by sea poses a unique challenge to the security forces in India owing to the ethnic and cultural similarity with neighbouring countries. Infiltration and/or ex-filtration of anti-national elements using the sea route has also become a contemporary methodology owing to the enhanced security over land borders.

(f) Overexploitation and unregulated fishing remains a major challenge in achieving sustainable fisheries in India. A regulation to enforce limits on numbers and accountability of the fishing boats operating poses a major challenge owing to its political influence and strong fishing associations.

(g) Intentional and unlawful damage to the marine environment which will directly impact the social and economic interests of the nation such as intended oil spill or explosion of gas carrier etc.,

The threats listed above are proven and well documented crimes against maritime activity. However, post the 26/11 attacks, it is evident that anti-national elements are resorting to asymmetric methods to inflict severe and catastrophic damage to the nations affecting peace and harmony. The International and national regulations to ensure maritime security is structured around the existing and proven technology. It must now take into account the rapid advancement in technology in shipping and associated fields and the reality that these technologies are easily accessible. This thought process may pave way to a whole new threat matrix which may include but not limited to:

(a) Exploiting uninhabited island to be used as a force building / rendezvous for anti-social elements and harbouring sleeping cells for prolonged period.

(b) Use of Maritime Autonomous Surface Ship to inflict damage.

(c) Undertake clandestine activities beyond maritime zones to avoid detection and enforcement by nations.

(d) Utilisation of security guards onboard ships and the floating armed vessel which ply adjacent to the territorial seas are challenges to international law and good practice. Though it is to promote security of the plying vessel probability of this leading to the possible spread of and an increase in violence cannot be ruled out[79].

(e) The deterioration of the marine environment due to climate change and pollution from land-based sources and garbage disposal from the municipalities will be a major challenge to be addressed by the nation wherein Coast Guard will be called in to monitor such changes at sea and to provide statistical data and logistical support.

Coastal Security

Coastal Security is another dimension of maritime security. Awareness about the need to strengthen India's coasts first arose in the aftermath of the 1993 Mumbai serial bomb blasts post establishing the fact that explosives used were smuggled in through the Raigad coast of Maharashtra[80]. The response at that time was limited to close coast patrolling conducted jointly by security forces using hired fishing boats due to the paucity of assets for such tasking. Further, these security measures were neither backed by shore-based surveillance, nor weaponry for such roles. The lack of actionable intelligence and coordination amongst intelligence agencies were other factors that put security agencies at a lower pedestal, compared to their adversaries. During the nineties, the situation along the sea borders continued to remain the same, with no major incidents. However, the situation started changing post Kargil war. In a nutshell, it can be summarized that the revival of coastal security concept started post Kargil, when the review committee of group of ministers in the year 2001 amply addressed the issue of strengthening maritime infrastructure. After these events, steps were taken to upgrade the coastal security project for installation of radar stations along the coast. The 26/11 incident further exposed the strategic vulnerability of India's vast and porous coast line and the lacunae in our coastal security. It was indeed a wakeup call for immediate measures to have new security mechanism. For the first time, the coastal security received the attention that it deserves.

Role of the Government

The Government of India constituted the Cabinet Committee on Security (CCS) in the year 2001 and issued various directives which included multi-agency approach, synergized and coordinated demand among the stake holders, organized and planned execution, capacity building of the maritime forces, real time intelligence sharing, optimum use of technology and launching of coastal security scheme to enhance the coastal security mechanism. The task of the Central Government was to define the responsibilities and the jurisdiction of all the stake holders who are party to coastal security, review and implement mechanisms to resolve gaps and vulnerabilities, liaison with the state government, allocate budget, position the central forces based on threat matrix, and finally promulgate the SOPs. It designated Indian Navy as the authority responsible for overall maritime security including coastal security and offshore security. The coordination mechanism to address the coastal security between the Centre and State government was also instituted.

The initiation and co-ordination of various operative measures and initiatives at the national level was being overseen by an apex committee called the National Committee for Strengthening Maritime and Coastal Security against threats from sea (NCSMCS) and is headed by the Cabinet Secretary. The main objective of the NCSMCS is to oversee implementation of CCS directives and resolve multi-stakeholder co-ordination issues.

The State governments have been tasked to implement the SOPs at the micro level, carryout liaison with the stakeholders, enhance surveillance in the coastal waters, respond to operations, institute technological and physical measures, conduct exercise to validate SOPs, provide infrastructural support to the forces both Central and State, and carryout quarterly and half yearly progress review.

In order to eliminate these threats from the sea, and secure nation's shores, there is a need to defend all the valuable assets in and around the coast, and within the Maritime Zones of India and also prevent access to the Indian hinterland by all types of anti-nationals and inimical elements by using ships, fishing vessels or other small craft. Hence, the security of the Maritime Zones of India and the coastline is indeed a daunting task, and there are many challenges and complexities involved.

Challenges and Complexities

The core problem of maritime security in general and coastal security in particular, is the ill-defined and complicated maritime environment. The situational awareness is the first and fundamental requirement of security. However, "Maritime Domain Awareness" or MDA, is exceedingly difficult to achieve, since both detection of a target out at sea and its identification are difficult tasks. There are many reasons - some common to the maritime environment and some specific to India.

(a) The sea-areas of interest are vast and enormous, which becomes highly opaque in adverse meteorological conditions resulting in disappearance of the ships and crafts in the vastness. Since all of the sea cannot be kept under surveillance on a 24 x 7 basis, detecting a small boat at night and in rough seas is therefore a daunting task. It requires considerable, sea and air-based surveillance to broadly monitor the seas. This is clearly an expensive proposition both in terms of Capital and Operational costs.

(b) Whilst the seas are vast, the increasing & un-regulated traffic also poses challenges of identification, not only for differentiating friend from foe, but also from neutrals, who by virtue of the right of innocent passage, legally use the sea areas of our EEZ and coastal waters.

(c) Any of the tens of thousands of fishing boats that returns from sea each day, to any point on the long coastline, may be a threat vector. The identification problem is not limited to fishing vessels alone, but also includes the thousands of container and cargo vessels that call at our ports, or ply the Sea Lanes of Communication (SLOC), which pass close to Indian shore.

(d) The effort to generate a 'recognisable maritime picture' by monitoring this maze requires high technology. Availability and access to modern technology, and the ability to share, fuse, and analyse large quantity of information regarding maritime activities in real time - and to disseminate the same information through a national common operating grid presents technological challenge of considerable proportions.

(e) The sea, by its very nature, is not amenable to borders, zones or any other demarcations. Due to the complexities of the Laws of the Seas, laying down boundaries is laden with disputes. India's International Maritime Boundary Line (IMBL) with Pakistan is not yet defined. Since the seas cannot be marked-out by pillars, fences, flags etc, there is only a diffused sense of straying into a prohibited zone or jurisdiction, especially on the part of the fishermen. Ethnic similarities are utilised by fishermen and terrorists alike, to cross-over with ease. This is a matter of grave concern as hundreds of fishing boats, most of them unregulated, can be effectively utilised by anti-national elements.

(f) The menace of piracy, armed robbery or theft is global by nature. It has been proven that it is not only a law and order problem, but also a social problem, especially in third world.

However, maintaining maritime and coastal security is complex and complicated issue, and all coastal nations find it difficult to streamline and optimise their security in the waters adjacent to their coasts, the challenge has to be and can be confronted. On the field, concerted and sustained efforts are being made by Central/State Governments and the plethora of security agencies, to address the challenges by a four-pronged approach i.e. Capacity Building, Coordination, Legislation and Deterrence.

Capacity Building

Post Mumbai attack, the immediate requirement for the security agencies was 'Capacity Building', which not only included augmentation of surface and air platforms, but also development of infrastructure & induction of manpower. All stakeholders involved in Maritime and Coastal Security have restructured their operations and are working together towards attaining synergy, including ICG.

The Indian Coast Guard is equipped with a wide inventory of assets to undertake surveillance of the EEZ of the 2 million sq m, which is its primary task. Beginning with two frigates on loan from the Navy 41 years ago, force levels of the Indian Coast Guard had reached 142 surface platforms and 62 aircraft by 2019. The Service is likely to achieve force level of 190 ships and 80 aircraft by 2023. To address force-level requirements, the Government has sanctioned in 2009, a large number of additional ships, boats, and aircraft. This has resulted in an accelerated and unprecedented growth of surface and air assets in the last one decade.

The number of Coast Guard Stations has also been increased from 27 in 2008 to 42 (at present) along the coast including in the Islands. The Government has sanctioned Regional Headquarters and air stations/ enclaves along with the requisite manpower in addition to CG Stations, to overcome the vulnerable gaps along the coast. At present there are two Coast Guard Seaboards; in the west at Mumbai and in the east at Visakhapatnam and five Regional Hqs at Port Blair, Kolkata, Chennai, Mumbai and Gandhinagar.

All coastal States and Union Territories have set up marine police stations equipped with boats. However, the training police personnel for marine activities is still a grey area and yet to achieve its optimal status. 182 police stations have been established under Coastal Security Scheme Phase I and Phase II equipped with 204 boats until September 2016. The state of Gujarat and Tamil Nadu have taken lead in setting up the effective marine police organisational structure. In addition, the Indian Navy has developed a force of Sagar Prahari Bal of about 1000 men with 95 craft. The Customs has added about 109 additional new boats in their inventory. The CISF has also recruited additional manpower for port security. Customs and Immigration are increasing presence at all ports and the BSF Water Wing is being strengthened by forming Creek Crocodile Commando unit equipped with 06 all-terrain vehicles and 30 fast patrol boats.

Additionally, Coastal Surveillance Network (CSN), comprising a chain of static sensors having radars, an automatic identification system (AIS), day/night cameras and metrological sensors has been established all along the Indian coastline provides surveillance for area of 'High Sensitivity' and 'High Traffic Density' apart from vessel traffic management system (VTMS) connectivity at the Gulf of Kutch and Gulf of Khambat, are being installed under CSN Phase II[81]. The aim of the project is to create fully integrated infrastructure to achieve real time coastal surveillance from remote locations. The data would be shared at different levels with all maritime operational authorities for responding to threats. Post implementation of Phase II, the coverage factor will be around 98 percent all across the Indian coast providing gap free surveillance.

The electronic monitoring and identification of smaller vessels, such as fishing boats, pleasure craft, and barges poses the greatest challenge. It would require an electronic device to be installed on every single object capable of generating an electronic echo. It is mandatory for all vessels above 20m in length to be equipped with Automatic Identification System (AIS) but implementing it has been a difficult task. Various other technology options such as Transponders for tracking of vessels less than 20m in length, and to record the departure and arrival at all fishing harbours & landing points are being explored by ICG in collaboration with ISRO.

As far as shipping goes, in keeping with a resolution adopted by the IMO, all nations are engaged in establishing Long Range Identification and Tracking (LRIT) Systems for merchant vessels traversing upto 1,000 nautical miles from their coastline. In India, the LRIT system has been implemented by the DG Shipping. However, the access to the data on real-time is limited and not available to all stakeholders. MoS, through the DGLL, has implemented measures to enhance maritime domain awareness along India's coastline. The national AIS and vessel tracking management systems, which have been initiated, have contributed towards enhancing the coastal security apparatus[82].

Coordination

Optimum surveillance, deterrence and interdiction require coordination of a high order by all stakeholders. Seamless coordination and synergistic cooperation at all levels between participating agencies is an essential ingredient, if coastal security measures are to yield success. Jointness of operational efforts has been deeply infused into the coastal security paradigm and has been accepted by all stakeholders. It is a regular practice to launch a co-ordinated joint effort in response to any specific information or intelligence on threats to coastal security. Since 2009, 397 joint operations and 188 joint exercises involving various coastal security agencies have been undertaken[83].

The Coast Guard has been specifically tasked to evolve Standard Operating Procedures (SOPs) in close consultation with all the stakeholders in coastal security, so as to facilitate coordination in Coastal States. A common understanding of shared responsibility has evolved after substantial discussions between the concerned Central and State Government agencies, and is now assimilated into the SOPs drafted by the Coast Guard. The Joint Operations Centres (JOCs), manned and operated by the Navy, have been established at Mumbai, Kochi, Visakhapatnam, and Port Blair. By virtue of being apprised of all operational activities pertaining to coastal security, the JOCs maintain complete situational awareness at all times, within their area of responsibility.

The DGICG has been charged with the responsibility for achieving overall coordination between all Central and State agencies in matters relating to coastal security. At the regional level, the Coast Guard Commanders, in consultation with the respective Naval C-in-Cs, iron out coordination issues with the State Administration, Coastal Police, Customs, CISF, Fisheries Authorities, Ports, etc. in each Coastal State in their area of responsibility. At the apex level, representation from all stakeholders at the highest level, addresses inter-ministerial, inter-agency issues related to coastal security. This committee called the "National Committee on Strengthening of Maritime and Coastal Security" (NCSMCS), is chaired by the Cabinet Secretary. The primary agenda of NCSMCS is to review the maritime security apparatus twice a year.

All states are in various stages of establishing State Maritime Boards for better co-ordination at the state-level. Maharashtra, Gujarat and Tamil Nadu are the only states to establish these boards, and the rest are following suit. These boards will not only co-ordinate coastal security issues, but also other vital maritime issues such as a Port and Fisheries Development, Marine Pollution Control, Marine Environment Protection etc. A sustained and coordinated approach including cooperation between Government agencies and private sectors is the need of the hour.

Legislation

A uniform fishing boat registration scheme, under the Merchant Shipping Act 1958, for all type of boats has been established. The National Information

Centre (NIC) has been given the task of developing the database of all fishermen and the scheme for the issuance of biometric identity cards to coastal fishermen launched by the Ministry of Fisheries. All the major ports have instituted waterfront security measures under the International Ship and Port Facility Security (ISPS) code.

Another important measure has been implemented by the DG Shipping for compliance by merchant vessels i.e., merchantmen intending to enter an Indian port are now required to submit a Pre-Arrival Notification of Security (PANS),96 hours prior to their Estimated Time of Arrival (ETA). This information is utilized for threat assessment and targeting of vessels for boarding operations by Customs and Immigration authorities before entry to the port.

Deterrence

Deterrence has been enhanced by vastly improved surveillance, patrol and joint exercises by all maritime agencies. The sustained presence of ships and aircraft of security agencies in any area holds the key to deterrence. Security awareness and alertness amongst the fishing community has significantly contributed towards 'Deterrence'. The community interaction programme in fishing villages by Indian Coast Guard with a view to sensitise them to act as eyes and ears for any illegal or suspicious activity that may come to their notice at sea has significantly assisted in closely monitoring the activities in the Indian waters. This has also resulted in certain fisheries associations have adopted a resolution to support the maritime security agencies in gathering intelligence at sea.

The first ever coastal security operations involving the Coast Guard was 'Op Tash' in the Palk Bay. Due to the increased activities of smuggling of arms, ammunition, contraband and illegal immigration across the India-Sri Lanka IMBL, joint patrolling in the Palk Bay was commenced by the Indian Navy and Coast Guard in 1990. This operation continues todate.

Three years later, Mumbai was hit by serial bombings in the year 1993. The response was a three tiered security system, code named 'Operation SWAN', under the auspices of the Indian Navy with participation of the Coast Guard. Moreover, considering the great vulnerability of the coast of Gujarat and Maharashtra, a Joint Coastal Patrol (JCP) involving the Navy, Coast Guard, State Police and the Customs was instituted under Op Swan for patrol of the coasts off these States upto the International Maritime Boundary Line (IMBL) with Pakistan.

Post 26/11, the patrolling and surveillance by the Coast Guard ships and aircraft has been enhanced exponentially. Despite limited assets, an average of 30 surface platforms have been kept out at sea every day on a continuous basis, and aircraft sorties flown every day for air surveillance in the Indian EEZ, in addition to specific security operations.

Further, to check the preparedness, and to impart experience to the other agencies involved in the coastal security, the Coast Guard and Navy have conducted regular exercises with all maritime agencies involved in coastal security. In addition, boarding operations is the key task undertaken by our ships and boats on patrol. There has been a significant increase in boarding efforts by 10 times since 2009[84].

The Marine Police have been equipped with boats under the ongoing Coastal Security Scheme for accomplishing patrols within its jurisdiction. Many of the states though are finding it difficult to run and maintain their boats, but this is a situation, which can be overcome with adequate funding and enhanced experience in marine operations. Besides patrol by Customs boats in the contiguous zone continue as hitherto, albeit in greater coordination with the Coast Guard. Within the waterfront areas in major ports, the CISF undertakes patrolling. The Port Facility Security Plans implemented and reviewed by DG Shipping, has added seriousness to the waterfront patrols at all the ports.

Intelligence gathering and sharing is also an important aspect of deterrence. A Multi Agency Centres (MAC) at the central level and Subsidiary Multi Agency Centres (SMACs) at state level were established by the MHA in 2001 for synergizing the national intelligence efforts. The MAC became fully operationalised post 26/11 when the Government through an executive orders gave a legal backing to this force for exchanging intelligence among all agencies including that of states directly without going into long procedural hassles. The state level representatives of R & AW, State special branches, Para Military Forces, Revenue Intelligence Agencies, Income Tax, Defence Intelligence Agencies (including Army, Navy Air Force) etc. were all co-opted as members. Presently the MAC daily Intelligence Sharing meetings are being attended by the nodal officers nominated by 22 intelligence agencies of the country. The Regular meetings at SMACs Centres based upon the broad guidelines issued by the IB Hqrs are being conducted.

Deterrence is also achieved through sensitization, in addition to sanitization. Recognising this, the Indian Coast Guard and the Navy conduct Community Interaction Programmes in the fishing villages dotting the coastline, wherein our personnel interact regularly with the coastal fishing populations with a view to sensitise them and to act as eyes and ears for any illegal or suspicious activity that may come to their notice at sea for intelligence gathering. Since 2009, a total of 7909 CIPS[85] have been conducted. In fact, certain Fisheries Associations have adopted a resolution to support the maritime security agencies in gathering intelligence at sea. The media has also been playing a large role in raising the awareness of the common man and merits acknowledgement.

Conclusion

By the very nature of the maritime environment, it is difficult to achieve fool-proof security. Any maritime arena or to say coastline is bound to be vulnerable to threats of attacks by non-state actors and other inimical forces. Preventing ingress of terrorists from the sea is a challenge. The use of non-state actors to carry out covert acts to bleed the innocent people can perhaps never be eliminated, but sensible hard steps can be implemented on fast track to reduce the probability.

The area required to be monitored is vast and the assets available with security agencies for surveillance are very limited. The problem is compounded by the thousands of fishing boats proceeding to sea each day, and is not yet fully bound by legal mechanisms that enable effective monitoring and control. Fortunately, our maritime and coastal security has witnessed a major overhaul, with legislation on the anvil. An energetic beginning has been made to address maritime and coastal security in a holistic manner, which is to be sustained by the concerted efforts of all stake holders, adequate funding, and most of all, the public awareness. The synergetic and well-co-ordinated efforts by all the stake holders are the key to ensure a safe and secured maritime environment.

Indian Coast Guard is at the fore front of the day to day activities in the maritime domain. The maritime security including coastal security is a complex maze, which has to be attended and is being done by ICG. The Capacity Building of the Coast Guard needs to continue with consolidation on each front. The capacity building has to be amplified with adequate legislations and effective coordination between all stake holders both at Centre and State levels. The participation of private stake holders to augment the resource will always be a win-win situation. Keeping pace with ever-changing dynamics of maritime security should always be on the horizon, while, nomination of one agency as the agency responsible for peace time maritime security.

The Japanese poet Ryunosuke Sataro said, *"Individually we are a drop, but together we are an Ocean"*. No one measure or agency can guarantee water tight security, a series of measures taken in totality would certainly serve to deter the intruders and exponentially increase the likelihood of success.

Chapter 5

Airpower Over Water: From Mahan to Mitchell

Group Captain Dr. A. V. Chandrasekaran

Introduction

The advent of maritime threats both conventional and non-conventional has been witnessing an upward swing in the vicinity of Indian waters. While Pakistan fuels maritime terrorism, a not too friendly Bangladesh playing second fiddle to China is also a worrisome indicator for the future. To counter this ever-mounting threat, the Indian Navy has its task cut out. However, given the agility and precision lethality of the aerial platforms available with the Indian Air Force, the able assistance of such a force would certainly obviate the threat. Both the services should pool in their resources to ensure no duplication of purchases takes place. The joint doctrines should focus on good intelligence gathering, adequate training and swift response to overcome any crisis.

Admiral Alfred Thayer Mahan of the United States Navy believed that national greatness was inextricably associated with the sea, with its commercial use in peace and its control in war and his book *The Influence of Sea Power on History*, is a grand testimony to this thought and emphasis on increased naval power. General William Lendrum Mitchell fondly known as "Billy" Mitchell was the father of the United States Air Force and was also titled as the Father of Military Flight. He argued that air power would become the predominant force of war, the assertion that air power should be the nation's first line of defence was proved by his bombing demonstration of scrapped ships including the massive German battleship *Ostfriesland*. His theory that no surface vessel can exist wherever air forces acting from land bases are able to attack them, stood vindicated. A classic case of an Admiral and General propounding theories in favour of the

Navy and the Air Force, both fighting for the same country. Both of them would have least imagined that in the present scenario a country would never be able to prove its might in the battle unless both the Navy and the Air Force work in tandem and supplement each other.

The ultimate yardstick of national power is its military capability. This is due to the fact that countries subsist in an environment where internal and external threats to security are both common and ever-present, the effectiveness of their offensive coercive arms becomes the ultimate measure of power. Military capabilities allow countries to defend themselves against all adversaries, foreign and domestic, while simultaneously enabling their leaders to pursue core national interests.[86] India continues to be vulnerable from its seas primarily due to vast area spanning three formidable water bodies from Bay of Bengal in the east, Indian Ocean in the south and the Arabian Sea in the west. After the 1971 India-Pakistan war, the eastern sea- space remained relatively calm due to a friendly Bangladesh and a not too hostile Myanmar. The Arabian Sea was considered the hotbed due to Pakistan's hostile intents and India continued facing both conventional and sub-conventional threats from this direction. The steady growth of the Chinese navy and its foray into the Indian Ocean has been viewed with caution by the Indian Navy. China continuously tries to entice India's neighbours through grants and aids and turn them against India. This continuous transformation has made India's own backyard very vulnerable. To add to this China is also building a submarine base for Bangladesh at Pekua and Chinese naval personnel presence in that area cannot be ruled out in the near future.[87] With growing vulnerabilities from all three sides the Indian Navy has its task cut out to launch both offensive and defensive operations. Though the Indian Navy is primarily responsible for countering threats from the sea, the deployment of the Indian Air Force and the Indian Army is also a necessity to jointly counter such threats.

With the spread of advanced military technologies and their exploitation by other militaries, especially China's People's Liberation Army and its sister services and to a far lesser extent by the Pakistani Navy, the Indian Navy's ability to preserve unfettered maritime access to two key areas of vital interest, the Indian Ocean and the Persian Gulf, is being increasingly challenged. While both countries profess benign intentions, it is an old military maxim that since intentions can change overnight, especially in authoritarian regimes. One must thus focus on the military capabilities of other states.

India as a "resurgent maritime nation," has myriad interests in the Indian sea lanes, ranging from energy security, economic growth, and safety of the sea lanes to its maritime ambition to play a leading role in shaping the security architecture in the oceans in its proximity. With its growing military and economic capabilities, India is poised to develop its blue economy to ensure inclusive growth and job creation. Intertwined with its national interests, its maritime strategy is centred on providing security and political stability to its "maritime neighbourhood" such as the Maldives, Mauritius, Seychelles, and Sri Lanka. In view of the overwhelming security challenges from diverse sources, including adversarial neighbours and non-state actors such as pirates, maritime terrorists and narcotics smugglers, India needs to adopt a more structured and holistic approach to address them at global and regional levels. For that, it will need to shape a long-term strategy not only to modernise, update and strengthen its naval sinews but also to plug loopholes in its decision-making on defence procurement and policy implementation. The role of both the Indian Navy and the Air Force is very vital for safeguarding the maritime interests of the nation.

Conversion Capability

While the availability of strategic resources is a critical ingredient of military capability, it is but part of the story. An effective military is one that can take these resources and "convert" them to create a modern force capable of conducting effective operations against a wide range of adversaries. This conversion process is critical because it determines whether the resources garnered from the country as a whole will finally produce a military force with operational competencies that make a strategic difference on the battlefield. Both the Indian Navy and the Indian Air Force have made great contributions to the art of warfare, but one blemish on the record is their continuing inability to work together as a team. Air Force wants unquestioned role in maritime domain which the Navy feels is unfair. In some cases, this has taken the form of factionalism and competition for resources within a single service. But at its worst it has pitted the nation's two airpower services, the Air Force and the Navy against each other in a decade-old roles-and-missions contest. This affects more as the resources available are scarce and there is a necessity to pool in and ensure optimum utilisation of resources. The Indian Prime Minister Shri Narendra Modi has been very vocal about the lack of coordination among the services in India and has been pushing for greater 'jointness'.[88] If the Air Force and Navy each learn the capabilities of the other and apply them objectively, the nation's airpower can't help but be strengthened. After all, land-based aviation has often been used against targets at sea, and vice versa. It is very important that both the Indian Air Force and Indian Navy will have to be rowing in the same direction. There is a need for all the three services to work in a spirit of togetherness and trust with national security interests being of paramount importance.

Latent Maritime Threats

The Indian Government is seemingly unconcerned about the possibility that maritime facilities and personnel might be at risk to armed violence. Not only are current maritime security efforts minimal, they feature a curious dichotomy: one thrust is directed toward occasional acts of terrorism, the other toward coastal defence in wartime. Despite a manifestly more interactive world marked by the ready availability of powerful, mobile weapons, no serious efforts have been directed toward protecting maritime facilities and personnel in India against special operations or unconventional warfare. It is not long ago that one of the biggest terror attacks perpetuated against India originated from the sea in Mumbai during November 2008. A while before that incident, the bomb blasts in Mumbai was also due to the delivery of explosives through the sea route at Dighi Jetty in Raigad. The second landing of RDX and other ammunition at Shekhadi a fishing village on the sun-soaked Shrivardhan coast in Maharashtra's Konkan region also contributed to the Mumbai bombings.[89]

India faces both conventional and transnational threats from the sea. The possibility of a Sino-Pak collusion to create trouble for the Indian Navy in the Arabian Sea is not a distant possibility. On the same grounds Pakistan sponsored maritime terrorists playing havoc on Indian assets also loom large. India must be operationally prepared to tackle both the threats in the same earnest. Though the conventional threats remain manageable, it is the transnational security threats that seek more attention. Transnational security issues are emerging as the top security challenge, for countries including India and pose even more long-term threat to state and regional security than inter-state conflict.[90]

Wings over waves

"*We can do it alone, without you, anywhere we please, at any time*" attitude is to be avoided by both the services to optimise success rate. Even with less defence spending in acquisition and procurement, the Air-Sea coordination is designed to enable such offsetting by jointly employing air and naval capabilities for cross-service and cross-domain synergy. Thus, the concept aims to counterbalance China's quantitative advantage in its periphery with the Indian qualitative advantage. Yet, to what extent the counterbalancing effect can be achieved remains to be seen, at least until concrete operational plans based on specific operational doctrines are developed. Further, a highly cost-effective approach to joint operation combining air and naval capabilities and new guidelines for armaments and force structure, entailing budgeting arms acquisition/procurement and military technology development, can be derived from the concept. Other proponents of the air-sea cohesion suggest that the existing approach is simply not sustainable because it is not suited to solve the problems of the future never mind how divorced it is from the reality of the current budget situation.[91] Without guidelines, the two services would compete for shrinking resources, optimizing their own organizational interests. They would even make redundant investments in weapon systems that could later be found non-interoperable between the services and, perhaps, even within a service. An issue for discussion is the procurement of shore based MIG-29 fighter aircraft which can be used by either service. On similar lines the UAVs operated by both services can also be effectively operated by either service. However, the concept still stands alone at the tactical and operational levels without being sufficiently connected to the strategies. This means that the discussion on the concept has so far failed to explore its implications for Indian national interests, goals, and priorities at the geo-strategic and geo-economic levels and to the higher security objectives derived from them.

Thus, it is essential to understand China's defence strategy and its military capabilities since a major war with the country is still possible, if not probable. China turned to the third strategy of 'Local War under High-technology Conditions.' It assumes that local wars are limited in geographic scope, duration, and political objective, and dominated by high-technology weaponry. The wars are conducted to achieve limited political objectives through relatively limited use of force, while military information systems have become increasingly integrated across command, control, computers, communications, intelligence, surveillance, and reconnaissance (C4ISR).[92] This is precisely what China is attempting in Ladakh where it is engaged in a border showdown with India. Ambitiously enough, China is also trying to transform a brown-water navy to a blue-water navy by including aircraft carriers. The above- mentioned factors are important pointers for India to devise its strategy of maximising results through inter services integration.

Traditional Threats

Another dimension of the growing challenge is the rapid modernization of the Pakistan Navy, including its decision to acquire eight Yuan-class Type 041 diesel electric submarines from China.[93] This development has the potential to upset the regional balance of power, leading to further power disequilibrium. The danger of "loose nukes at sea" also increases with the Pakistan Navy's decision to deploy nuclear weapons on its naval platforms. Al-Qaeda's September 2014 attempt to capture PNS Zulfikar at the Karachi naval base provides forewarning of the vulnerability of deployed nukes to terrorists.

As elsewhere, the expanding Chinese footprint is visible in the growing frequency of Chinese naval patrols, including by submarines, and the expanding scope of China's Maritime Silk Route (MSR) projects. The growing Chinese naval presence in the Indian Ocean has balance of power ramifications that may destabilize the maritime system, given the inadequacies of the existing governance mechanisms. The Chinese government does not have an officially articulated policy on the Indian Ocean. However, its 2015 white paper on military strategy represents a doctrinal shift from "offshore waters defence" to a combination of that objective with "open seas protection," and the abandonment of the "traditional mentality that land outweighs sea," so that "great importance has to be attached to managing the seas and oceans, and protecting maritime rights and interests." According to Ryan Martinson, in the Chinese text of the white paper, the relevant concept translates more accurately as "strategic management.[94]

An important aspect of this endeavour is to invest significantly in a political sense in IOR littoral and island countries, especially in the form of maritime infrastructure projects carried out under its Maritime Silk Route (MSR) programme. Some of these projects, when executed in financially weak countries, have resulted in Chinese acquisition of equity participation, yielding greater control over their management. Because of these projects' strategic locations, there are apprehensions about them being used for military purposes, although China has not stated explicitly any intention to have naval bases in the Indian Ocean. However, given China's tendency toward "changing the facts on the ground" in the South China Sea, such apprehensions are not groundless. Djibouti offers an example worth considering.

Likely Targets in Conventional Operations

There are a number of targets that the enemy would try to neutralize and cripple our war making effort through surprise strikes. India must be able to defuse crises and/or defeat aggression early to prevent escalation and limit damage. Thus, a requirement of flexible, rapidly deployable forces with sufficient depth and strength to sustain multiple, simultaneous operations is an absolute necessity. The Air Force in consonance with the naval planning must be geared and be the first to fight. The following needs to be protected at all costs and under all circumstances.

1. Shore based establishments like Naval Command HQ & Maritime Air Operational centre.
2. Military Ports & Harbours.
3. Ships, Submarines, and aerial assets.
4. Coastal Air Stations.
5. Coastal Batteries.
6. Logistics hubs.
7. Counter Minefields from Deep to Shallow Water.

Strategic Context

The targets have to be adequately defended against enemy surface, subsurface and aerial attacks. The Indian Navy has submarines, warships and an aircraft carrier with offensive aeroplanes like the MIG-29 on board to take on any aerial attempts by the enemy. The MIG-29 variant of the aircraft is primarily an air defence weapon and the Indian Navy requires the assistance of the Indian Air Force to carry out punitive bombing attacks of both ships and other enemy coastal targets. To obviate the enemy's threat, the Indian Air Force has bases all along the western, southern and eastern coasts for speed, flexibility and agility. The shore based Jaguars primed for the maritime strike role are positioned along the coast of Gujarat and the maritime strike SU-30s are positioned along the western coast and southern coast including Thanjavur for immediate strike operations. On similar grounds there are a number of operational military airfields in the eastern coast to counter any threats to Indian assets in the Bay of Bengal. The Indian Air Force has to perfect the three Cs — Challenges, Concepts, and Capabilities to usher in an expeditionary culture in tandem with the Navy. The attacks by both the Pakistani Navy and the PLA (N) can be countered in a calibrated fashion by identifying the theatres of war and theatres of operation. The combat and communication zones need to be operationalised. It is to be borne in mind that both our adversaries are nuclear armed and the response will have to be accordingly tapered. Both the services through regular Joint exercises have sharpened their swords and are gearing up for joint stratagem. The Indians should follow the Capstone Concept for effectively mastering joint operations.

Capstone Concept

The Capstone Concept for Joint Operations (CCJO) was first introduced in the United States of America and can be effectively utilised in the Indian context. The CCJO heads the family of joint operations concept that describes how joint forces are expected to operate across the range of military operations. Its purpose is to lead force development and employment primarily by providing a broad description of how the future joint force will operate. The CCJO focuses on a strategy for achieving military objectives while contributing to broader national objectives through unified action integration with other interagency and multinational partners. It postulates potential areas where the joint force and other elements within the government may find common ground in which to best integrate their efforts. On similar lines the three services in India should formulate target fodders, draw out common targets and plan on maximum utilisation of the scarce resources. The central idea describes in aggregate what the future joint force will do to overcome future challenges. The supporting ideas provide more specificity in how the joint force will resolve the stated military problem. The future joint force's key characteristics include being knowledge empowered, networked, interoperable, expeditionary, adaptable/tailorable, enduring, precise, fast, resilient, agile and lethal.

Targeting Philosophy

The Indian Air Force will have to take out certain targets of the enemy to facilitate naval operations. It is assumed that China would either use Pakistani ports of Gwadar or Karachi to launch coordinated attacks on the western coast. The possibility of an attack on the Eastern Coast is remote as Bangladesh may not allow the use of its naval facilities for offensive operations against India. On similar lines using the Djibouti base to attack and fight in the Indian Ocean would be difficult to logistically sustain operations far away from the parent base. On the other hand, India will be waging a war from its own bases and can respond rapidly. Pakistan has already tasted the wrath of Indian air and naval operations against Karachi in the last war between both the countries. The following would be the Air Force tasks in the maritime operations;

1. Destruction of enemy naval command & control infrastructure.
2. Destruction of enemy ships afloat & ashore & amphibious assembly areas.
3. Bombing coastal defence systems including radars, Surface to air missile sites, fuel & ammunition dumps.
4. Interdiction of enemy bombers.
5. Aerial mining of enemy waterways.
6. Recce of uninhabited islands.
7. Slithering ops.

The combat Air Umbrella of the IAF for the maritime operations would consist of the following variants of the aircraft;

1. Jaguars maritime strike aircraft.
2. Sukhoi-30 multirole aircraft.
3. MI-17 v5- maritime role helicopters.
4. IL-78 air to air refuellers.
5. MIG-21 & 29 Air Defence & Interception roles.

Once IAF successfully carries out its operations it would have achieved the following;

1. Degrading enemies air power.
2. Reducing enemies capability to interfere with own surface forces.
3. Constraining enemies manoeuvrability and mobility.
4. Create imbalance in enemies force disposition.
5. Destroy & damage enemies communications & logistics.
6. Multiple moving maritime targets can be hit simultaneously.

Advantages of Air power

The deployment of airpower in the maritime domain has its distinct advantages and can quickly turn the tide of the battle in quick time through an array of offensive actions.

1. Dominate, Destroy & Devastate.
2. IAF's ability to carry out concurrent ops.
3. Ability to conduct multiple ops simultaneously.
4. Can have a 360-degree eyeball.
5. Can overcome adversary in physical, cognitive & virtual domains.
6. Air power's flexibility, speed, reach and precision enables it to concentrate force rapidly at different areas, thereby creating a range of effects.
7. Air force has the advantage of being able to rapidly cover a relatively larger area even beyond the immediate theatre than any other force projection capability.

The above discussed points amply bring out that any conventional battle between India and her adversaries can be effectively managed through a series of joint operations. The Air Force assets allocated for the maritime missions are exclusively earmarked for the joint operations and this usage would not render the Air Force in its western and Northern theatres short of aircraft. Assets have been set aside for each sectors with a wartime reserve as well. However, the difficult proposition would be employing airpower against the non-traditional targets.

Trans National Threats

Pakistan based Lashkar-e-Taiba and Jaish-e-Mohammed terrorists are increasingly getting trained in underwater sabotage and terrorism. These tactics are imparted by Pakistani marine commandos who has been seconded to the Lashkar.[95] Terrorists have already expressed their intentions to continue their aggression towards India. Their goal is to inflict maximum economic damage, cause mass casualties, spread unprecedented fear among citizens, and thus destabilize the nation to further their agenda. Ports, nuclear facilities, liquid natural gas (LNG) facilities, urban areas, bridges, chemical plants, and other critical infrastructure are all elements of this complex targeting system.

Challenges

1. Terrorist networks today are more dispersed and less centralized. They are more reliant on smaller cells inspired by a common ideology and less directed by a central command structure.
2. While the Indian security agencies have thwarted many attacks, it has not been able to prevent them all. Terrorists have struck in many places from Pathankot to Pulwama.
3. While India has substantially improved the air, land, sea, and border vulnerability, the heartland is not immune from attack.
4. Terrorists have declared their intention to acquire and use weapons of mass destruction (WMD) to inflict even more catastrophic attacks against India.
5. Some states, such as Pakistan and Turkey, a recent hostile addition against India continue to harbour terrorists at home and sponsor terrorist activity abroad.
6. The ongoing terrorist operations in Kashmir has been twisted by terrorist propaganda as a rallying cry by feeding a steady diet of manipulated information.
7. Increasingly sophisticated use of the Internet and media has enabled the terrorists to communicate, recruit, train, rally support, proselytize, and spread their propaganda without risking personal contact.

Threat Assessment Memo

There are six basic types of tactics that terrorist groups are likely to use against India: hijackings, kidnappings, bombings, assassinations, armed assaults, and barricade-hostage incidents. A group's objectives and organizational capabilities dictate which tactics it uses. Terrorist organizations typically use hijackings, kidnapping, and barricade-hostage incidents when the group wishes to force the targeted company or government into negotiations. India has been a victim of almost all of these operations. The IC 814 hijack on 24 December 1999 leading to release of hardcore prisoners is an ignominy India had to face. The Kidnapping of Rubaiya Sayeed the daughter of the Indian Home Minister on 08 December 1989 who was released after Indian Government released hardcore prisoners was also yet another slap in the Indian face.[96] The terrorist group frequently is able to obtain the release of prisoners or extort money using the sentiments and political compulsions prevalent then. Such incidents increase the level of risk to the terrorist organization and require a mature planning, operations, logistics, and intelligence capability to successfully conduct the operation. Bombings, assassinations, and armed assaults are less risky and generally require less organizational capabilities. These tactics tend to be used to accomplish the following goals:

1. Create a climate of fear in a targeted group or nation through a sustained campaign of violence
2. Impose huge costs on the state for an effective counter-terror mechanism thereby draining the state financially
3. Negatively affect processes that the terrorist organization sees as against its interests
4. Eliminate specific individuals or groups.

The Geography of threat

1. **Floating Armouries**- The unrestrained spread and the associated illicit trafficking of small arms and light weapons is not a new phenomenon in itself, but has attained a new dimension threatening many countries. The Arms Trade Treaty (ATT), the leading international instrument on arms trade, restricts and regulates the methods and types of arms that may cross international boundaries, but does not apply to the international movement of arms where the arms remain under one party's ownership. As a result, the phenomenon of "floating armouries" was created. The LTTE had many such floating armouries for illegal transportation of weapons and this also leads to running rackets. The possibilities of Pakistani floating armouries using a false flag for the supply of arms to India for nefarious activities cannot be ruled out. Floating armouries are typically commercially owned vessels that carry weapons, ammunition, and other equipment, such as body armour, food, and medical supplies and they are often anchored in international waters, and are sometimes referred to as logistic support vessels. Most are concentrated "in the Red Sea, Gulf of Oman, and the Indian Ocean." Further, some states that do license floating armouries, such as Sri Lanka and Djibouti, do not make licenses publically available.[97] This is problematic because the legitimacy of these licenses cannot be scrutinized. As the armouries are moored in waters close to unstable states, such

as Pakistan, there is a fear that pirates or al-Qaeda-linked groups could seize the weapons, hijack the vessels or blow them up. India has raised its concerns with the United Nations shipping agency, the International Maritime Organization (IMO) on more than one occasion. In a document submitted on 19 August 2014, India said it stood "exposed and seriously threatened due to the presence of largely unregulated floating armouries with large amounts of undeclared weapons and ammunition". The IMO's Maritime Safety Committee said that while it was "sympathetic to India's concerns" it "noted different views expressed by Member States on the legal implications of the proposals" and has not initiated any actions till date.[98] The presence of these armouries in the vicinity of Indian coast is a potential danger to Indian vital installations.

2. **Clandestine movement of cadres from one safe sanctuary to other-** The terrorist cadres are moved by Pakistan from one country to another fearing retaliation by Indian security agencies. The number of terrorists who were hitherto hiding in Pakistan have been moved out to the Gulf and other friendly countries. They rely on illicit networks to facilitate travel and often obtain false identification documents through theft or in-house forgery operations. Meanwhile, Indian intelligence officials have also pointed out that Pakistan-based terror group Lashkar-e-Taiba's (LeT) charity, Idara Khidmat-e-Khalq, has been radicalising Sri Lankan Muslim youth and these youths crossing the ocean to perpetuate acts of terror in Indian soil in Tamil Nadu and slip back unnoticed is a definite possibility.[99] The Pakistani ISI can subsequently ship the perpetuators to safer sanctuaries.

3. **Narco Terror-** The several decades long 'war on drugs' and the more recent 'war on terror' have found common ground in countering the threat of narco-terrorism, thus combining two threats that have traditionally been treated separately. In the western Indian Ocean as in the southern and eastern Indian Ocean the threats are rooted in inadequate enforcement capabilities. The concept of narcoterrorism originates from an understanding that the two phenomena of narcotics trafficking and terrorism are interconnected and subsequently that a coordination of anti-drug and anti-terror policy can be used, and is necessary, to effectively deal with both threats.[100] This results in human trafficking, drug smuggling, terror financing, and the movement of terrorists and

criminals both on land and at sea. This region is affected by illegal, unreported, and unregulated (IUU) fishing activities that deprive those countries in the region that have legitimate maritime claims of an important resource for their socioeconomic progress. From March 2019, there has been regular seizures of narcotics and other banned drugs leading to almost a dozen recoveries from Pakistani narcotics smuggling gangs. In March 2019, the Gujarat ATS and the Indian coast guard arrested one Afghanistan national following seizure of 100 kg heroin. Six Pakistanis were arrested in May 2019 when a Pakistani fishing boat 'Al Madina' was caught with 218 kg heroin off the coast of Kutch in Gujarat. In March 2020, eight Pakistani nationals were arrested after 400 kg heroin was recovered from two foreign vessels operated by the Sri Lankan navy. The Maldivian National Defence Forces and the Sri Lankan Navy through joint operations have made many seizures in the ten months of 2020.[101] What is equally worrisome for the Indian agencies is the routing of the opium which is being sourced from Afghanistan and then processed by the criminal syndicates based in Faisalabad and Lahore before being dispatched to Karachi or Gwadar for sea transportation or smuggled inside Indian territory from across the border to sponsor terror activities of groups like the Lashkar-e-Taiba (LeT).

4. **Acts of economic terrorism to disrupt economy & energy supplies-** Terrorist organizations have always been interested in targeting oil and gas facilities. Striking pipelines, tankers, refineries and oil fields accomplishes the desired goal. Terrorist attacks on remote infrastructure like oil pipelines are hard to defend against, and are increasingly being seen by violent terrorist groups as "an opportunity to weaken economies, undermine the authority of governments and exploit local grievances.[102] The growing importance of the sea is not always fully appreciated. The sea holds a central place in economic planning because it carries the vast bulk of trade and communication, provides food supplies, source of substantial energy resources and it promises even greater mineral wealth. Moreover, the sea is an important focus for both security and insecurity.

5. **Surreptitious movement of materials for WMD-** The number of containers that enter Indian ports is mind boggling. It is just unfortunate that India does not have the wherewithal to screen

all these containers. The number of Radiation Portal Monitors that have been installed are negligible. Further the terrorists know the ports where these monitors are involved and would invariably avoid those ports. Once the radioactive substance is smuggled in to the town or city the effects can be catastrophic.

These factors coupled with the help of state actors may facilitate the terrorists to carry out a major attack on a country. A Country like India is highly vulnerable to these attacks and India affords ample opportunities to the terrorists due to the presence of a large number of vital installations which feature regularly in the crosshairs of the terrorists. The following would be the likely targets of the terrorists;

1. Explosions in the vicinity of ports.
2. Off shore oil platforms.
3. Oil refineries.
4. Nuclear power stations.
5. Missile testing establishments.
6. Stationary war ships & submarines.
7. Luxury cruisers & oil tankers in mid-sea.
8. Vital maritime choke points.

Specific risk scenarios

To execute these attacks with precision the terrorists need equipment's, and actionable intelligence. The following tools are available with the terrorists to mount an operation.

1. Domestic use of waterborne improvised explosive devices (WBIEDS);
2. Waterborne platform for conducting a stand-off attack (e.g. man-portable air defence system (MANPADS) attacks);
3. Use of a small vessel as a stand-off weapon platform provides greater operational security, improved access to targets (bypassing shore-side security measures), and a ready means of escape;
4. Attacks by UUVS (under water drones);
5. Airborne drones;

6. Hijacked vessels compromised below the waterline as a means to forcefully collide with a target ship;
7. Cargo containers to act as a vector;
8. Trained underwater divers well versed on sabotage;
9. Trojan horse tactics-use of 'Trojan horse' tactics, concealing weapons or other explosive devices, in seemingly harmless looking vessels as such fishing trawlers, tugs or re-supply ships. the international ship and port facility security (ISPS) code exclude vessels less than 500 tons, it also provides exclusion for all fishing vessels regardless of their size;
10. Scuttling a ship at a chokepoint or narrow sea lines of communication (SLOC) (e.g., Malacca straits) to disrupt commercial trade and shipping movement;
11. Hijacking LNG carrier and using it as a floating bomb;
12. Cyber-attack to spoof auto ID system.

Consequence Assessment

It becomes the responsibility of both the Indian Navy and the Indian Air Force to counter these threats and may have to pool in their resources to seek and destroy these threats. The requirement is to identify hostile crafts at a longer distance than in the vicinity of the target and take them on. Both the services have the following air borne platforms to take on the challenge. It ranges from the unmanned aerial vehicles to the rotary variants and the fighter bomber variants.

Ability to verify: UAVS

1. Currently being used for non-lethal assignments
2. Drones operate at close vicinity of target
3. Difficult for humans to get close access to the hostile target
4. Reduces costs, improves safety, & better assessment
5. Inspection & identification by drones are relatively easy
6. Target vessels can be monitored and real time intelligence passed to ships or off shore observers

7. The size of the drone varies in sizes and the variant of a micro drone will make it impossible to be taken out by the terrorists
8. Drones can be operated by a single person
9. Drones can be launched from ships or shore
10. Identification and relaying information to a waiting Air Force bomber to take the target out
11. Armed drones can take targets out

Detect & Deter

1. Armed UAV of the Predator models have emerged as extremely lethal platform that could be employed in a standalone mode.
2. The UAVs ability to loiter and gather intelligence before a strike, is the key in its employment
3. The basic concept underlying the employment of the armed UAV is to quickly kill an emerging target before it disappears back into hiding
4. Kill chain is the process that prescribes the sequence of events needed to locate, identify, and destroy the target
5. The tactical advantage in arming the UAV was that the sensor and shooter were resident on the same platform and no dissemination of information was required resulting in a speedier response from the moment of sighting a target to the delivery of the weapon

Fighters and Bombers

1. If it is confirmed that the terrorists are operating in a big way beyond the range of the ship's guns or even missiles the maritime strike aircrafts of the Indian Air Force can be launched to take on the targets.
2. On specific intelligence inputs that the terrorists are operating from an island and using it as a sanctuary the target can be taken out by the fighter bombers and the destruction of the target can be confirmed.
3. When an oncoming aircraft has been identified as a potential suicide bomber the same can be taken out by both Indian Navy and Indian Air Force fighters using air to air missiles.

4. On similar lines big sized trawlers or smaller ships if not identified and display inimical intention can be taken out by the bombers of the Indian Air Force.

Role of the Rotary

The helicopters which are used extensively by both the services can be effectively utilised against any non-traditional threat envisaged. The pilots of both the services can interchange and operate each other systems to know the nuances and exploit the machines to their fullest potential. Their slow speed facilitates easier spotting and in case fired upon has enough armament to respond in kind. In addition, it offers a plethora of choices for the users. It can also identify hostile submarines and carry out anti-submarine operations. It also has the following distinct characteristics that make it the favourite weapon for anti-maritime terrorism operations.

1. Excellent flexibility, ability to respond
2. A multirole platform, coastal patrol, search, seek & destroy capabilities
3. Can be both land & ship based
4. Can carry our regular Armed patrol
5. Can indulge in Fast reconnaissance
6. SEA KING, KAMOV 28 IN, ALH MK III ICG, MI-17 V5 variants available with both the services
7. Can drop/facilitate commandos to land on board hostile ships

Combat Pair

In the realm of doctrine, there was an emergent Navy acceptance of the value of strategic air campaigns involving the Air Force and the idea that naval air forces must become more influential players in the decision making realm. For its part, the Air Force also embraced the new demands and opportunities for working more synergistically with its Navy counterparts both in peacetime training and in actual combat. The single most influential factor that accounted for bringing the two services ever closer together in strike-warfare tactics, techniques, and procedures (TTPs) and is evident today was when the Naval MIG-29 have been deployed in the air force bases in the north to take on the Chinese. The experiences suggest that the Air Force and naval aviation should now consider each other as natural allies in the roles and function as a Combat Pair. The Evolution of Air Force–Navy Integration in Strike Warfare resources arena should function in full bore, since they do not have to compete but rather mutually support and reinforce the other in the achievement of joint strike warfare goals.

India increasingly requires precision strike capability against Pakistan's, and China's ground based war-fighting and war-supporting targets, thereby deterring its escalatory options at the conventional levels. The capability is essential to destroy or at least neutralize China's military's networks, weapons platforms, long-range ISR and strike systems that may deny the freedom of Indian Navy in the Indian Ocean at the beginning of conflict.

India would also face threats from sea borne terror attacks sponsored by inimical neighbours, pirate attacks on its merchant ships or even attacks on vital installations by adversaries using conventional means. India has to attribute adequate importance on non-traditional challenges such as human trafficking, Illegal, Unreported and Unregulated (IUU) fishing, climate-induced crises and maritime pollution. The counter mechanisms to take would be possible when both the services synergise in unison, pool in their resources and take on the enemy together. The aim of joint operations between the two services should be

1. Speed in execution.
2. Flexibility in organization, logistical support, and employment.
3. Agility in thought and intellect.

Concluding Thoughts

The usage of aerial platforms to confront both conventional and non-conventional threats has a huge advantage. The country using these platforms can exploit the fear psychosis created by the aerial platforms to their benefit. It is no doubt that a low-level screaming fighter would certainly strike terror in the heart of the enemy. The multi-directional operating capability facilitates approaching the target from any direction to catch the terrorist's unawares leaving very little reaction time to counterattack. On similar lines adequate training is to be imparted to the aircrew to use hostile measures after due identification with solid intelligence as the killings of innocents can create a huge international furore. The acquisitions have to be weighed carefully to avoid duplication of resources. The advice of seasoned operators in the field may be obtained for an accurate employability of resources. The services should shrug away the 'my machine' concept and should be willing to pool in resources for the common cause. The threats are not going to decrease any time soon. With volatility being witnessed world over, it is envisaged that the situation would deteriorate with a huge advent of terror-based violence creeping in all over.

Chapter 6

Oar Steadying the Boat: India's Maritime Security Architecture

Dr. S. Utham Kumar Jamadhagni

India's National Security rubric rests on the bulwark of civilian control, in reality, bureaucratic control, over military. This entails a non-participative primary stakeholder namely the armed forces in policy structure where the military instead of bringing to the table its concerns, strategic analysis and future vision is often reduced to a secondary role of following directives. Identified as one of the issues in India's prevailing Higher Defence managerial system greater say of uniformed personnel in matters military has been attempted in recent times though in fits and starts.

The creation of the post of Chief of Defence Staff towards integration and greater synergy of the armed forces is indeed welcome. This post which had fallen vacant after the tragic demise of the first Chief of Defence Staff Gen Bipin Rawat has now been filled.

India's maritime security both as a topic of policy making and implementation has garnered significant interest of late. While this has been long overdue, the catalyst for change has definitely been the 26/11 Mumbai terror attacks via the sea. Even earlier after the Kargil War, the Group of Ministers in its report suggested the creation of an "apex body for management of maritime affairs should be formed for institutionalised linkages between the Navy, Coast Guard and the concerned Ministries of the Central and the State Governments", and had asked the Defence Ministry to "take necessary action to constitute the apex body".[103]

However, 22 years later, part of it has only just been realised. The 2022 appointment of National Maritime Security Coordinator is a culmination of a long-awaited transformation. Reporting directly to the National Security Advisor, the NMSC will perform the much-needed synchronisation role for a variety of agencies ranging from central ministries and departments (external affairs, defence, home, shipping, fisheries, etc) and state governments to the Navy, Coast Guard, customs, intelligence agencies, and port authorities, dealing with maritime security in general. Acting as the principal advisor to the government on maritime security domain, he would be the interface between civilian and military authority over the seas.

The National Maritime Security Coordinator (NMSC) must now work with the National Committee for Strengthening Maritime and Coastal Security (NCSMCS)—the apex review mechanism for maritime and coastal security. While he would be the point man for all things maritime to the political structure, his task mainly lies in balancing competing focus on coastal security, traditional threats and other non traditional threats apart from Terrorism that have not received much needed attention till date.[104]

The yet-to-be-passed draft Coastal Security Bill, creation of a Maritime Advisory Board or even the setting up of a Central Marine Police Force only heighten the imperative for an NMSC to carve out extensive interactions with various stakeholders to provide a holistic picture of the needs, challenges and mechanisms for a robust maritime security architecture.

Civil control over military matters has been the topic of discussion in India's Higher Defence Organisation since independence. Though the rationale for this imbalance in the early years is understandable, 75 years later the growing need is for greater stakeholder participation in defence decision making and execution. While many of the defence related structures have been newly established the emphasis is still on coordination and jointness which go a long way in realising the complete potential of defence preparedness and strategy.

Change thy name blue

With the Maritime Theatre Command expected to be announced at the 76th Independence Day celebrations this year, the move towards according wider integrated preparedness amongst the three forces spearheaded by the Navy in this case has raised expectations. This tactical outfit would focus on response to threats to India's peninsular region as well the island territories present on either side of the mainland. Three more Theatre Commands are to be set up in the near future.

Interestingly, China has been making changes to its western Theatre command to improve its jointness capability. Its foray into Indo-Pacific in a big way including establishing its first off-shore naval base at Djibouti and feared in the process of setting up another in the Solomon Islands in the Pacific Ocean are indeed developments of special concern. The rapid naval modernisation plans aimed in principle to achieve blue water capability add yet another aspect to Chinese accruing of strength.

With the growing currency of India's international status the onus of overhauling her Higher Defence management machinery gains added weight. In this, instead of just creating new posts or responsibilities the emphasis must be on the effectiveness of such tinkering in the wider scheme of strategic outlook and its impact on ground realities. The NMSC could expected to play a vital role in reorienting focus on the adjoining ocean space and accord it a rightful place in the scheme of things while attempting to retain enduring interest in policy circles for primacy of maritime realm in India's security matrix.

Chinks in the armour

India's political ascendancy in the world arena together with her expected improving economic growth in a challenging geostrategic environment warrant significant course correction in policy matters. Evaluation of strengths and weaknesses in preparedness not only at the tactical level but at the larger policy framing, analytical and execution strata is thus imperative. In this, a closer and more thorough examination of Higher Defence organisational positives and negatives could go a long way in improving the overall system.

Bequeathed as a colonial legacy, the Higher Defence Organisation of India like many other management systems must be amenable to modifications and adjustments in tune with rapid transformations in global order, regional dynamics and national priorities. In order to point out the lacuna in the present security architecture, a retrospect on the journey of the HDO in India's post independence path is mandatory. Prior to independence the Commander in Chief was a member of the Viceroy's Executive Council and also the *de facto* Defence Minister. The Defence Secretary was ranked under the Principal Staff Officers and the defence department was confined to solely issuing orders in the name of Government of India. It is to be noted here that the Defence department neither examined proposals nor was above the Army headquarters.

The contribution of the Indian Armed Forces towards India's freedom has been clouded by the shadow of doubt about loyalties by the then political class. The colonial masters employed both the Indian police and armed forces in quelling freedom fighters fuelling the perception of politicians that the British Indian Army was a symbol of imperialism and repression. Lest it be forgotten, the Indian Naval mutiny of 1946 that later spread to other arms of the military truly propelled the Indian freedom movement towards the ultimate aim of independence. General Wavell, the C-in-C admitted in a secret report remarked, "It is no use shutting one's eye to the fact that any Indian soldier worth his salt is a Nationalist…" [105]. The words of Former Chief of Naval Staff (Admiral) Arun Prakash warn that "*To forget the sterling role played by the armed forces during the violence and turbulence of partition, and in integrating the recalcitrant Princely States would be an act of rank ingratitude*".[106]

Regrettably, this distrust seeped into policy making post-independence as well. Upon independence, India was left with a Commander in Chief in charge of each of the three services and a Chiefs of Staff Committee that would take up inter service coordination and with that of the Ministry of Defence. What should have naturally progressed to a greater role for the three services within the ministry culminating in them turning into separate departments turned into a shocking relegation of significance to the status of "attached offices" leaving them completely out of the loop in the ministry throwing a permanent wedge in the services–bureaucracy relationship. In fact, the dynamic between the two pillars of policy namely the bureaucracy and the services ever since independence, according to Defence Analyst Nitin Gokhale, is that it "*has been in a constant state of tension between the 'generalist' bureaucracy and the 'specialist' military leaders, with the political executive watching and sometimes encouraging the bureaucracy to keep the military under control*"[107].

A drastic reduction in powers of the service personnel vis a vis civilian bureaucrats was witnessed during the years that followed. General mistrust of the military despite their laudable performance during independence years and the total lack of interest in defence matters of the political class propelled the movement of complete subsuming of the military organ in national security matters to the extent that according to the Transaction of Business Rules (ToB) that are often cited, The Defence Secretary a generalist administrator is bestowed the task of security even war whereas the specialist military are mere spectators from the sidelines.

While many democracies have retained civilian control over armed forces, "few militaries have been subjected to the kind of overwhelming civilian bureaucratic dominance that the military in India has endured"[108] making a complete overhaul an imperative.

After a series of starts and stops the Chief of Defence Staff finally saw the light of day two decades after the maiden proposal was made in the Arun Singh-led Task Force on Management of Defence report of September 2000 to examine the existing structures for the management of defence[109]. The appointment of CDS was indeed welcomed but the seat of the CDS has fallen empty after the tragic loss of Gen Bipin Rawat in December 2021.

Issues

The latest proposal of the government to recruit IAS cadre specialisation-wise[110] has brought to the fore the subject of competencies. While other areas of global affairs are tipping towards super-specialisation, India's national government administrative machinery has lagged far behind. The dearth is further accentuated by the reality of disproportional reliance of a majority of the political executive on bureaucrats especially in matters military not only for knowledge inputs but more seriously on the entire thought process. This does not bode well for the armed forces leadership who though professionally trained and competent to advice on National security problematique are at best spectators in the policy planning and review stages. Crises periods have time and again thrown glaring focus on this gap. The unjustified primacy accorded to 'generalist' administrators over 'specialist' service personnel has worked as a catalyst in at times undermining India's strategic capability and even in handing her humiliating defeat.

The grievance nursed by the uniformed services in this quarter, is aptly described in the words of Admiral Vishnu Bhagwat in his book *The Soldier and the State*,

"By selective usage, omission and interpretation of language, it (civil services) has continuously imposed a variety of constraints, checks and curbs on the very functioning of the armed forces in general, and the business of service headquarters in particular. This has virtually isolated and marginalised the defence forces from all processes which go into the formulation of national policies and agendas, even in the cardinal sphere of national security."[111]

In contrast, on occasions when political leadership sought or heeded military acumen victory or success was indeed assured. The 1971 Indo-Pak war victory is an appropriate example.

While concerted efforts at reformation like the Kargil Committee Review or GoM were afoot, constant hurdles were laid by the bureaucracy in propelling the wheels of change to their logical progression. It however must be acknowledged that measures like One Rank, one pay and the creation of the office of Chief of Defence Staff (CDS) and the Tri-Services Command at A & N have seen the light of day, albeit after a long gestation period.

Other than this there are concerns[112] relating to the overlapping of responsibilities of the myriad agencies involved in maritime border management. Often this leads to delay in response or lack of intelligence coordination among the various stakeholders. Just as in the case of land-based security, maritime apparatus is also inordinately trained on terror aspect alone rather than the comprehensive coverage including all possible mainly non-traditional threats such as human trafficking, narcotic smuggling, illegal fishing, marine pollution etc.

The repeated haul of drugs from various ports along Gujarat brings forth the threat of narco smuggling to the fore.[113] Tracking of non-military vessels through the Information Management and Analysis Centre of the Indian Navy and the establishment of Information Fusion Centre - Indian Ocean Region IFC-IOR have helped in surveillance and coordination within India and between countries. A coastal tracking surveillance system is in place consisting of a network of radars and sensors, an automatic identification system, and various other communication measures. However the inability to cover the entire coast with existing systems and the problems related to fishing vessels identification continue. It just points to the fact that vast improvement in incorporating technical solutions to surveillance challenges needs to be undertaken. Optimal utilisation of resources both man and machine especially in the coastal security aspect is sorely needed.

A wide range of ministries, departments and other government agencies are involved in various aspects of maritime security. Coordinated response could well be attempted if the NMSC serves as a balancer in assuaging the needs, aspirations, responsibilities and roles of the various agencies related to maritime security to offer a synchronised and appropriate approach to countering emerging concerns by preparedness enhancement and effective implementation of strategies.

In its first meeting in June 2022 the NMSC took up the discussion on "mapping of existing orders and policies on maritime security to identify gaps, review of standard operating procedures for maritime contingencies, security of ports and coastal infrastructure, creation of a national maritime database, capacity building of coastal states and UTs".[114]

Capacity building of the stakeholders in raising maritime domain awareness has also been part of the mandate of the NMSC. Towards this end, the maritime coordinator office has been seeking inputs from academic institutions, think tanks and researchers as contribution in the form of workshops, certificate programmes and other educational exercises that could further this goal.

Conclusion: Path of Progress

The current maritime environment elicits operational and more importantly ideational adjustments from countries like India. One of the persistent problems is the profusion of ministries and departments that deal with various aspects of maritime security. This has not resulted in seamless coordination in the fields of information sharing and plan implementation. The effect has been less than optimal responses to challenges and the fear of repetition or oversight due to multiplicity of authorities and decision makers.

The emergence of new factors and conditions both at the international and regional levels warrant organisational structure adaptability. The increasing presence of China in the waters of the Indian Ocean and the ever-rising pressure on the resource aspect of maritime areas prop up the attention for a comprehensive approach in managing maritime security architecture. The National Maritime Security Coordinator with the prospect of offering unified focus and direction to strengthening India's maritime structure is certainly a step towards a glorious future.

Chapter 7

Role of Merchant Marine in India's Maritime Security

Captain Swarup Bhangara

Introduction

The Merchant Marine plays a modest role in contributing towards securing India's Maritime neighbourhood or for that matter for any Nation. Comparably, its indirect contribution to security – largely through Economic Dimension is significant. This chapter seeks to explore the economic dimension of merchant ships and in doing so, endeavours to bring out the resultant contribution to maritime security.

Shipping is the life blood of global economy. Without shipping, intercontinental trade, the bulk transport of raw materials, and the Import/export of affordable food and manufactured goods would simply not be possible. The international shipping industry is responsible for the carriage of around 90 percent of world trade.[115] Seaborne trade continues to expand, bringing benefits for consumers across the world through competitive freight costs. Thanks to the growing efficiency of shipping as a mode of transport and increased economic liberalization, the prospects for the industry's further growth continue to be strong.

There are over 50,000 merchant ships trading internationally, transporting every kind of cargo. The world fleet is registered in over 150 nations, and manned by over a million seafarers of virtually every nationality. Ships are technically sophisticated, high value assets (larger hi-tech vessels can cost over US $200 million to build), and the operation of merchant ships generates an estimated annual income of over half a trillion US Dollars in freight rates. Globalization has had the effect of further propelling shipping to even greater prominence, that of a catalyst for world peace and Prosperity. The reality, however is that ships operate in a very fragile marine environment with an inherent perilous nature, which creates social cost detractors of safety and environment protection.

Analysis, Actors & Capacity Building

Shipping is the least environmentally damaging form of commercial transport and, compared with land based industry, is a comparatively minor contributor to marine pollution from human activities. The International Maritime Organization (IMO) tasked with the responsibility of minimizing the social cost of shipping, has established a clear mandate to strive for cleaner oceans and safer ships. Ships that operate outside these standards are deemed to be substandard and therefore pose the greatest risks.[116]

Flag state, port state etc. have the most stakes in the event of a Maritime catastrophe, therefore along with the shipowners have an explicit legal responsibility to enforce the provisions of conventions. The IMO has produced a profusion of regulations that have been tailored to promote quality shipping. However, there are several impediments. As has been observed generally there is knee jerk reaction on the part of some Governments in the wake of a disaster caused by real or perceived public pressure.

Added to this is the fact that few states confer nationality on vessels for the sole purpose of economic benefits-commonly referred to as "Flags of Convenience".[117]

The Indian shipping Industry plays a crucial role in the Indian Economy. Around 95 percent of India's trading by volume and 70 percent by value is done through Maritime Transport. It is pertinent to note that ONLY 8 percent of our Exim Cargo is carried by Indian Ships. Hence, it is important to put this in the right perspective whilst deciding on future policies and more so whilst our "unaccountable" bureaucrats deal with prospective Foreign investors and Shipping Lines. It is important for policies to be put into place basis India as a Country and not due to political or state compulsions. As the former Chairman of a Multinational Ship Owning Container Company which owned and operated 135 Container ships on worldwide trade, the author was privy to painful experiences existing in our bureaucracy that would easily deter any foreign investors from participating. Having said that it is heartwarming to see Prime Minister Shri Narendra Modi trying to make changes in attitudes and on ease of investments, which I hope will take us to even greater heights.

India has a coastline spanning 7516 kilometres, forming one of the largest peninsulas in the world. It is serviced by 12 major ports, 200 notified minor and intermediate ports. More Ports and Terminals are being put into place.[118] In 2018, Indian ports handled about 16 million TEUs (Twenty foot equivalent Units) of containers, of which nearly 70 percent was gateway container cargo and 25 percent trans- shipped enroute to a different destination. Trans-shipment is the act of off-loading a container from a large container ship (generally at a hub port) and loading it onto a second, smaller feeder ship to be carried to the final port of discharge.

Global vessel sizes have significantly increased in the last decade and most main liner vessels have capacities of 10,000 TEUs or more, with the largest vessel reaching a capacity of 23,000 TEUs. It is indeed tragic, that despite consistent inputs from professionals, urging India to focus on developing suitable trans-shipment hubs on both East and West coast, India continues to depend on trans-shipment ports like Colombo, Jebel Ali, Singapore etc. it is obvious that decisions made in developing ports and terminals are more due to state driven politics rather than country driven necessity. Lack of consultation with professionals coupled with lack of understanding by policy makers has contributed to this lacuna. The only project that might be of any significance in the immediate future is Vizhinjam which is controlled by the Kerala State Government and is being undertaken by Adani Ports. The advantage that Vizhinjam has over the other ports is the natural deep water depths of 20 metres and hence can accommodate the largest Container ships servicing global trade. It is indeed ironic that Colombo already has a Container terminal (CICT) which can handle these mammoth carriers, which call regularly. Colombo is in the process of adding East container Terminal and subsequently West Container terminal in the next couple of years, both have required depths.

Options for India

Large container ships need deep-draft ports offering a depth of around 18 metres to berth. India's terminals offer maximum of about 14.5 to 15 metres depth on the berth- and that too only in a few terminals- a quarter of all containers are trans-shipped through ports in other countries. Colombo (Sri Lanka), Singapore and Klang (Malaysia) handle more than 80 percent of India's trans-shipment cargo.

Over 70 percent of Transhipment volumes handled (in/out) in Colombo is of Indian Origin! It is interesting to note that Colombo achieved a throughput of over 7 million TEUs in 2019- which is their highest so far.

As you all are aware, Sri Lanka has very few exports and the Container Terminals rely heavily on Transhipment, which is a huge source of revenue for them.[119]

Trans-shipment adds to the cost of handling cargo because of the extra port-handling charges. It has been estimated that the Indian port industry loses up to Rs 1,500 crore per year in revenue on trans-shipment cargo that is either originating from or destined for India. The additional cost is about $80-100, or Rs 5,600-7,000, per TEU, which would not be incurred, if the container could be imported/exported directly from an Indian port. Through its ambitious Sagarmala project, the Indian government wants to transform the country's ports and reduce logistics costs for domestic and import/export cargo by optimizing infrastructure investment. Maritime Development Fund, Maritime India Vision 2030 are part of this focus.

Whilst Government is focusing in the right direction with Sagarmala and Inland waterways, may I take the liberty to offer possibly a politically unacceptable view that though we have proposed and have set up numerous terminals, we have consistently ignored the connectivity to these terminals? Those in the shipping Industry are painfully aware of the congestion, bottle necks and lack of connectivity in the past- and above all the bureaucratic hurdles and the lack of understanding and support rendered by both Bureaucrats and Regulators. Why cannot professionals be given a free hand to make policy decisions and improve efficiency and performance?

The International Ship owners have the CHOICE to call ports that are commercially viable - more so during such challenging times. [120] The Vizhinjam port is about 225 km from the government-owned Vallarpadam port, where the Dubai-based company DP World has been operating, India's first container trans- shipment terminal for the last six years. The author was on the Board of Cochin Port as a Trustee for 3 years during the development of this project- and hence has a firsthand knowledge of the efforts that the Port Management and the Board, had to endure to convince all concerned . It is beyond reason why India could not have concentrated in developing Vizhinjam port atleast 10 years ago as competition to Colombo, which would have certainly benefitted trade, we were instead permitting states to propose and allocate thousands of crores on terminals which could only eat into each other volumes and yet not offer facilities to accommodate largest container vessels thus avoiding transhipment as far as possible. For good order sake, I must clarify that it is envisaged that future growth in import/export volumes might offer sufficient volumes for not only Indian Ports and Terminals but also neighborhood transhipment hubs- but the immediate focus should be on India overcoming the over-dependency on transhipment ports like Colombo, Singapore, Jebel Ali etc.

Economic Potential

Tariffs play an important role in our Terminals being competitive and offering efficient service. Quick turnaround and above all minimum depths for mega carriers to call our ports directly should be a priority. Though our transhipment tariff is lower than Colombo, the vessel-related charges or marine charges at Indian ports are four times more than in Colombo. For instance, the marine charges for a 24-hour stay for 5,000-TEU capacity ships are about US$40,000 in India vis-a-vis US$10,000 in Colombo. The marine charges are low in Colombo because the Sri Lankan Government funds basic infrastructure, including dredging- "unlike in India". The Indian Government expects Ports to pay for dredging which is in fact a huge component of the tariff- and hence this is inevitably passed on to the end users- and there is a need to make our tariffs practical for Shipping Lines to call our terminals and will consequentially result in lower costs to our shippers and importers to compete globally. Existing Ports offering high tariff and then offering discounts to Lines, does not make sense. We must ensure that our Tarrifs are in line if not better than our competitors.

If coastal shipping is used to complement road and rail transport in India, it could therefore lead to significant logistics cost savings. It is heartwarming to observe that the present Government has realized this and is in the process of according priority to Inland Waterways, Coastal Shipping etc.

The Government of India's proactive initiative in recently holding the Maritime India Summit 2021 will go a long way in improving logistic costs for trade "Sagar Manthan", setting up of Mercantile Marine Domain Awareness Centre ,Major Port Authority Act 2021 will all contribute to enhancing our growth and hopefully reduce Logistics costs.[121] It is pertinent to note that Cost of Logistics in India is around 14 of GDP vis-a-vis Europe's 8 percent of GDP. The Utilization of inland waterways would result in huge overall savings in Logistics cost. India offers potential concessions in Ganges-Bhagirathi Hooghly Rivers, Brahmaputra, Rivers in Goa, backwaters in Kerala, inland waters in Mumbai and the deltaic regions of the Godavari-Krishna rivers.

Impediments

Whether the powerful Road Transporters lobby will permit this to succeed is another issue of concern. We can expect them to resort to periodical strikes and hold the various Governments to ransom. Besides from a political perspective, implementation of road infrastructure is more "visible" to the voters than improving Inland waterways or terminals- so will the Government have the political "will", to expedite Inland waterways projects and emulate projects in Belgium, Nederland and rest of Europe, only time would tell.[122]

A cause for concern is that from 01 January 2020, the IMO Marpol Annex VI regulation on limiting sulphur content of bunker fuel to a maximum of 0.5 percent will enter into force. At present, the global sulphur content cap on bunker fuel is at 3.5 percent, a level considered easy to comply with for vessel operators. This will bring significant increases in fuel prices - expected to increase fuel costs by one third hence Freight rates are expected to rise correspondingly. Though COVID had initially exacerbated the Maritime Sector, the subsequent shortage of containers globally, has resulted in huge increase in Ocean Freights (freights at times have increased by four to seven fold!) which has placed the importers and exports worldwide in a very difficult situation.

Regional Security

Merchant Navy is traditionally considered as a second line of Defence for a Maritime Nation - after the Navy. Merchant Navy also contributes in the economic defence of our nation. The challenges facing maritime security in the Indian Ocean region, however, have significantly broadened. Traditional threats include the military presence of belligerent powers and the consequent strategic rivalry, and terrorism, piracy, and illegal smuggling; non-traditional threats include the challenges of climate change, such as increasing natural disasters and loss of traditional livelihoods. These disruptions severely impact the island nations in this part of the world. A close partnership between these island nations and larger littoral countries thus becomes a practical necessity and plays a critical role in maintaining stability in the region.

A strong governance and security architecture in the Indian Ocean is necessary and ought to be a global priority. New Delhi's Indian Ocean policy, enshrined in "SAGAR – Security and Growth for All in the Region," articulates India's vision for building a secured regional architecture, which includes "safeguarding mainland and islands, strengthening capacities of maritime neighbours and advancing peace and security" in the Indian Ocean Region. For a country like India, the island nations of the Indian Ocean hold immense strategic value in shaping the geopolitical contours of the region and ensuring maritime security and order.

The Indian islands of Andaman and Nicobar, and Lakshadweep, have significantly helped the country in enhancing its maritime capabilities. The Andaman and Nicobar Islands are positioned close to the Strait of Malacca and are less than 90 nautical miles from Aceh in Indonesia. This enables India to closely observe military and economic activities in and around the Strait of Malacca and also overlook the maritime entry point of western Pacific countries in the Indian Ocean. To its west, India enjoys rights over nearly 400,000 square kilometers of exclusive economic zone (EEZ) due to the Lakshadweep islands.

Farther west from India, the islands of Socotra (Yemen), Madagascar, Mauritius, and the Seychelles have gained strategic importance, standing at the crossroads of Europe, Africa, and South Asia. While Socotra is strategically located at the opening of Gulf of Aden, which connects the Suez Canal with Indian Ocean, the maritime zones of Madagascar, Mauritius, the Maldives, and Seychelles span over 1 million sq km, which allows them greater rights in ocean waters. However, it is with the island nations of Mauritius and the Seychelles that India primarily seeks to bolster its economic and strategic relations in order to influence the dynamics in Indian Ocean. Focus on QUAD has certainly improved the chances for India Ocean Region to contain China. Involvement of India in the Chabahar Port Project in South Eastern Iran is a good strategic move as well.

Sri Lanka

Sri Lanka presently has 5 Container terminals in Colombo Jaya container terminal (JCT), East container terminal (ECT), Unity container terminal (UCT), South Asia gateway terminal (SAGT), and Colombo international container terminal (CICT), and is working on setting up the additional infrastructure in Hambantota. Unable to repay its debt, Sri Lanka gave China a controlling equity stake and a 99-year lease for Hambantota port, which it handed over in December 2017.[123] The economic rationale for Hambantota is weak, given existing capacity and expansion plans at Colombo port, fueling concerns that it could become a Chinese naval facility. However, the Chinese are setting up an SEZ in Hambantota, and also bunkering facilities. This besides the enhancement of port facilities.

Likewise, Indian and Japanese interest in port facilities in Trincomalee, on Sri Lanka's east coast, should be tempered by Sri Lanka's debt levels and the existence of competing ports in the region. Though India was initially accorded the East Container Terminal Project, basis a Tripartite Agreement signed between governments of Sri Lanka, India and Japan, it was shocking to see Sri Lanka renege on this due to pressure from Trade Unions and some local politicians with vested interests.

Adani Ports, appointed by India was supposed to handle this project with its local partner "John Keels Holdings" of Sri Lanka. Subsequently the Sri Lankan Government tried to appease by offering the West Container Terminal instead- and strangely went ahead with direct negotiations with Adani Ports basis a BOT proposal for 35 years-without the involvement of either the Indian Government or the Japanese Government.[124] This project is presently under negotiations. Understand that Adani's APSEZ has just received an LOI on 15th March 2021, from Ministry of Ports and Shipping of Sri Lanka and Sri Lankan Port Authority for the development and operations of "West Container Terminal" in Colombo. For this project Adani will partner with John Keels Holdings PLC and Sri Lankan Port Authority to build, operate and transfer basis for a period of 35 years as a PPP. WCT will have a quay length of 1400 Mtrs and alongside depth of 20 mtrs

Seafarers

The worldwide population of seafarers serving on internationally trading merchant ships is estimated at 1.65 million seafarers, of which 774,000 are officers and 873,500 are ratings. Which means that merchant navy generates quite significant employment opportunities worldwide. Additionally, a career at sea pays much better than a career on shore and therefore, merchant navy further contributes to the global economy by increasing the purchasing power of those employed by it.

The Shipping Industry and its relevant stakeholders cannot expect there to be an abundant supply of qualified and competent seafarers without concerted efforts and measures to address key manpower issues, through the promotion of careers at sea, enhancements of Maritime Education and training worldwide and addressing the retention of seafarers.

Conclusion

In order to truly become a player of consequence in Regional Trade and make any impact in the Indo-Pacific Theatre, India needs a merchant fleet, competitive and commensurate in size to carry not only its national export trade, but also across trades of other countries, thereby earning freight income for India while assuming the role of provider of those services. India stands 17th in the World Merchant Fleet in deadweight terms.[125] Indian Government recently announce a new scheme of providing Rs. 1,624 crores over a period of 5 years, which is a great initiative and will enable better training and employment opportunities for Indian seafarers besides enhancing Indian Companies share in Global shipping.

One can only hope that the Government and its bureaucracy continue to remain focused on improving the ports, terminals, inland waterways and coastal shipping and accord logistics costs, the priority that it deserves.

Chapter 8

Privately Contracted Armed Maritime Security: Should India Be Wary?

Dr. Ramakrishnan Ramani

Introduction

This chapter focuses on Privately Contracted Armed Maritime Security (PCAMS) and its role in protecting the merchant marine. It takes a look at the global trends that drive this industry - particularly piracy and armed robbery on the high seas. Owing to the remote geography of operations and the murky scenarios in which protective action sometimes happens, the details of engagement are often translucent. Of course, there are also clear anecdotes that showcase the high-handedness of maritime armed guards. The chapter, in this respect, looks at two popular incidents that have made waves in the Indian media. Highlighting salient regulatory points from the Indian perspective, it focuses on the challenges of leveraging PCAMS. The chapter is not definitive but requests the readers to consider various facets of this growing industry.

Piracy: A Brief History

The phenomenon of piracy and armed attacks on the high seas has been a constant shadow for merchant marine since the earliest days of sailing. Perhaps the first recorded act of piracy dating back to the 14th century BC involved the 'Sea People' a group of raiders focusing on mercantile ships in the Aegean and Mediterranean seas. The story of Julius Caesar being taken hostage by Cilician pirates leading to their annihilation by General Gnaeus Pompeius Magnus in 67 BC is another popular example.

Piracy is not new to Indian waters. There have been tales, documented and undocumented, of the prevalence of piracy in Indian waters. Often these maritime brigands feasted from the ever-fomenting strife between the dominant kingdoms in India, such as the struggle between the Deccan sultanates and the Vijayanagar Empire. Horses, being a much-prized commodity, were often the subject of raids by pirates off the Konkan coast. Even today ballads are sung on the exploits of pirates, such as Timoji (also known as Timayya), who had his base at Anjadip Island (near present day Goa). He was notorious both as a privateer who and as a pirate. He harassed the Deccan Sultans by seizing the supply of horses and passing them on to Vijayanagar. He also made a pretty penny siding with the Portuguese whenever favourable. As a pirate, he also attacked merchant ships carrying pepper from Kerala to Gujarat. The Maratha Admiral Kanhoji Angre is also a name to be remembered in a similar vein – a relentless privateer too in harassing and capturing European merchant ships till his death in 1729. The merchant ships of the Mughals were considered a catch prize for European adventurers in Indian waters and near the Arabian coast during the 16th and 17th centuries. The South Indian coast (Coromandel Coast) too had its fair share of piracy. Historical records reveal that the Chola kings harnessed the skills of 'pardoned' pirates and used their services in the Chola navy (Kallarani) in duties that ranged from sanctioned piracy to reconnaissance of the enemy coast.

While these examples may conjure pictures of swash-buckling pirates of yore, the phenomenon of piracy has only become more complex with evolving geopolitical dynamics and technological force multipliers. Let's see how the numbers speak in this part of the world. Statista, the global statics and research company states on its website that "contemporary maritime piracy reached its peak level in 2010, with around 445 reported incidents. The regions most likely to come under threat from pirate attacks include Indonesia, Malaysia, and Nigeria. Here, pirates are attracted by the abundance of natural resources in the countries themselves or in adjacent areas. Strategic passages for oil transport such as Bab-el-Mandeb, near Somalia, or the Strait of Malacca off the Indonesian coast have become notorious targets for maritime crime. In 2013, oil tankers shipped 15.2 million barrels of oil per day through the Strait of Malacca; this exceeds the daily volume of oil imported into the whole of the European Union. With oil prices hovering around 70 U.S. dollars per barrel in 2018, the hijacking of a crude oil tanker sounds like a promising deal for pirates. In 2017, Venezuela was thrust into the limelight: Here, the number of incidents rose from five to 12 between 2016 and 2017."[126] The report also states that around 100 pirates were killed by armed maritime security personnel "who are increasingly seen to be of central importance to the protection of merchant ships."

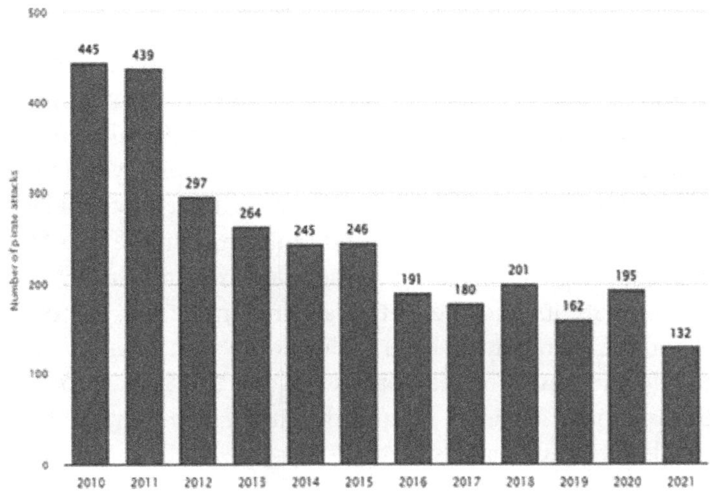

Number of pirate attacks worldwide (2010-2021). Source: statistica.com

In Indian waters, analyst reports state that during the initial year of the Covid Pandemic alone there have been six piracy attacks which included actual boarding of merchant vessels. This is stated to be an increase in attacks when compared to immediately preceding years.[127]

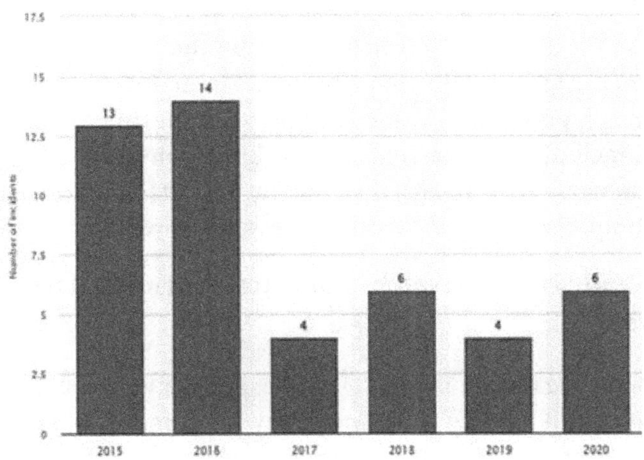

Number of actual and attempted piracy attacks in India 2015-2020. Source: statistica.com

Here to Stay

The global economy is dependent on the vast international shipping lanes. This holds true for shipping in the Indian Ocean region. Reports highlight an increase in piracy especially during the COVID-19 pandemic. The Maritime Union of India (MUI) states that there is a 26 percent increase in piracy-related attacks due to the domino effect of the pandemic - job loss and economic downturn among others. India is especially concerned. In its statement, MUI said, "The menace of maritime piracy is a major cause of concern for over two lakh Indian seafarers as India now provides around 9.35 per cent of the global seafarers and ranks third in the list of the largest seafarers supplying nations to the world maritime industry."[128] Along with the Singapore Straits and the waters around Indonesia, the other major hotspot for the merchant marine includes the west coast of Africa near Guinea, and the waters of the northeast along the Somali coast. There is data to show that the waters around the Indian sub-continent, especially the west, also witnessed attacks.[129]

The General Secretary MUI, Amar Singh Thakur states, "It has become a political issue unfortunately as governments of certain countries are unable or not willing to extend their control over various groups of pirates who manage to procure arms and ammunition without much difficulty." It takes no major sleuthing to connect the relationship between actors in such economically poor societies with terrorists and guerillas across the region and beyond. The relationship is symbiotic - money for guns, information exchange, even manpower support when required.

This statistic is also reflected in a report by the United Kingdom-based International Maritime Bureau, The ICC. Their report reveals a higher percentage of piracy and armed robbery in the initial months of the pandemic including a 40 percent increase kidnapping in the Gulf of Guinea over the previous year. The MUI states that 132 attacks in since the start of 2020 in comparison to 2019 which witnessed 119 such incidents.

Do We Really Need Privately Contracted Armed Maritime Security?

Government organizations such as the navy and coast guard play a significant part in fighting maritime piracy and armed robbery on the high seas. The role of the Indian Navy has been stellar in this regard.

For over a decade the Indian Navy been deployed across all hotspots in the Indian Ocean Region. It has been at the forefront in combating maritime piracy. It has shared this role with the navies of other friendly countries. An article on MoneyControl states that, "As many as 72 Indian Navy warships have been deployed till March 2019, safely escorting more than 3,440 (including 413 Indian-flagged) ships with over 25,062 mariners on board... The Navy has thwarted 44 piracy attempts and apprehended 120 pirates till April 2019, it states." This is as per the Ministry of Defence's annual report for 2018-19."[130]

Acting on the matter, the Government of India has introduced 'The Anti-Maritime Piracy Bill (2019)'. If enacted it will enable Indian agencies to become more effective in combating piracy and administer punitive action wherever necessary. As per PRS legislative Research, "The Bill enables Indian authorities to take action against piracy in the high seas. The Bill brings into law the UN Convention on the Law of the Sea. It applies to the sea beyond the Exclusive Economic Zone (EEZ), i.e., beyond 200 nautical miles from India's coastline."[131]

Despite the Pandemic and military actions, such as the Russian war on Ukraine, economies will grow, trade will go on and the seas will continue to be the platform for large volume logistics. India's merchant marine alone can boast of a total deadweight tonnage that ranks 15th in the world and in terms of human resources, it supplies around 13 percent of officers and around 14 percent of ratings to the global seafaring community. This implies that despite national and international laws and the increasing role of military units in and around piracy hotbeds, there will be a void that would have to be filled. This, especially, holds true for merchant ships of all kinds from General cargo vessels to Container ships, Tankers, Dry bulk carriers and Multi-purpose vessels. To protect each ship would not be operationally and policy-wise possible by various government forces. Thus, the need for private maritime armed guards will only increase. Such a scenario provides a lucrative picture for privately contracted maritime security companies globally. In India too, the number of private security services companies has increased. Many new security organizations have come up since 2008 and many others are including maritime security in their portfolio. Some of the prominent names include:

- Seven Seas Maritime Security Services.
- Superior Marine Security Consultants Pvt. Ltd.
- Seashell Integrated Services Private Limited.
- Bhagyodya Consultants and Agrotech Private Limited.

- Inter Protect Marine Pvt. Ltd.
- Alphard Maritime.

The industry is indeed boosted by the popular saying that "no ship with armed guards has been taken by pirates." However simplistic that this statement may be, it is a fact that is undeniably proven in confidential reports published across many years. As David Isenberg states in his article 'Rise of Private Maritime Security Companies', "When this paradigm fails and pirates do overpower or outwit an armed security crew, the media will be the first to point out the exception."[132]

In short, there are advantages of having highly trained and highly skilled armed men on board a merchant vessel. Adequately staffed, such vessel would be more than sufficiently neutralize any pirate attacks. Panos G Moraitis, Managing Director at Aspida Maritime Security, states, "When the vessel is properly hardened and the security team along with the watches perform their duties and we have an attack, usually a couple of well-placed warning shots are enough to avoid an attack."[133] Armed men bring the 'active' element to defence in case passive security measures fail. This double phased protection paradigm ensures the master of the vessel greater piece of mind and his men - officers and others - the luxury of focusing on what they do best - run the various operations in the ship. From the financial and brand perspective, adherence to such practice may help in lower insurance premiums.

There are, however, challenges in this approach. Using privately contracted armed maritime security does come with its challenges especially when it comes to the regulations of certain countries that do not permit armed men on board merchant ships in their ports. In fact, there is a government and industry thought that armed maritime security should adhere to greater regulation on board ships, on the high seas and definitely when in a country's territorial water. While most of the fears stem from exaggerated accounts, there have been less than pleasant incidents such as unintentional killing of fishermen or others often due to doubt of intent when smaller vessels approach a merchant ship. When in waters notorious for piracy, mistaken identity could cause the death of local fishermen even when the private maritime security personnel have had military or maritime police experience. However, due to various safety measures, such unintentional killings are not as high as those of land-based security operators.

Operating high velocity weapons are permitted under law - especially for self defence on the high seas. But legal approval tends to far from forthcoming when in the vicinity of ports and in territorial waters. This forces "security companies require creative workarounds to avoid the stiff fines and penalties levied by developing and often rightfully paranoid nations in Africa and the Middle East."[134] Today there are a plethora of regulations that private maritime security providers need to adhere to wherever they may port. These include mandatory disclosures to UN Arms Embargo inspectors and other regulators. After all, private security companies need to also be in the right side of international regulatory agencies and international watchers.

IMO Secretary-General Koji Sekimizu sums it up aptly when he stated before the 90th session of the Maritime Safety Committee (MSC) on 16-25 May 2012, "The carriage of firearms on board merchant ships is a complex legal issue with Member States taking diverse positions. The Committee has determined that the carriage of armed personnel is a matter for flag States to authorize, however it has also accepted that their carriage has legal implications for coastal and port States, particularly with respect to the carriage, embarkation and disembarkation of firearms and security equipment in areas under the jurisdiction of such port or coastal States."[135]

Regulations

Such adverse perception on the potential hazards that armed maritime security personnel in port or in coastal waters has accelerated the creation of stringent legislation in many seafaring countries. While the United Nations Convention on the Law of the Sea under Article 17 permits innocent passage in a nation's territorial waters, the scope of weapons for 'self defence' that can be carried is at logger heads with the constraints as elucidated under Articles 19 and 21. This picture gets even more convoluted when one considers the multiple stops/transits that vessels would have to make. Each nation's maritime regulation affects the export and import affect weapons and equipment disembarkation in ports.

The Indian government too is wary of the potential hazards that such personnel pose. Naturally, any information regarding security-related incidents occurring in India's territorial waters, such as those that include encounters between privately contracted armed maritime security personnel and pirates or mistaken fishermen within India's Exclusive Economic Zone, is to be shared at the earliest.

The Indian government mandates specific notification regarding the presence of privately contracted armed maritime security personnel and the firearms and security-related equipment used by them that are presently carried on board ships intending to enter in or depart from Indian ports, anchorages, roadstead or offshore terminals. At the outset, Indian law is very clear that non-authorized military and law enforcement personnel and citizens are not permitted to carry lethal weapons. It also mandates all pertinent information regarding flag state authorization for use of privately contracted armed maritime security personnel including their equipment.

There are stringent requirements on ships, carrying private armed security personnel, entering ports, anchorages, offshore terminals and others. Under Section 30 of the Customs Act (1962) mandates that before a cargo ships carrying goods enters a port, it will share with the appropriate custom's official or officials an 'import manifest' in the prescribed form that enumerates and elucidates arms and ammunition and other security-related equipment and material carried and used by the private maritime security personnel onboard the ship. If the manifest is not delivered to the appropriate officer within the stipulated time and/or if any part of the document does not meet the requirements specified in this sub-section leading to the dissatisfaction of the officer concerned, the person-in-charge of the vessel will be held liable and a penalty will be applied as per law.[136]

The law is also clear about the security and control of weapons and other security-related equipment that are stored on board ships especially when private security personnel have disembarked at a port or roadstead. The law emphasizes that all weapons, especially firearms of all caliber and other related equipment should be secured in a strong room while entering Indian waters. It is mandatory that the strong room in the ship should be sealed with the appropriate seal by the customs officer on arrival at the port after due inspection. Such a secured room will be considered as a customs bonded store room.

Challenges Posed by Privately Contracted Armed Maritime Security

The use of PCAMS does have many advantages from stymying pirate attack to obvious insurance cost benefits and everything in between. However, in the real world, such benefits do come with its share of potential challenges - after all, PCAMS is an unregulated business operating in murky waters. The source of the challenge stems from the fact that the industry is largely self-regulated. This is compounded by the fact that strong international laws on PCAMS are largely missing. Consider, for example, the use of force. There is an obvious chasm in the legislation in this area leading to much criticism. However, that has not led to any legal developments.

This security concern starts from the organizations themselves. They regulate themselves with minimal, if any, reporting concerns to external authorities. Training, personnel and equipment management and standard operating procedures on the high seas in response to threat are company specific. As PCAMS is a highly competitive business, there is no stopping them from training guns against each other. This question becomes even more acute when one considers the fact that large swathes of the open ocean can be devoid of any naval influence – thus making PCAMS a law of their own.

Another grey area is the standard operational procedure of PCAMS. How are the personnel onboard a merchant vessel supposed to respond to a perceived threat? What actions are they allowed to take if a potential threat is perceived? Are they permitted to fire warning shots across a suspected pirate ship? Can they be preemptive and neutralize suspect pirate vessels? Can they use lethal force? On these premises, law is vague. In the high seas, when it comes to protecting merchant vessels from potential pirate attacks and armed robbery, are these personnel considered equivalent to those under the Armed Forces (Special Powers) Act (AFSPA)? James Brown (Director, Alliance 21, University of Sydney, US Studies Centre) states, "There is a legitimate role for private companies in fighting piracy, possibly half of ships travelling the Indian Ocean are employing them but private naval fleets are operating in a legal vacuum". Brown also states, "Private armed guards on ships seem to have been effective in reducing piracy but already shootings at sea have led to accidental deaths and international disputes."[137]

The case of floating armoury ships, such as the Sierra Leone flagged MV Seaman Guard Ohio that was detained off the coast of Tuticorin in October 2013, is another threat dimension that PCAMS pose to littoral states. Carrying arms and ammunition is not only dangerous due to inappropriate storage leading to possibilities of onboard accidents, but due to the dubious nature or the organizations – even legitimacy – due to which there is a real possibility of these floating armouries supplying high-powered weapons to non-state actors, such as pirates and terrorists, with malevolent intentions on regional states.

The murky nature of agreements between PCAMS and various merchant marine organizations, desolate areas of operation, lack of externally imposed regulatory control, existing gaps in international law and incapability of the smaller navies of many Indian Ocean littoral states to effectively monitor and, if necessary, control may lead to the following opportunities (not limited) to misuse PCAMS' capabilities.

One primary concern is the overwhelmingly asymmetric response that they could offer to threats that disregard or that are even ultra vires to established protocols on the high seas. Such exhibition of disregard can be witnessed in cases such as the Enrica Lexie.

Another concern - one with a larger strategic impact - is due to the lack of credible physical presence of government agencies, such as coastal police, coast guard or navy. This gap could embolden PCAMS to use territorial waters for activities that are not in accordance to their 'stated' purpose, such as illegal arms transfers. The presence of floating armouries provides a credible opportunity for such activities. In fact, there is no auditing of the types of weapons that PCAMS carry with them. In effect, they could carry anything from high-powered assault rifles to shoulder-launched surface-to-surface missiles, anti-ship limpet mines, even tactical nuclear weapons.

If illegal weapons transfers are a risk, the opportunity for PCAMS personnel themselves to serve as mercenaries poses an even greater threat. Often with many years of 'active' services in the armed forces, there is virtually nothing to deter these veterans to offer their tactical skills to bidders - irrespective of cause. This could also be extended to the floating platforms themselves, such as the MV Seaman Guard Ohio.

The above mentioned threat possibilities are not unfounded. Much to the the discomfort of global governments there are many instances that showcase the threat that PCAMS pose that narrate against their purpose and spirit.[8] Indian waters too have not been spared of such incidents. The two most published episodesz being that of MT Enrica Lexie and the American MV Seaman Guard Ohio.[138]

A decade ago, on February 2012, the Italian oil tanker MT Enrica Lexie, which was sailing from Singapore to Egypt caught the media's attention for wrong reasons. About 20 nautical miles, two marines on-board the oil tanker fired 'warning shots' over a suspected approaching motor boat. However, this killed two men onboard the craft. It, unfortunately, turned out that the boat was a fishing vessel and the 11 men onboard, including the two killed, were fishermen from the South Indian state of Kerala. What makes the incident a matter of concern is the perception of Italian vessel's captain who believed that it was not necessary to report the shooting. Reports state that a few hours later, an Indian Coast Guard ship intercepted the vessel and escorted it to Kochi for investigation. The ensuing long-drawn legal process between the governments also impacted bilateral relations and the case was taken to the International Court of Justice in The Hague.[139] While the Enrica Lexie case may seem to be an aberration to the current narrative as the two armed men on board the Italian vessel were Italian Marines, it does have questions relevant to us.

The first is the failure to report the incident as it had happened in what THE Italians authorities states as a 'contiguous zone' and that there was not no regulation that mandated it. However, the Indian Shipping Ministry stipulates (SR-13020/6/2009-MG (pt.) dated 29 Aug11) that it is mandatory for all merchant vessels, Indian or foreign, to disclose weapons and guards on board and to hold a legitimate Pre-Arrival Notification for Security clearance document before entry into India's Exclusive Economic Zone Search and Rescue Region.[140]

However, the incident does highlight the murkiness of operations on the high seas. As on July 2020, the Permanent Court of Arbitration has "recognized the functional immunity of the two Italian marines, noting that they were engaged in a mission on behalf of the Italian Government, and thus ruled that the process continue in Italy. However, Italy was required to find an agreement with India in order to compensate for the two deaths and for the physical and moral damages suffered by the crew members and the vessel.[141]

The second incident is that of the floating armoury ship MV Seaman Guard Ohio. Sierra Leone flagged, the ship belongs to a private American security company, AdvanFort. The vessel's purpose is to serve as a storage for weapons and PCAMS personnel serving private anti-piracy contracts. The ship was caught off the coast of Tuticorin (tamil Nadu) without adequate mandatory documentation. Reports state that it had on board "35 automatic weapons and nearly 5,700 rounds of ammunition during seizure. The captain of the vessel obviously violated Pre-Arrival Notification for Security requirements.[142] After due investigation the the ship and its crew were set free by the Madras high court which stated that "it (was) an unintentional, accidental act and not one of criminal conspiracy"[143] These two incidents bring to the fore the challenges that PCAMS personnel and vessels could bring in the wake of their presence.

Conclusion: What Should India Consider?

It is obvious that PCAMS will continue to wield their guns for those who require their services to stave off pirates or armed robbers. But, in no way, is there any assurance that the 'guns for hire' will be used as per law.

What recourse does India have? While the shipping ministry has not approved the use of PCAMS on merchant vessels, it permits their use. It has laid out regulations for private shipping companies to follow, but are there other areas that need to be monitored and tightened to ensure better control ensuring that PCAMS personnel and vessels abide with regulations as laid by the authorities? At the outset, India needs to tighten its regulatory and enforcement frameworks to ensure accountability. It also needs to ensure that the system isn't compromised by corruption which would bring the efforts of the government to a nought.

The ministry is clear that the contracting company will be held responsible if there are any issues by PCAMS personnel. Hence, it lays the utmost importance on risk assessment and due diligence by shipping companies. Shipping companies should be aware of the contracted PCAMS organization and its history.

Operationally, it emphasizes that the command and control of the merchant vessel remains with the ship's captain (master) and its complement of officers. Clear distinction on the chain of command is to be made clear when employing PCAMS personnel onboard. The ship's captain will be ultimately held accountable. Thus, this would mean that he should be have constant situational awareness. This means that the captain cannot delegate his duties to PCAMS personnel. The captain decides the ship's maneuvers to ascertain the intent of suspicious vessels approaching it. Based on the threat perception he commands the security personnel to fire warning shots or directly at the threat.

For PCAMS personnel, regulations are categorically clear. Personnel should understand that their primary duty is prevent pirates from boarding the vessel with minimal use of force. The use of lethal weapons is permitted only for self defence and for the protection of others on the ship that is being threatened.To ensure this, the shipping ministry can adhere to ISO directives (ISO PAS 28007: Part 1 & Part 2) clearly dictates that deployed PCAMS, in conjunction with the master of the ship, need to adhere to disclosure rules. For example, the number of personnel on board a merchant ship and their identities, the types of weapons on board and their details, what types of weapons are not permitted. While the Navy may not be able provide ship-by-ship security and as small convoys may not be operationally possible, it is possible to involve the Central Industrial Security Force (CISF) for this role, without dismissing the role of PCAMS.

Chapter 9

Sailing into Unchartered Waters?: Legal Aspects of Privatisation in Maritime Security

Mahathi. U

Public International Law (PIL) has been deemed transformative by many for its dynamic nature - in attempting to adapt to changing relations between States. Yet, there are many areas and practices which though not very recent, have had very little effect on PIL. One such developing practice is privatisation in maritime security. The reasons why PIL has not been able to keep up with such a practice are layered, and cannot be oversimplified. Privatisation striking traditional notions such as state control of security and related services seems to lie at the very heart of these reasons.

With this issue in perspective, the chapter *first* turns its focus to popular and unpopular ideas on state monopoly of security. Here, it also evaluates possible questions of sovereignty that arise due to privatisation. *Second*, it attempts to analyse if there exists a general security gap which necessitates privatisation in the maritime sphere. *Third*, it seeks to examine the legal regulation and issues surrounding such privatisation, looking into international law. *Fourth*, the chapter provides thoughts on how India must proceed in this area, and whether adopting privatisation practices at sea, is the only way forward.

Security and the State – Does Privatisation fit in?

States are surely the primary political actors in the international arena but not the only ones. The increasing involvement of actors who are not the State and nonetheless, influence the political scene just as much, has led to questions on exactly how much the State controls.[144] Questions that pertain to economy, ones that pertain to security, and many more, arise.

As opposed to the economy which is still a private-public tussle, security has traditionally been seen as something the State has monopoly over.[145] Deviations from this 'rule', in the form of privatisation, remained deviations and did not initially affect how national security was viewed, from an international standpoint. What was affected first, was how individual States viewed national security. Some thought of militias and other private companies as undercutting the State's monopoly and the idea that a State 'needs to be in control of any use of violence or force'.[146] Some thought of it as a compromise of legitimacy. These beliefs have seldom changed.

On the academic front as well, there are a variety of views on this matter. They go as far as to offer an integrated perspective stating that collective measures by individual actors and States' higher-ups are necessary if they are to achieve security.[147] Neoliberalists believe that geographical fragmentation of control will best curtail the power of different actors, whereas the Classical liberalists advocate for competition between State and market.[148] At the centre of these claims and opinions on the control of force, is the international construct – sovereignty. Sovereignty, although without a definite meaning, has been consistently viewed as a permanent and rigid principle. Any changes to sovereignty have therefore, meant its decline and not that it has merely changed form. Ironically, it had long been accepted that violence by a non-state actor is legitimate only for developing States to then delegitimise the practice. This period became a decisive milestone in bringing the State control of force under the sovereign State.[149] But the *status quo ante* only goes to show that this supposed challenge to sovereignty has recurred, signalling the need to recognise an important change in construct.

The Need for Privatisation

To assess why a need has arisen to accommodate in law, a change in practice, we must look at the gap that privatization seeks to fill. As soon as the Cold War ended many private actors began to threaten State-centered security. A number of other examples that involve private threats include militias, mafias, vigilantes and insurgents to denote the erosion of state power. Such weak governments in effect, disrupted order requiring the intervention of private security actors.

Over time, private actors began to show potential in providing tools to fill in gaps left by incapable governments and other international institutions like the United Nations. This is especially true of the Eastern Bloc and in other countries like Angola, Sierra Leone, etc. But today, there are other additional considerations that contribute to the increase in demand for private security. For instance, *concerns relating to Somali-piracy compounded by defence fund reductions have fueled the use of private actors in maritime security.*[150]

Since pirates did not limit themselves to the more familiar coasts of Somalia or that of the Gulf of Aden, and intruded into the Indian Ocean Region, the extent of these attacks and their intensity became harder to predict. This in turn forced ship operators and owners off the relevant coast to formulate alternative plans to mitigate risk considering the reluctance on the part of governments to fund anti-piracy operations.[151] As a consequence, naval forces became unreliable where protection at sea was concerned and refusal to take up underwriting obligations became prevalent in the absence of armed security aboard the ships. The market for private security companies in the maritime sphere seems to have emerged in this manner.

From experience, therefore, as opposed to traditional state forces, these new actors are better expected to meet new challenges that may arise in the future.[152] This is primarily due to the private actors' individual financial capabilities and relatively lesser resource constraints resulting in State forces incurring less costs in their operations while preserving security.[153] As inferred from the above-referenced material it is clear that the issue of privatisation is neither new, nor undeliberated. But it is undecided. The problem with this uncertainty is simply that the rate of division of coercive capabilities world-wide, especially in the maritime realm, does not permit it. It demands consensus on long-contested matters in the form of a single set of rules, much like with the development of any other area under the law.

Whereto? – The Law on Privatisation

Determining the legal position of private actors generally, and specific to maritime law is imperative in order to accurately attach liability in cases of breach of international obligations but to also determine whether their existence is permitted and whether there are legal voids to be filled. It has always been the case under international law that responsibility for acts committed by private, non-State actors is attributable to States solely based on the functions they carry out.[154] The entity must be a state organ, have legal personality accorded under the municipal law, carry out a sovereign function or act under the instruction, direction or control of the State.[155]

In this regard, there is one main concern that has come to light. What if the objective of the State in establishing the private maritime security company was to forego international obligations and perform otherwise illegal acts under international law? The answer to this under the existing framework involves references to the *function test* but is not conclusive.

Theoretically, the nature of 'privatisation' of security, is such that it defers to the already 'public' or 'regulatory' character of the function. The semantics of the term (-isation) denotes that a public function is now *being made private,* not affecting its predominantly 'public' character. To put it simply, contracting firms for maritime security (a matter which has remained under a State's sovereignty) does not imply that the security function no longer remains in the State's domain. It has been argued that it merely augments state forces and does not replace them.[156]

The comments of the Draft Articles on State Responsibility gain importance here.[157]

Draft Articles on State Responsibility

Comment 6 under the Chapter 'Attribution of Conduct to a State' reads that,

> "*...the conduct of certain institutions performing public functions and exercising public powers (e.g. the police) is attributed to the State even if those institutions are regarded in internal law as autonomous and independent of the executive government*"

Further, Comment 2 to Article 5 reads that,

> "*...in some countries private security firms may be contracted to act as prison guards and in that capacity may exercise public powers such as powers of detention and discipline pursuant to a judicial sentence or to prison regulations.*"

From a reading of the generally accepted comments and the term 'privatisation', it may be argued that more often than not, all acts of the private security personnel or company will be attributable to the State. It would then follow that if private actors are being recruited to commit breaches of the law, the State cannot simply wash its hands away when challenges to such breaches are raised, owing to the seemingly low threshold for attribution. Moreover, considering private actors' significance not only to the State's regional affairs, but also to its international standing, their acts can seldom be completely autonomous or unregulated.

On the other hand, it could also be argued that, for practical purposes, a contractual relationship does not always infer that they are acting under the direction of the State or under its control.[158] In such cases, allegations of international law violations might not prevail without these entities being subject to them in the first place unless the State's due diligence fails international standards.[159]

In line with this approach, it is interesting to note that no state has till date been found responsible for the illegal acts of private entities under PIL. This is also because onerous responsibility on the State for these acts would be unjust, especially if the entity's clients also include non-State actors. This has resulted in advocacy for a shared responsibility regime.[160] But no single or concrete set of rules has emerged from it.

The developing standards under the Montreux Document[161] and the International Code of Conduct for Private Security Companies[162] (ICoC) are the closest available codified regulatory mechanisms on the matter apart from the occasional directions from the International Maritime Organisation (IMO) which are specific to issues at sea.

Montreux and ICoC

The Montreux Document is a first of its kind intergovernmental statement of existing legal obligations with regard to a State's private security actors. Whereas, the ICoC aims to ensure that private security industry standards are uniformly improved, and that human rights standards are met using a certification or audit process in addition to oversight measures. Obligations under these documents, however, are not many and are more self-regulatory than mandatory.

International Maritime Organisation

According to the IMO the use of private and armed security beyond territorial sea limits is of concern only to the Flag state. Although the stance of the IMO clarifies that any issue associated with private actors aboard vessels must be addressed by respective flag state, and this is endorsed by the US, UK etc., many others have a different view, including countries like Portugal. Many States did not consent to the implementation of a self-regulation process like the one envisaged in the ICoC and called on the IMO to establish a standard. Two standards were developed, in response.[163]

The common problem with all existing frameworks and these documents, is this: Shipping companies' concerns with respect to hiring private security personnel remain unresolved and waters made murkier due to the presence of two geographically-based standards and possibly more to come. A comprehensive international document seems to be the inescapable solution.

Municipal Law

From a municipal law standpoint, some might argue in favour of context while interpreting existing rules or in the creation of new ones. They may contend that the position will differ from State to State or that every fact situation is open to interpretation. These arguments cannot be rejected summarily and must be accounted for. To tackle such potential legal and logistical challenges and avoid unnecessary disputes, the relevant country must ensure that a law is enacted to cover the extent of autonomy of such private entities, their exact functions and objectives consistent with internationally developed principles.

India and IOR

In a discourse on contemporary maritime issues such as privatisation and steps to be taken regionally, it is not only appropriate but also necessary to include a section on India and the Indian Ocean Region – both forming a part of the most maritime-forward areas in the world. India has increasingly incurred costs of the previously mentioned Somali piracy due to its large coastline. Once the Arabian Sea was effectively deemed infested with pirates, ships were re-routed through the Indian shores leaving maritime safety in jeopardy due to congestion. The positioning of armed personnel on merchant vessels also burgeoned causing a snowball effect in the presence of unregulated floating armouries near India. The recent incidents in the Indian Ocean Region bring to light the risks surrounding such unregulated entities.

In the *Enrica Lexie* case, for instance, the vessel in question was a commercial merchant vessel carrying armed guards. It has been argued that vessel protection detachments were involved here and that there is substantial ambiguity on their legal status and identity. Further, after the Seaman guard Ohio case, the possibility of terrorists disguised as private guards was considered.

India has consistently taken the stance that the lack of legal provisions and intelligence about ships carrying combatants acting as security personnel endangers not just its fishermen but also its security.[164] It has since been pushing for the development of regulations for the rapidly growing industry.[165] On a national level, although we already have the *Guidelines on Deployment of Armed Security Guards on Merchant Ships*[166] India could introduce comprehensive regulations on detachments, armed security in general, and on the use of weapons, enumerating strict and exhaustive compliance requirements for each. This could be carried out after gauging India's ability to enforce these laws in collaboration with State agencies. In terms of policy measures in the path towards privatisation, India has already acted positively in asking the Central Industrial Security Force and private agencies to provide security to industrial and manufacturing sector units.[167] With maritime security, the decision is not as simple and must be taken after considering with utmost sensitivity as to whether India can sufficiently control its own private actors and accordingly demarcate the security functions of the Navy, Coast Guard and Private entities.

Conclusion

In *status quo*, the regulation of maritime security issues is based in customary international law and *opinio juris*. Newer issues that arise as a result of privatization however, seem to be square pegs in these round holes. That privatisation of security at sea has become the need of the hour, has been accepted across jurisdictions. Despite this concept having gained a lot of traction in academia and in many ways having contributed to policy development especially in States with a growing maritime foothold, regulation in the field has been sparse both internationally and regionally. Keeping this and building maritime tension in the Indian Ocean Region in mind, India must carefully begin its voyage into privatisation and avoid bad weather at sea.

Chapter 10

Ebbing Green Tide Blues: The Future of Maritime Bio-Terrorism

Dr. Ashutosh Mukherji

Introduction

Maritime security constitutes a critical domain of homeland security and especially for India. It was through the sea that Indian cultural and political influence spread to South east Asia, the Near East and Eastern Africa. With respect to the medical domain, the effect on maritime security includes contraband control and denial of access to waters by foreign powers and using the sea to reach out during medical emergencies and humanitarian missions. Contraband here, can mean people or living agents afflicted by diseases or carrying harmful radioactive isotopes which if left free in the hinterland would cause severe human loss of life and ability and severe economic loss. Moreover, targeting India's economic zone in the sea by dumping toxic waste or by smuggling nuclear contraband can not only endanger life but also cause the destruction of valuable natural and economic resources and coastal environment. Hence, Maritime security as a domain, should cover not only the threat of foreign aggression over the deep sea, coastal waters and economic zones but also deter narco-smuggling and terrorist ingress limiting the risk of bioterrorism through the spread of diseased people, animals, vectors or contraband from entering the country. Lastly, the use of sea power can help project soft power in the medical domain by its use during moments of humanitarian crises and for medical missions to friendly countries. It is vital in understanding the Maritime environment, which requires gathering data for the compilation of threat analysis and the implementation of a comprehensive approach to Maritime Security. Issues related to the spread of disease, using disease germs and medical technologies to attack a country or its maritime assets have been known from ancient times, and in the present era of non-state actors carrying out the activities of States which use terrorism as an instrument of State policy, this threat has not only multiplied but also diversified.

A nation which aspires to grow must be mindful towards its security needs which include external and internal threats, threats to its trade and foreign relations, threats to its culture and way of life and to its environment and natural resources. Maritime security constitutes a critical domain of homeland security and especially so for India. The Indian subcontinent through the ages has been the centre for trade plying between East Asia and the Near East with remnants of well-designed dockyards seen in cities of the Harappan Civilisation such as Lothal and Dholavira. The Greek work "*Periplus of the Erythrean Sea*" attributed to Arrian chronicles the trade links between the Greco-Romano-Egyptian world and the rim states of the Indian Ocean, focussing on the Indian subcontinent. This document thought to have been written between the 1st century BCE to 1st century CE describes ports on the western and eastern Indian coasts and the volume of trade and items passing through these ports. It was through the sea that Indian cultural and political influence spread to South east Asia, the Near East and Eastern Africa. The maritime history of the Cholas, the Arabs and later the European Powers is replete with stories and accounts of how decisive maritime control has enabled continental control. The growth and establishment of the colonial empires of the various European States and the later Supremacy of the NATO over the Warsaw Pact has further underlined the importance of maritime power in maintaining a decisive advantage over competing States.

Maritime Security does not just mean preventing foreign aggression or infiltration through sea routes or coastal areas, or infringement of territorial waters. It also means access to natural resources from the sea and protection of the country from "*medical invasions*" in the form of infected people or livestock or vectors.

An important example of this was Siege of Jaffa in 1346 by the Tartar Mongols. The Mongols unable to get into the city for nearly 3 years tossed in dead bodies of people and livestock infected by the plague bacilli which lead to an outbreak of Plague in Crimea. From there through refugees fleeing to Constantinople, the Plague reached Constantinople (Istanbul) and thence to the whole of Europe and the Near East killing nearly a third of the then population. This instance highlights the need for controlling ingress to a nation from the sea. In recent times, similar events have come up in Europe of people in genuine distress fleeing the civil wars in Libya and Syria not to their neighbouring countries but to countries in western Europe.

Months later these countries face increased incidents of inter-community violence or even hate crimes from many refugees not willing to integrate into the host country's culture but wanting to impose their own culture in areas where the refugees are congregated. Other examples of "medical invasions" were those of the Spanish conquistadors introducing small pox in South America or the early European settlers introducing diseases in Australia and New Zealand. This chapter does not deal with the need or importance of Maritime Security but how medical issues can impact Maritime security.

Spread of diseases from sailors or refugees

Plague, Cholera, Smallpox and Anthrax: Throughout human history there have been instances when a small group of explorers have been able to take over entire civilisations helped often by the pathogens they have carried aboard their ships. The spread of Plague from the Crimea to the rest of Europe and the Near East as explained in the Introduction is one such instance. It has often been quoted that the victors in any war are often not the ones with best weapons or training but the ones with the deadliest pathogens[168,169]. Plague is caused by the bacterium Yersinia pestis which is transmitted by rats and fleas. These vectors often breed in conditions of low sunlight and bad hygiene or public cleanliness. Between the 14th to the 17th centuries, an estimated 200 million people have died of this disease[170]. In fact, the spread of plague during the 4th century AD has often been cited as one of the major reasons for the fall of the Western Roman Empire. Ships infested with rats and fleas affected by the bacteria would cause outbreaks in port cities, from there the general atmosphere of bad public health practices helped spread the disease to the hinterland, eventually affecting two-thirds of Europe's population. The basic rules of quarantine and health checks of incoming ships crews had never been followed and these resulted not only in widespread deaths but also a complete clampdown on the economy. India's 1994 outbreak resulted in just 52 deaths, but cost the developing economy over 1 billion USD in economic costs, threatening the very existence of the Surat diamond industry and endangering the economic health of important states such as Maharashtra and Gujarat[171].

Similarly, Cholera is caused by another bacterium called Vibrio cholera infection by which results in individuals passing out nearly continuous thin watery stools and eventually dying of dehydration and shock. There was little or no treatment except giving oral fluids with salt, lemon and sugar mixed with it. This disease has been described from ancient times with eastern India being an endemic area especially Bihar, Bengal and Odisha. With the advent of colonialism and disruption of rural economy in India, there were regional and then global pandemics of Cholera reaching out from India to South East Asia, China, Southern Russia, the Middle East and Europe and North America through trading, troop and ships carrying migrant[172,173]. Anthrax and Smallpox have been other diseases that spread through cattle and human which have travelled with humans through sea voyages and infected virgin populations. In some cases, such as in Meso-America and with the Incas in South America, small numbers of Spanish soldiers were able to simply wipe out extensively developed native civilisations because of the susceptibility of native populations to these diseases[174,175].

Thus, unsecured maritime domains open up an entire domain of ingress to a society which cannot be controlled or predicted. Ingress of diseases leads to blacklisting of such ports as unsafe thus limiting trade from these areas. Loss of trade would reflect in economic loss which is a vital contributor to national power. Also, the spread of these diseases into the hinterland will lead to disease and deaths in the population, disruption of daily life, loss of trade and law and order issues. The nation affected would lose human resources which could affect vital industries, the resultant social chaos would disrupt economic productivity and public order; requiring realignment of security forces towards maintaining public order and enforcing social quarantine and blockades to limit people-to-people contact and thus limit the spread of the disease. Realignment of the security set-up of the country towards quarantine control and disease control and quarantining of security personnel themselves from diseases would add costs towards maintaining homeland security, diluting efforts towards deterring external aggression and protection of borderlands.

Refugees as a Maritime Medical Threat

India is located in a dangerous neighbourhood with many of its surrounding countries exposed to internal strife. There is also the danger of terror organisations using people or groups of people as weapons to transmit deadly diseases. While our society by large is cosmopolitan and pluralistic, and we have had a tradition of welcoming people seeking shelter and safety; yet it would be prudent in the present times when there are a lot of non-state actors being guided by inimical foreign powers to pull down a growing India, to have proper safety processing protocols in place before openly accepting all refugees. These considerations should be in addition to demographic, social and economic considerations. A simple example was the recent movement of the Rohingya refugees by sea from the Arakan coast in Myanmar into neighbouring Bangladesh and thence into India. These refugees numbered more than a quarter of a million and while there were demands by some political parties to allow these refugees, both India and Bangladesh wisely indulged in realpolitik. The refugees were first isolated on uninhabited islands in the Bay of Bengal where Indian and Bangladeshi medical teams could process these people. Criminal elements amongst these were identified. Even then many of these refugees were able to bribe their way into mainland India and quite a few have been arrested for involvement in various criminal activities.

From the medical point of view, an unrestricted acceptance of these refugees would have created a lot of problems for India's North East and coastal Bengal as happened after the 1971 war. Many of these people would not have had the immunization coverage available to most Indians and could have led to viral and bacterial diseases native to their original homeland starting here in India. Especially there could have been issues with India's efforts to achieve polio-free status. A similar event in the near future could be used by forces inimical to India to transmit deadly diseases to groups of refugees who would be then persuaded to come to India mainly by the sea, as the land borders are now well demarcated and manned with quarantine and processing facilities. Further, entering through land borders puts the onus on the neighbouring country through which the refugees may come. From the sea on the other hand, a diverse group can simply be launched at the country in the shape of political or religious refugees fleeing persecution. In such a situation, India would be morally bound to care for these people and if proper initial segregation is not followed then there is a high likelihood of the disease spreading into the country from these asylum seekers.

Case Scenario 1: An unknown origin high class yacht washes up on a beach near Ankleshwar in Gujarat. The local people from the nearby villages go up into the yacht and find dead and dying people. They inform the local police who take over the site and find that most of the bodies have pus filled ulcers on the skin and armpits or face with bleeding from the nose, mouth and ears. The local health department is called in while the bodies are sent to the morgue. The local health authority in charge arranges for autopsies, while the local media gathers to cover the event. In 3-4 days, the report of the autopsies is that the people in the yacht died of bubonic plague and that the deaths were very recent. Also, from the nearby villages, there are increasing reports of people falling sick with pus filled sores forming on their bodies. Many of the policemen, district health workers and media personnel are also affected. Within days large areas of the State are affected and the refineries at Ankleshwar and Hazira are shutdown as are nearby ports. Central response teams and those from the military are brought in, the local police are by now largely ineffectual and affected. Military moves in to the area in protective gear, the illness is confirmed to be a bubonic plague of a very virulent sort and suspected to be produced in a laboratory. The ship's log is checked and there are parts relating to sudden diversion of course and taking in of unscheduled passengers who vanish also suddenly.

This above scenario looks fictional but could well happen. There are tourist cruises on the western coast of India which could be hijacked and converted into a medical bomb. The result is a catastrophic spread of a highly infectious disease which ties down the local administration and if not controlled well in time has the potential to shut down the entire industrial and manufacturing corridor in South Gujarat causing heavy economic loss to the country in addition to losses in human resources. The country would have to devise ways in which such hijackings or any movement of a registered vessel off course is immediately picked up by coastal defence authorities and the coast guard. Police posted in coastal areas also have to be trained to look out for potential biological and medical attacks and use of dirty bombs.

"MALSINDO" is an agreement concluded in 2004 between Singapore, Malaysia and Indonesia which deals with permanent sea surveillance and advanced information sharing and is the air equivalent to the "Eyes in the Sky" program with the same task and agreed "Terms of Reference" and "Standing Operational Procedures". This was done as it was estimated that sinking a single mega-container ship in the Malacca Straits or in Singapore port would be more catastrophic than 9/11 with economic losses alone more than 200 billion USD[176]; not considering medical attacks if these ships being sunk were also loaded with infected people or livestock or nuclear waste.

Case Scenario 2: Indian naval destroyer on patrol in the Northern Bay of Bengal picks up an unidentified vessel moving towards Haldia port. The vessel from its movement vector seems to have originated in Bangladesh. The destroyer sets course and intercepts the said vessel. It discovers that the vessel is an ordinary mechanised fishing trawler but filled with people, many of them women and children. These people look distressed and seem to carry no weapons. The vessel is boarded by naval personnel who find out these are Hindu Bangladeshis who are seeking asylum in India. The Personnel direct the vessel to an office at Haldia port where these refugees are then screened by intelligence and immigration officials. Within 4-5 days of this event, many of the involved sailors, officials and their families start developing high grade fever with vomiting and seizures for 1-2 days before collapsing. Within a week, contacts and their contacts of the initially affected people are also down. Haldia port and Kolkata city are affected. Most of the batch of the refugees have also developed this sickness and died.

While this scenario also looks straight out of a movie, it is very much in the realms of possibility and would require a high degree of suspicion on part of our agencies. As explained before, refugees also need to be screened as potential carriers of harmful diseases and then they need to be educated about relevant Indian laws and customs. While events may not be as drastic or dramatic as explained above, refugees from another nation should undergo mandatory health screening and should be considered potential carriers of highly transmittable infections before being allowed entry into the country. Therefore, as at land borders, on the sea also, domain awareness and interoperability between the navy, coast guard and local coastal authorities both military and civil is an essentiality.

Bioterrorism And Nuclear Terrorism

Bioterrorism refers to the use of biological agents such as bacteria, viruses or living particles or even diseased individuals as weapons of war to bring down an otherwise stronger or better defended enemy. The most potent weapons are those for which there is no native immunity such as diseases which have been thought to be wiped out such as smallpox and anthrax or diseases which are so new that no immunity has been developed such as the ongoing Corona virus Pandemic. Also included in such agents are those with heavy mortality rates for which there is no treatment such as the Viral Haemorrhagic fevers such as West Nile virus, Ebola, Lassa virus and Hantaan virus.

Common threatening infectious agents include botulism, influenza, plague, tularaemia, viral haemorrhagic fevers (Eg. Ebola, Marburg and Lassa fevers), anthrax and smallpox[177,178]. To many military and counterterrorism planners, anthrax and smallpox have represented the greatest bioterror threats[179] before the development of molecular biologics and designed viruses. Smallpox's case mortality rate of around 30 percent and high transmissibility confer on it the desired properties to use this virus as a potent bioweapon. There are officially only 2 samples left for research purposes which are stored in WHO accredited BSL-IV labs namely the Centers for Disease Control and Prevention (CDC) in the United States and the State Research Center of Virology and Biotechnology VECTOR in Koltsovo, Russia but the existence of other sources, particularly from the 1970s Soviet research programme or from US Cold War samples as happened in Atlanta in 2014, cannot be ruled out. There could also be instances in which using online available Smallpox virus genetic code and having a good molecular lab, maleficent powers could redesign the virus. The use of anthrax bacilli as recently as in early 2000s as letter bombs in the US mailed to important people in public administration highlights the threat of these "*bioweapons*" which spread fear about the safety of the US Postal System.

It is also possible that bioterrorism take on a nuclear dimension in which a "*dirty bomb*" or "*low yield suitcase nuclear weapon*" can be smuggled in from a coastal area into a densely populated zone usually a target of economic vale such as a busy port and be exposed to the public. While an explosion may not kill a lot of people or cause a lot of damage, the resultant nuclear exposure and contamination would result in widespread civilian radiation exposure treatment of which would tie down large numbers of medical personnel and a lot of infrastructure. Lots of people who after exposure to large doses of radiation do not die immediately but suffer for between 1-4 weeks requiring intensive care as in 2nd and 3rd degree burns before the vital systems of the body shut down. Only in case of whole body receiving significantly high doses or high doses to vital areas such as brain, abdomen or bone marrow, does death occur relatively faster. According to radiobiological experiments, it has been noted that exposures higher than 50 Gray at a single shot to the brain can cause death in 48-72 hours while doses above 10 Gray to the whole abdomen as a single dose can cause death in 2-3 weeks. Doses to whole body below 10 Gray can cause bone marrow failure and depending on the dose received, there may be occasional survivors who develop long-term toxicities.

As we can see a single such attack in a crowded port will not only cause large scale human death and suffering and tie down medical services, it will lead to a contamination of that area and its complete isolation and shut down, affecting the local and national economy besides triggering a nation-wide or State-wide panic. This type of an attack comes with high deniability for the perpetrators and some cam even blame nearby local nuclear installations for such a catastrophe. If one such attack can be so catastrophic, one can imagine the effect of 4 or 5 such coordinated attacks at the same time on different ports or nuclear lower plants located in coastal areas by attackers coming in from the sea in small teams of 1-2 people. Similar attacks can be made by "lone wolf" attackers bearing chemical agents such as Nerve gases. An example of such an attack was the Sarin gas attack in the Tokyo subway network.

Case Scenario 3: In this scenario, we explore the modalities of "bioterrorism" and "undeclared war" with a medical point of view on threats coming in from the sea. Coastal radar at Vizag port picks up an underwater signature heading straight towards port. On analysis, it is found to be a Chinese Xian class submarine making towards Vizag port and is less than 50 Km away. The submarine breaks surface and rises. It sends a distress signal to Indian authorities about fire on board which has disabled the rudder and steering systems. Also, the reactor is overheating. There are many Chinese naval casualties onboard and the captain is requesting permission to beach the submarine. Transmission is however patchy, and the submarine is making straight for Ramakrishna beach. The Indian navy deploys destroyers at the entry to Vizag port to prevent entry of the submarine. The submarine however beaches in nearby RK Beach and there is a meltdown of the reactor and rupture of the hull. Military personnel cordon off the area, but not before there is exposure to dangerous radioactive effluents. This scenario while painting a doomsday picture raises several administrative and strategic questions.

What should be the first response from the Indian navy to such an intrusion even by a vessel giving distress signals which could cause a potential catastrophic disaster when such a vessel nears the Indian coast. Should the Indian navy establish a red line away from the coast at which the danger if it has not been contained be destroyed to prevent coastal contamination. What would be international implications of such action. Whether this action by this stricken Chinese vessel constitutes an act of war when evidently the submarine's steering was damaged and the resulting nuclear disaster was an "accident".

How can such "accidents" be prevented? As we can see from the scenario, the "other side" can cause significant damage to Indian security, economic and public infrastructure in the guise of an accident and later even ask to be allowed to help in the rebuilding. In addition to a nuclear accident from a vessel, if there is a dangerous leak of radioactive effluents and chemicals into the sea, this would create another dimension of an ecological and public disaster which could even cause closure of all facilities in the area and largescale evacuation from the area. However, such action while causing damage on a scale comparable to 9/11 would still be termed as an accident according to established norms. Therefore, maritime security concerns for India dictate that the country draws trip lines at distances from its coast or important sea based or sea facing vital infrastructures and lays out standard operating principles for violation of each of these trip lines.

These trip lines could be at variable distances from targets such as at 200 km, 100 km, 50 km and 20 km or even further depending on the type of response envisaged. These "redlines" should be backed up by naval force, intelligence, fast decision making and efficient coastal and civil defence. Intelligence is a must to sift genuine disaster cases from bioterrorist actions. Finally, as the Soviets and the Americans repeatedly did during the cold war, having a ship accidently sunk is a far better alternative than losing a coastal city or port and its hinterland to the risk of infectious disease or nuclear / chemical disaster.

Maritime Medical Diplomacy And Humanitarian Missions

An essential component of securing a domain is to win the hearts and minds of people involved. Maritime security does not therefore mean just policing the entire stretch of the sea entrusted to India. This would not be physically possible and would certainly result in failure. India has since its Non-Aligned days been a net provider of security to countries in Africa and Asia though under a UN umbrella. In the last 2 decades it has increased its outreach to the Indian Ocean Rim States and has set up friendly missions in many of these countries such as Seychelles, Mozambique, Kenya, Tanzania, Madagascar, Indonesia, Myanmar, Maldives, Oman and South Africa. It has helped conduct hydrographic surveys, provide training for coast guard and naval personnel and set up facilities for weather monitoring, anti-piracy control and repair and refitting of ships.

From the medical point of view India has time and again demonstrated its ability to respond quickly in times of natural calamities or human strife to provide relief, medical aid and evacuation to coastal states and island territories both those which are part of India and foreign countries. The Indian Navy was the first responder after the 2004 Bay of Bengal Tsunami not only to its own affected coastal and island regions but also to affected areas in Sri Lanka, Bangladesh, Indonesia and Malaysia. It has provided medical aid and evacuation facilities not only to its own citizens but also to those of 18 other countries during Operation Raahat in 2015 from Aden in Yemen. India has also sent time and again hospital ships to war zones or countries with civil strife such as East Africa and has thus earned a lot of goodwill.

Conclusion

Ensuring Maritime Security requires domain awareness to create a comprehensive picture of maritime activity based on all accessible information from various sources such as naval, satellite, HUMINT, telecommunications, SIGINT. This situational awareness has to be layered and multi-dimensional including the high seas to territorial waters, including littoral areas and port facilities. The availability and management of information, data and spatial planning is vital to understanding the Maritime environment, the compilation of a threat analysis and the implementation of a comprehensive approach to Maritime Security. Issues related to spread of disease, using disease germs and medical technologies to attack a country or its maritime assets has been known from ancient times, and in the present era of non-state actors carrying out the activities of States which use terrorism as an instrument of State policy, this threat has not just multiplied but also diversified. Coastal areas remain a porous entry point for the Indian subcontinent and its security from various threats can be carried out on the surrounding waters and high seas. India has to learn to draw trip lines in the high seas around it and establish domain awareness and control if it wants to prevent bioterrorist events from happening. The 26/11 attacks would pale in comparison to a nuclear or biologic attack.

Chapter 11

Dragon in the Sea: A Postcolonial Approach to China's Quest for Power

Dr. R. Srinivasan

Introduction

Nations as entities are organic beings and, in that sense, are subject to the same laws of nature that individual species are subjected to. Herbert Spencer (1820-1903), perhaps the most notable but little read and much less studied sociologist far ahead of his times, is credited with the phrase "survival of the fittest" in discourses on theories of evolution. Spencer developed an extraordinary theory of geopolitical and dialectical dynamics in his monumental works – *Descriptive Sociology* and *The Principles of Sociology* (Turner, et.al, 2002)[180].

In contrast, well adored Charles Darwin did not consider the process of evolution as the survival of the fittest; he regarded it as survival of the fitter, because the "struggle for existence" (a term he took from English economist and demographer Thomas Malthus) is relative and thus not absolute. Instead, the winners with respect to species within ecosystems could become losers with a change of circumstances (Brittanica, n.d.)[181].

Deriving from Spencer and Darwin, however, is a quintessential lesson that applies to species and nations which we would like to state in these terms: Nations that learn from their history lessons that have endangered their very survival, attain those capabilities that are essential to outlive similar environments.

This chapter attempts to examine Chinese history briefly, albeit in the navy dimension, to see whether it has made an attempt to learn from it. To do so, a post-colonial approach to geopolitics has been adopted in which we have relied on Oxford History of China which we believe will reflect the western perception on Chinese capabilities and PLAN document published by the Ministry of Defence of PRC which conveys the perceptions and philosophies that have guided them in building their naval capabilities.

China and the Opium War 1839-1842

We visit the following instances from the Opium War to assess China's experiences vis-à-vis the British naval power, before attempting to draw lessons from that experience. The Cambridge History of China, Vol 10, Late Ch'ing 1800-1911, Part-1 (Twitchett & Fairbank, 2008)[182] has been relied upon to draw up these instances:

- (On) 21 June 1840, **sixteen British ships of war, four armed steamers and twenty eight transports carrying four thousand soldiers** had assembled off Macao. On 05 July, British ships bombarded Chusan which routed the garrison after which the British looted the city. (British Prime Minister) Palmerston had expected the capture of Chusan to shock the Chinese into immediate surrender. This did not happen. Since Chusan's garrison had been routed by naval artillery, the loss of the island did not destroy the myth that Englishmen could not fight ashore. (P-195)
- On 21 May 1841, I-shan (Emperor's cousin), sent flaming rafts downriver toward the English fleet anchored at Whampoa. In the ensuing battle, **seventy-one Chinese war junks were destroyed and sixty shore batteries seized**. Then, protected by the Nemesis, troopships moved around the city to land forces which occupied the northern heights just outside Canton's old walls. (P 202)
- Pottinger reached Hong Kong on 10 August 1841 to direct an expeditionary force … that, by the end of the war, would include twenty-five ships of the line, fourteen steamers, nine support vessels and troopships carrying ten thousand infantry. He soon led the first two thousand men and part of the fleet north to the important Fukien port of Amoy. The commander of that region, Yen Po-shou, should have been eager to see them, because he had already persuaded the emperor to spend two million taels on defences there. **Fifty large junks, three 'impregnable' forts and nine thousand infantry were supposed to shatter the English forces** as soon as they approached. When the expeditionary fleet anchored off Amoy's approaches on 26 August, Admiral Parker

did find the granite ramparts impenetrable to his shells, but the Chinese gunners could not keep a concerted fire going long enough. Amoy was taken the next day at a cost of two British dead and 15 wounded. (The city was looted, women raped and defenders massacred). (P-204)

- The British then moved on to Chusan, Ningpo and Chin-hai. **The long-held myth that British could not fight on land was literally blown to smithereens during the counter-attack on Ningpo in which the British field artillery got sick of killing the Chinese**! The Yangtze Campaign that followed lasted from 07 May to 20 August 1841. Having taken virtually undefended Shanghai and Chinkiang, by August, British guns and ships had sliced China into half. (P-206)

- Treaty of Nanking was signed on board Pottinger's vessel, HMS Cornwallis, on 29 August 1842. Its main provisions were: (i) an indemnity of $21,000,000 to be paid in instalments: (ii) the opening for trade of the five ports of Canton, Amoy, Foochow, Ningpo and Shanghai; (iii) equal intercourse between officials of corresponding rank; (iv) British consuls at each port; (v) abolition of the Cohong monopoly; (vi) a uniformly moderate tariff to be imposed on both imports and exports; and (vii) cession of the island of Hong Kong to be British territory. China's door had finally been opened but the negotiators had still to arrange the terms on which the British could move in. (Pp 211-212)

In short, it took 25 British ships of the line, 14 steamers, nine support vessels and troopships carrying ten thousand infantry to dispel the long held Chinese belief of the invincibility of their naval and ground troops. It is also important to note the following events precipitated by these military defeats shattered the Chinese empire, forcing China into what President Xi Jinping referred to as the Century of Humiliation (Ching, 2018)[183]:

- The May (1841) attack on Canton was not of immediate military significance for the English, but it was to carry great consequences for the Chinese. First, in the wake of the assault, with its looting and disorder, the normally rowdy local robbers and pirates of the delta became much bolder than before. Large portions of the Liang-Kuang - especially the hilly border area between the two provinces - were soon almost lost to bandit gangs. The years from

1841 to 1850 thus saw *a crescendo of social disorder that actually precipitated the Taiping Rebellion.* (P-202)

- Second, a tradition of antiforeign resistance was created which profoundly affected China's later relations with the West. While the English and Indian troops north of Canton were waiting for the Chinese authorities to fulfil the conditions of the ransom agreement, they despoiled some of the local temples and raped several women in and around the rural marketing centre of San-yiian-li. Such specific incitements, together with pervasive popular anxieties about the war, *helped to transform relatively benign stereotypes about foreigners into xenophobic racism.* (P-202)

However, during the First and Second Opium Wars, not everything Chinese was as ineffective as one would presume about their ability and tactics. For instance, American Commodore Josiah Tatnall, who was present and eventually got involved in rescuing the British from utter annihilation is reported to have penned exhaustive memoirs. Charles Jones (Jones, 1878)[184] who studied his life, presented the following observation:

- The Second Battle of the Dagu Forts is significant because it considerably extended the length and scope of the Opium War. The British loss not only caused a costly 13 month delay, but the fighting force went from 3,000-4,000 troops to a fleet of over 18,000 strong. Even if the Manchus could not defeat such a vast fleet, as was assembled in 1860, the cost to assemble the force alone is a loss for the invaders. The Qing didn't need sophisticated machinery or professional soldiers to win the battle, instead it was a basic tactic that had been around and perfected since the times of Sun Tzu: **deception**. The Manchus used the invaders misperceptions against them, as the British had seen Manchu soldiers flee fortresses countless times before invasions, and the British and French did not expect to be challenged at the Dagu Forts. The Manchu soldiers sprung their trap, defeated the British, and this one false move by the invaders cost them dearly.

- The aftermath of these defeats and the Rape of Nanking by burning down the Yuan Ming Yuan (Winter Palace of the Emperor) in 1860 appear to have become living memories of the Chinese people (Bowlby, 2015)[185], influencing their special drive to rectify the weaknesses that led to their downfall.

Having visited Chinese experiences during and after the Opium War, we will now survey what China has done to imbibe these lessons into developing its PLA Navy.

Growth Trajectory of Chinese Naval Capacity

In the years after the Treaty of Nanking, China went into a progressive decline. The Treaty System imposed by the British led to similar concessions granted to US, France and other foreign trading nations that took advantage of the clauses of the treaty to maximize profits from tea trading. Within two years of the Treaty of Nanking, US and France had even obtained the concession of Extra Territoriality by which citizens of these nations remained outside Chinese judicial powers for prosecution even for crimes committed on Chinese citizens. Such dilution of control and increasing abrasive behaviour by foreign merchants, troops and clergymen became the seeds of resentment against Manchu rule leading to successive rebellion. Taiping (1840-1868) in South East China, Nian (1851-1873) in Northeast China and Muslim Revolts (1855, 1868-1873) in West and Northwest China had weakened the Empire into a collapse. At the heart of the trouble was the outflow of silver due to opium trade which had exceeded nine million Taels (one Tael approximately weighs one ounce of silver), to cater to which the Empire had to exorbitantly tax the farmers and citizens. In this general economic scenario, Chinese navy received a little more than cursory attention for development.

However, between 1861 and 1875, Emperor Tongzhi attempted to revive Chinese power through what he called "self-strengthening" measures. Part of these measures taken under his minister Zeng Guofan was an attempt to obtain machinery for building new weapons and arsenal. Zeng commissioned Yung Wing (who had graduated from Yale in 1854) to the United States to buy machinery necessary for opening an arsenal in China capable of producing heavy weapons comparable with those of the western powers. The arsenal later became Jiangnan Shipyard[186]. Due to such measures[187], by 1868 China had begun to produce rifles and steam ships!

The reforms initiated by Emperor Tongzhi were not pursued when Cixi (Dowager Empress) ascended to power. Even then, Chinese Navy expanded into four distinct navies, Nothern, Southern, Foochow and Canton navies.

The realization of technological deficit vis-à-vis British, French, and American ships and farsighted initiatives like the one by Zeng Guofan translated into acquiring western technology and propelled innovation in

China. Hsien-Ching Wang (Wang, 2009)[188] in studying this aspect notes in his abstract that:

This paper examines how China tackled the technological differences between itself and the West in the process of acquiring steam technology. It begins in the First Opium war (1839-1842), when the Chinese people witnessed British paddle-wheel steam warships. Having misunderstood the steam mechanism, they worked instead with the technology available to them in order to combat British naval forces. In the 1860s, they experimented with steam-powered ship technology again, but in a different environment in which foreign machine tools and knowledge of the steam mechanism were available. Through trial and error they realized the importance both of machine tools in turning the principle of steam power into a workable engine and of technical drawings in diffusing technical knowledge. Thereafter the Chinese government established arsenals and shipyards that used steam as their source of motive power. Along with foreign machine shops, they marked the beginning of radical changes in technology and society in China

However, Wang also found that "Chinese engineers lacked the requisite machine tools and technical drawing to replicate the steamship effectively" (P. 43-47). Scholars in Chinese history like Jenny Huangfu Day (Day, 2015)[189] even observed that this change in approach to adopt and innovate western technology had to face the challenge of deep rooted notions of cultural superiority and overcome it through innumerable observations and evaluations by Chinese diplomats, admirals and travelers. As Day notes, the initial Chinese belief was that the western "fire ships" (huo chuan) or "boats with cartwheels" (chelun chuan) could be easily sunk by using water which is fire's natural enemy!

Notwithstanding such cultural barriers and the eternal corruption in its elite bureaucracy, China under the Tongzhi and Cixi empires went on to build a formidable steam propelled navy from the 1860s onwards. In about three decades, Chinese had built four navies.

Amongst them, The Northern (Beiyang) fleet was the best of the whole Empire of the late Qing dynasty. From 1880, China started to order ships abroad, modernize its training, with the aid of a few British Officers. The modernized Foochow fleet however was entirely sunk by the French Navy over Indochina in 1884, and it's later rebuilding was largely supported by British and Germans, while Japan was at that time purchasing ships from France. It should be noted also that the fleet lacked ammunitions and more modern ships, as funds were embezzled by corrupt officials (even during the war), the Empress Dowager Cixi even spending military funds on renovating the Summer Palace.

The Battle of the Yalu River (1894-95) or the First Sino-Japanese War again was to test the mettle of this modern navy, especially its Beiyang Northern Fleet. For comparison, the Beiyang Fleet was led by her flagship, Dingyuan, and her sister ship, Zhenyuan, which were the biggest in Asia; German-built armoured turret ships, they were armed with four 12in guns and two 6in guns, plus six smaller guns and three torpedo tubes. The Japanese fleet, including the Matsushima and her sister ships Itsukushima and Hashidate, were each armed with a single 12.6in Canet gun and 11 or 12 4.7in guns, plus smaller guns and four torpedo tubes (Lai, 2019)[190]. The far superior Beiyang fleet was shot out of the waters on 17 September 1894 by a much smaller Japanese fleet, which forever changed the context of Sino-Japanese relations. While the superiority in ship size and weaponry favoured the Chinese, agility and leadership won the day for the Japanese. For example, knowing the iron hulls of Chinese battleships as impregnable, the Japanese concentrated on the super structures setting the battle ships and ammunition stores ablaze. This battle is to prove the superiority in tactics and leadership as crucial lessons. Ironically the Chinese had even employed British and American naval officers of rank to command or co-command their ships. The Japanese too had employed French naval officers in their ships.

The intervening years from the close of 19th century till the Mao led revolution in 1949, had kept China preoccupied with Japanese aggression, leaving little room for improvements to its navy. Thus in 1949 when PRC came into being, the maritime capabilities of the Navy were rudimentary, confined as it was to its coastal protection. In the aftermath of World War II, Britain sought to sell a number of its war ships owing to the impracticality of maintaining them. China stepped in to buy nearly 26 British naval ships. Though in the emerging Cold War scenario, China was forbidden to buy the ships with complete weaponry, the arrival of these ships marked the beginning of the expansion of the fleet again. At the peak of the Cold War in 1976, China entered into an agreement with USSR to buy 36 ships with necessary technical assistance for rebuilding/refitting them with Soviet assistance. By 1980's China set about forming the culturally important four navy format.

In parallel, China also drafted for itself a clearly spelt out policy framework defining the purposes for which PLA (N) would be created and deployed.

We will now visit the Report of Ministry of National Defence, PRC, in its most recent document (2019) to understand these aspects. We draw below mentioned inputs from the Ministry of National Defence, PRC (Li, 2019)[191]:

> The PLAN has a very important standing in the overall configuration of China's national security and development. It comprises submarine, surface ship, aviation, marine, and coastal defence forces. Under the PLAN, there are the ETC Navy (Donghai Fleet), the STC Navy (Nanhai Fleet), the NTC Navy (Beihai Fleet), and the PLAN Marine Corps. Under the TC navies there are naval bases, submarine flotillas, surface ship flotillas and aviation brigades. In line with the strategic requirements of near seas defence and far seas protection, the PLAN is speeding up the transition of its tasks from defence on the near seas to protection missions on the far seas, and improving its capabilities for strategic deterrence and counterattack, maritime maneuver operations, maritime joint operations, comprehensive defence, and integrated support, so as to build a strong and modernized naval force.

The Ministerial document further goes on to explain how PLA and PLA (N) gone about building 'mutual trust, mutual benefit and win-win cooperation in carrying out pragmatic exchanges and cooperation with foreign militaries'. The document amplifies how, beginning 2008, PLA (N) task groups achieved cooperation with multiple naval forces across the globe, especially in the Sea of Aden to safeguard international SLOCs. It further provides instances of China's armed forces taking an active part in the international efforts for HADR.

The Ministry's Document also lays down the undermentioned principles for promoting 'Defence and military developments' in all respects:

- **Promoting innovation in defence S&T and military theory**. China's armed forces are accelerating the implementation of the strategy to develop the military through S&T in a bid to maintain and enhance the strength of the areas where they lead, and intensify innovation in emerging areas. *They have made great progress in independent innovation in some strategic, cutting-edge and disruptive technologies, and succeeded in developing strategic hi-tech products such as the Tianhe-2 supercomputer. Focusing on war and fighting wars, China's armed forces have innovated in military doctrines and delivered outcomes in military strategy,* *joint operations and informationization*, which have provided a theoretical support to defence and military development.

- **Establishing a modernized weaponry and equipment system**. China's armed forces are optimizing the overall composition of weaponry and equipment, coordinating the efforts of all services and arms in this regard, *promoting the balanced development of main battle equipment, information systems, and support equipment, with a view to comprehensively raising standardization, serial development and interoperability*. Old equipment is being phased out, and a system created that mainly comprises new and high-tech weaponry and equipment. Type 15 tanks, type 052D destroyers, J-20 fighters, and DF-26 intermediate and long-range ballistic missiles have been commissioned.
- **Building a combat-oriented modern logistics system**. China's armed forces are putting in place a support mechanism combining centralized and decentralized support, and general and special-purpose supplies, with *PLAJLSF as the backbone force and service logistics units as supplements*. They are also building a joint, lean and efficient logistic support system with the strategic and campaign level forces as the main force, the affiliated forces as the support, and the civil sectors as supplements. Logistics units have been incorporated into TC-level joint training, trans-theater training by services and arms, and joint exercises and training with foreign militaries to strengthen the integrated training of logistical and operational forces. *China's armed forces have acquired a rapid, multi-dimensional and precise support capability*.
- **Strengthening strategic management**. Adopting demand-oriented planning and planning-led resource allocation, China's armed forces have established and improved the *strategic management procedures of demand-planning-budgeting-execution-evaluation*. They have completed a system of strategic plans and programs composed of the development strategies of the military as a whole, and its key areas, branches, and the PAP. They have regulated military strategic planning, promulgated and implemented the *Outline of the 13th Five-Year Plan for Military Development*, and optimized the mechanisms for evaluation, supervision and control.

In order to appreciate whether Chinese policies and programs have bequeathed to them a credible maritime power based on their experiences through stated historical narratives, it is necessary to revert to contemporary western perceptions and analyses, which we feel may not fully portray the capabilities[192] but will still afford greater understanding.

Western Conceptions about Contemporary Chinese Naval Capabilities

United States has had an abiding strategic interest in the Pacific and specifically with reference to China in a pronounced manner after the infamous Japanese attack on Pearl Harbor. The fortuitous absence of the US carrier fleets in Pearl Harbor on 07 December 1941 helped America to declare war and launch counter attacks, eventually culminating in the Japanese surrender in 1945. While mounting the counter offensive in the Pacific Theatre against Japan, United States also mounted a mammoth operation known as the Hump to assist Chiang Kai Sheikh in countering Japanese land forces which had practically over run Han China. It had built numerous airfields in the northeast of British India and deployed hundreds of aircraft that flew thousands of sorties across the Himalayas providing military hardware and supplies to Chiang. In the aftermath of the Japanese surrender, US also undertook to protect Chiang's Nationalist Forces and eventually helped in establishing Taiwan as Republic of China. When Mao emerged as the strongman of continental China and established the PRC, US assistance to Taiwan became the impediment in establishing normal ties with PRC that persists till date. The Korean and Vietnam Wars as a result of Cold War perceptions contributed in furthering mutual distrust and suspicions, initially on ideological basis and subsequently in no small measure by the increasing bonhomie between USSR/Russia and PRC. China's overtures to Pakistan specifically from the late 1980's is also essential to be kept in mind owing to the developments concerning Afghanistan in the pre-and-post 9/11 era. China's economic growth and outreach under Deng and Hu Jintao during these periods and now Xi Jinping, are a matter of contemporary history on which volumes of scholarly studies are available.

We feel that this brief narrative linking the past to the present is relevant and is to be viewed in perspective. In order to study developments concerning PLA (N) in the post-Mao era, we draw from a 2009 document published by United States Office of Naval Intelligence (ONI, 2009) [193].

From its inception in 1949 until the mid-1980s, the PLA (N)'s primary strategic concept was one of *"coastal defence."* This strategy focused the PLA (N) on defending China's coast from the Soviet Pacific Fleet as a small component of what would primarily be a land war. By 1982, despite the lack of resources and continued focus on continental threats, PLA (N) Commander Admiral Liu Huaqing directed the PLA (N)'s naval research toward *"offshore defence." (P-5)*

Offshore defence is a regional strategy that does not advocate replicating U.S. or Soviet "blue-water" naval capabilities. Instead, it calls for naval capabilities suited for China's specific regional maritime interests. While offshore defence has often been generically described as operations within China's 200 nautical mile (nm) Exclusive Economic Zone, Admiral Liu defined China's offshore areas as the Yellow Sea, East China Sea, South China Sea, the seas around the Spratly Islands and Taiwan, the areas inside and outside the Okinawa island chain and the northern part of the Pacific Ocean. This includes areas outside of the "First Island Chain" and the more traditional coastal waters. (P-5)

Events of the 1990s, including the U.S.-led operations against Iraq and Serbia, U.S. intervention in the Taiwan Strait crisis of 1996 and the ongoing modernization of both Japan's and Taiwan's navies, highlighted to Chinese strategists both the weakness of China's maritime flank and China's vulnerability to long-range precision strike weapons. Specifically, *the success of U.S. weapons combined with the willingness of the United States to intervene in regional conflicts made it clear to Beijing that China was not prepared for the realities of modern warfare.* (P5)

The CMC charged the PLA with developing the ability to fight "local wars under modern high-tech conditions." In order to do so, the PLA introduced two key concepts to help guide its modernization: "informationization" and "non-contact warfare." (P-6)

Chinese scholars and PLA (N) strategists now advocate a new strategy for the 21't century, termed "distant sea defence." This new strategy would not bound operations geographically, but rather be defined according to China's maritime needs. In addition to the continued protection of maritime interests, advocates of distant sea defence see a respected modern navy as a necessary component of China's rising international status. (P-6)

Concepts behind Chinese Naval Strategy

The ONI document also delves on the doctrinal concepts that in its assessment the Chinese Communist Party leadership had mandated to PLA (N). ONI (2009, p.7)[194] lists three concepts that appear to be the foundational doctrines on which PLA (N) would be developed viz., Informationization, Non-Contact Warfare and Distant Sea Defence:

> "**Informationization**" describes China's military effort to incorporate modern technology into all aspects of operations. It recognizes that modern, long-range weapons require fast and accurate means for coordinating data over long distances. A military adept in informationized warfare would be able to effectively control and coordinate forces with speed and precision, while inhibiting the enemy's ability to do the same. Thus informationization includes means to protect one's own information, such as modern command and control systems, and means to disrupt the information of the adversary, such as cyber-attacks and electronic jamming. The greater coordination between multiple naval units and "smarter" weapons enabled by informationization gives rise to a key element of modern warfare referred to in the PLA as non-contact warfare.
>
> "**Non-contact warfare**" involves employing platforms and weapons in precision strikes from outside of an enemy's "defended zone," reducing the risk to friendly platforms. Similar to U.S. doctrine that emphasize s parallel attacks against key node s with in an enemy's system, Chinese writings on non-contact warfare stress non-linear attacks against the entirety of an enemy's operational and strategic depth, causing an opponent to lose the ability and will to resist. From a naval perspective, non-contact warfare is demonstrated by the PLA (N)'s development and acquisition of long-range weapons to be launched from ships, submarines, aircraft, or shore-based platforms and the associated detection and targeting capabilities required to employ these weapons to their fullest capacity.
>
> "**Distant sea defence**" While coastal defence and to a certain extent offshore defence have either an explicit or implied geographical limitation (that the PLA (N) would only operate a certain distance from China), distant sea defence has no such limitations regarding distance from the mainland. The PLA (N) would be required to be able to defend China's maritime interests whether they were close to home or on the other side of the world. This is not to say China

> will develop a global navy like the United States, but that the PLA (N) would be required to have a basic global reach to defend China's specific needs, such as the anti-piracy patrols in the Gulf of Aden.

A decade later, in 2019 James Fanell (Fanell, 2019) [195] cited ONI of US extensively to draw up the below given perceptions:

> The PLAN's expansion from 2000 to 2018 far exceeds the buildup in any other nation's navy in the post–World War II era, save for the U.S. Navy under President Ronald W. Reagan during the 1980s. *For China's leaders to achieve their vision of a rejuvenated and restored China, they need a fleet that can expand China's interior lines out into the maritime domain. In other words, they need naval, air, missile, and expeditionary forces that can take China's regional military dominance and intimidation to the global realm.* Because of atrophy of U.S. naval forces over the last decade, Beijing's goal is expected to be realized by 2020. Concurrent with the PLAN modernization has been the changing pattern of its operations. Instead of continuing its role as a coastal naval force operating within fifty nautical miles (nm) of China's coast, today the PLAN has pushed out into the blue water of the Pacific Ocean and beyond. An examination of PLAN blue-water operations during the past fifteen years reveals that "*China's ambitious naval modernization has produced a more technologically advanced and flexible force.*" This evolving naval force will provide Beijing with the capability to conduct a military campaign successfully within the first island chain (for instance, to take Taiwan or the Senkaku Islands).

Survey of Lessons and Their Practice

Having surveyed the Chinese historical experiences between 1940 till 1949, China's stated policy objectives and the contemporary western assessment of China in maritime power dimensions, we will proceed to list lessons first of what the Chinese are perceived to have learnt. Thereafter, we will also attempt to evolve some lessons for the rest of the world to facilitate greater understanding of the Chinese mind.

Survey of the Opium Wars and the Yalu Campaign appear to be giving forth the following lessons to the Chinese:

- The importance of a powerful navy (commensurate if not above the capacity of foreseeable opponents,
- The importance of amphibious capability, and

- The need to acquire extra-regional or even global operational capacity which is independent of homeland, if China were to meet challenges to its aspirations.

There are also certain other lessons available through these narratives that are useful in understanding the Chinese mind in the contemporary world. These could indicate strengths and inherent weaknesses:

- **A powerful and centralized government that is focused on increasing military capacity is necessary**. Manchu dynasty's failure to have a centralized military equipped with contemporary weapons and tactics was the single most reason why the Opium Wars resulted in 'shaming' China. Reliance on sword wielding troops, relying on fixed battlements with aging cannons that could only take on massed frontal attacks, mobilizing regional overlords to supplement troops hastily drawn from peasant population, and disjointed attacks without realistically assessing enemy capacity, for example, are some of the portent lessons that come from the Opium episode.

- **Underestimating the foreign powers** – The cultural perceptions, notions of superiority (Heavenly Mandate) and lack of battle proven leadership were serious pitfalls. This is not to say that Manchu army was not battle worthy. At least some elements of the army were professional soldiers with theatre experience. However, their critical strength was advantageous in land battles. With the vast hinterland where home troops were more proficient, had the Manchu drawn the British into running battles across Han China, the story of Opium War could have been differently. This view was also held by avid Chinese scholars including an advisor to Mike Pampeo (Yu, 2018)[196]. Instead Chinese decided to use fixed batteries to take on British frigates and anticipated classical frontal attacks (them being masters of siege warfare) from their enemies. In other words, they expected the British to play the war by the Chinese book!!

- **Over reliance on cultural perceptions** – for example, believing that Taoist tantric divers could stay under water to place mines on British battle ships; the invincibility of Manchu army based on victories in battles with tribes and marauding armies who had similar weapons and tactics, perhaps far inferior; the belief that "Heavenly Mandate" of the Emperor by itself could dispel

British guns; tactics based on cultural beliefs like 'water is the nemesis of fire'. Hence fire spewing British ships could be sunk by flaming rafts; etc. It is important to note that the Ministry of National Defence document refers to the cultural superiority of Chinese society, while carefully tempering it with the necessities of adopting to prevalent technological environments.

- **Mandate of Heaven in a new format** – Universal peace, order and framework of values based on Chinese beliefs is the underlying theme of every policy and program that the Ministerial document states.

- **Acquiring Knowledge and Innovation** – the building of navy and arsenal as evidenced from Yung Wing Biography, writings of Jenny Huangfu Day and other scholars cited gives ample evidence to the inherent understanding about importance of credible maritime power derived from their experiences. More importantly, sending students across to study in western universities, utilizing diplomatic and civilian voyages as opportunities to acquire contacts, information and technology – these appear to have been done systematically rather than incidentally. Chinese ability to replicate and improvise Soviet designs for their aircraft and ships is a matter of public knowledge. We are also aware that Chinese students and scholars of Chinese origin are part and parcel of the scientific community in any nation that claims an iota of technical knowhow.

- **Loss of Tribute paying neighbours** – The events and weakening of the Empire in the course of the stated wars and Treaty System imposed by western powers (resulting in reversal of fortunes by which wealth started flowing out), led to the loss of Tribute paying neighbours viz., Korea, Vietnam and Burma. This rendered the Manchu Rule hollow, resulted in even their successor, the Qing Empire finally dissolving in 1912 and rise of nationalist and communist forces in China. These again point to the constant Chinese attempts towards territorial aggressions and expansions like annexation of Tibet, Xinjiang, acquiring Karakoram/Aksai Chin and bullying India over Arunachal Pradesh. China's engagement with North Korea and ill-fought war with Vietnam in 1987 are also to be seen in this light. Mao's famous Five Finger Policy, when seen from this assessment, lends greater appreciation of Chinese intent.

Has US been a great source of learning for China?

The short answer is 'Yes'. However, we would like to qualify it a little more.

The interest with which United States views developments concerning Chinese can be assessed by the volume of studies that US institutions publish about things concerning China – Naval War College, Universities, Departments of Government, Think Tanks, individual analysts, authors… the list is endless. Curiously, Chinese interest US is reciprocal. It would be easy to say that this interest is because they are the only contestants for domination of the world order. But we do not subscribe to that view entirely. In our view, China's actions are driven by an urge for redemption through domination and restoration of the glory of Chinese culture. The redemption aspect has two components – redeem what is perceived as 'lost prestige' and the prosperity that China enjoyed through trade which was lost in the aftermath of Opium Wars.

It may be of interest to note that when the initial hostilities in the Opium War appeared in the horizon, especially when Commissioner Lin succeeded in pushing the British to Macau in an attempt to isolate them, the American traders were spared. When Elliot (Factor of Canton) appealed to Americans to join the British, he was rebuffed in these words:

> Robert Bennett Forbes, the leading North American trader, had answered in turn that, 'I had not come to China for health or pleasure, and that I should remain at my post as long as I could sell a yard of goods or buy a pound of tea. . . . We Yankees had no Queen to guarantee our losses.'[197]

As a matter of fact, the Elliot himself had realized from the beginning that *the mere principle of extraterritoriality might seem less important to merchants than their profits* - especially if their competitors, the Americans, picked up their annual tea contracts. As a record of history, Gladstone who was a Tory MP at that time, had condemned Palmerstone's appeal to the British Parliament to approve of a war on China in the following words:

> A war more unjust in its origin, a war more calculated to cover this country with permanent disgrace, I do not know and I have not read of. The right honourable gentleman opposite spoke of the British flag waving in glory at Canton. That flag is hoisted to protect an infamous contraband traffic; and if it were never hoisted except as it is now hoisted on the coast of China, we should recoil from its sight with horror.[198]

To the Chinese mind, this would (should) be an important lesson in understanding the western mind – that behind the veneer of principles of their national or international laws, western governments were driven by their merchant class which in their turn were driven by no greater motive than profiteering. We would believe that this lesson about western minds should have been absorbed by the Chinese since we see the same principles manifesting in the actions of the Chinese in the most recent developments concerning RCEP in which, despite vociferous demands for investigations into the origin of Corona virus and joining the QUAD, Australia enlisted itself with RCEP in its 'national interest'[199].

That America stood behind Taiwan right from 1949, but continued expanding its trade ties with China in the post-1991 in spite of the ideological difference and growing evidence of Chinese footprints in SE Asia, Africa, Pakistan, Middle and East, Central Asia and Africa could perhaps serve well to reinforce the surmise that Chinese did indeed have made a probing analysis of the western mind. Our surmise is also based on statements like "We already have slipped. If we fall any further, we may not recover" by Fanell.[200]

Apart from these understandings of the western mind with reference to mercantilism, America's resounding victory against Japan in World War II was brought about by its navy in the Pacific. In the Cold War era, US spread its naval presence in the oceans of the world through its carrier groups. Moving the 5th Fleet to Indian Ocean forcing India to warm up to USSR in 1971, The Libyan War, Yugoslav-Serbian episode, Iraq 1991, hounding Osama by sea based attacks, blockade of Iran, and other such instances where US Navy and its carrier fleet played the clinching role are not merely a fact of history. They are of immense interest to strategic analysts everywhere else, including China in view of its policy commitment to protect its interests beyond domestic seas.

Carrier Fleets and China

The lesson that again stands out from these contemporary instances is the importance that maritime capabilities, especially of the aircraft carrier class, play a crucial role in furthering what we may say 'national interest'. To presume that this lesson has not been of interest to China would amount to the proverbial cat closing its eyes to drown the world in darkness. Again the Chinese attempts to acquire blue water capabilities in terms of a carrier fleet is an important dimension to understanding Chinese mind. In our analysis of the Chinese aircraft carrier program, following lessons were found (Srinivasan, December 28, 2020)[201] :

Lesson 1:

With two US carrier groups standing at its doorstep, especially of the Nimitz class, use of the entire Second Artillery Corps and fleet of J-7s would have only repeated what happened at Canton in 1841 which President Xi Jinping specifically as the Century of Humiliation. Adventurism tempered with wisdom. So, lesson number one is: **Learn from your history**.

Lesson 2:

It took Chinese ten years to refit and induct Riga as their own Liaoning. The point to note is the rusting old float that was towed 28000 km over two years, became China's credible aircraft carrier through their own technical, homegrown expertise at the port of Dalian (Vavasseur, 2019)[202]. Lesson number two: **Grow your technical expertise to cater to FUTURE needs, before the future arrives**.

Lesson 3:

Liaoning even went through a refit after six years of service bringing new lessons. The third Chinese aircraft carrier is being developed now reportedly will come with CATOBAR (Catapult Assisted Take-Off But Arrested Recovery) design equipped with electromagnetic catapults). Lesson number three: **Learn again from your weapon system and involve R&D in improvising them**.

Interestingly, India's story of procuring INS Vikramaditya runs on a similar dateline to Liaoning. Rest is open to deductions.

Lesson 4:

The second carrier, Shandong, was launched in less than six years from the scratch. An ability to assimilate and focus research to produce what the country needs. Lesson number four: **Remain focused and constantly upgrade skills**.

Lesson 5:

The political scenario in China through the late 1990s to 2012 went through as many incidents and events as could draw parallel from India. Just to mention few events: in 1996, China launches Shanghai

Five that became SCO later; in 1997, death of Deng Xiaoping witnesses riots, bombings and killings; in 1998, Zhu Rongji launches reforms, creating economic turmoil in and outside Party lines; in 1999, NATO bombs Chinese Embassy in Belgrade; in 2000, the purging of corrupt officials starts; in 2003+ SARS hits China and the Hong Kong rebellion breaks out; in 2005, China adopts new law that calls for Taiwan calls for use of force should Taipei declare independence from mainland China; 2005-06 witnessed rising tensions with Japan; in 2007-08, new Bishop chosen by China is approved by the Pope in Rome and the worst ever snowstorms kill over 100 million people; 2008-09 mark the global financial crisis impacting China too; 2010-12, notwithstanding allegation of Chinese cyber hacks and resultant trade issues with the US, it emerges as the world's no.2 economy; in 2012. The Bo Xilai scandal rocks China... (BBC, 2019)[203]. Lesson number five, and most important of all: **Internal or even externally assisted turmoil will come and pass over. As they say-Even This Shall Pass. The country's political, a bureaucratic mechanism must be proofed against such vagaries of the times.**

Conclusion

We turn to Robert Dahl for an interesting perspective on the concept of power. Dahl (Dahl, 1957)[204]observed, "*Unfortunately, in the English language power is an awkward word, for unlike 'influence' and 'control' it has no convenient verb form, nor can the subject and object of the relation be supplied with noun forms without resort to barbaric neologisms*".

China's experiences during the Opium War underwrote the necessity to acquire power by whatever means which would force likely opponents to look for conciliatory approach in settling bilateral or multilateral issues on terms that China desires. That the Chinese navy today has grown to be a credible instrument of national power has been accepted by experts even avowedly critical of China. That deployment of such a 'power' would be seen as hegemonistic does not appear to be a concern to the Chinese mind. Its actions in bringing Sri Lanka, Pakistan, Bangladesh, and Djibouti to cede important concessions in maritime dimensions in Indian Ocean region through debt-trap diplomacy appear to support such a conclusion.

In its own domestic waters (SCS and beyond that China claims as its own), creation of militarized islands, deployment of PLAAF and PLA (N) in force to a level that has come to be of strategic concern to all nations of the world is yet again an indication that the lessons of history are being learnt, revised and improved upon with a consistency unaffected by domestic or international pressures. In the most recent instance when sabre rattling reached a high pitch compelling the US to pull out USS Nimitz from the Gulf to SCS, commander of USS Theodore Roosevelt made a pertinent remark:

> *"We're seeing larger number of aircraft, larger number of ships available to the Chinese military being utilised on a daily basis. So the capacity has clearly increased," Verissimo told reporters via phone from aboard the USS Theodore Roosevelt (Sevastopulo & Hille, 2021)*[205].

When read again, the underlying meaning of the statement by Admiral Verissimo indicates that due cognizance is to be taken of the demonstrable capabilities that Chinese have acquired in the maritime dimension. In addition, the power that they display now makes the most powerful navy in the world take caution!

Apart from the expanding physical assets including a carrier group, considerable attention appears to have been paid to enhance leadership and operational philosophies through extensive frameworks with other countries. It is to be noted that the cooperative frameworks were achieved through internationally accepted best practices in military/naval diplomacy. To recall the activities in multifarious dimensions of maritime diplomacy, we again draw from the report of the Ministry of National Defence (PRC) (Li, 2019)[206], which lists:

- Since 2012, China has held over 100 joint exercises and training with more than 30 countries. These engagements have covered traditional and non-traditional security fields, in locations extending from China's periphery to the far seas, and the participating forces have expanded from land forces to multiple branches including the army, navy and air force. Cooperation and exchanges in personnel training have intensified. Since 2012, *the PLA has sent over 1,700 military personnel to study in more than 50 countries. Over 20 Chinese military educational institutions have established and maintained inter-collegiate exchanges with their counterparts from more than 40 countries. Meanwhile, more than 10,000 foreign military personnel from over 130 countries have studied in Chinese military universities and colleges.* (Italics supplied)
- In line with relevant UNSC resolutions, since December 2008, the Chinese government has dispatched naval ships to carry out regular

vessel protection operations in the Gulf of Aden and the waters off the coast of Somalia. Chinese *PLAN task groups cooperate with multiple naval forces in the area to safeguard international SLOCs. In the past decade, over 100 vessels and 26,000 officers and sailors have been regularly deployed in 31 convoys, each consisting of three to four ships, in vessel protection operations. They have provided security protection for over 6,600 Chinese and foreign ships, and rescued, protected or assisted over 70 ships in distress.*

- China's armed forces take an active part in the international efforts for HADR. Military professionals are dispatched to conduct disaster relief operations in affected countries, provide relief materials and medical aid, and strengthen international exchanges in this respect. Since 2012, *China's armed forces have participated in the search for the missing Malaysian Airliner MH370, and in the relief operations for Typhoon Haiyan in the Philippines, the Ebola epidemic in West Africa, the water scarcity in Maldives, the earthquake in Nepal, and the flood caused by a dam collapse in Laos.* Since it entered service a decade ago, the PLAN's hospital ship Ark Peace has fulfilled 7 voyages coded as Mission Harmony and visited 43 countries. During these visits, it provided medical services to the local communities, organized medical exchanges, and helped over 230,000 people.

That the Chinese have taken to diplomatic, military and personal engagements to appropriate knowledge and technology is a lesson that stands out through the threads of history and contemporary affairs.

We would like to conclude with the opinion that there is something distinctly Chinese about learning from history. While CCP leadership repeatedly calls for reinforcing their culture as the basis of nation building, it appears that they have drawn extensively from that very culture an ability to remain committed to learning from history.

Chinese scholars like Chan (Chan, 2014) also observe that "The importance of understanding China's historical approaches to international law cannot be understated"(Chan, 2014)[207]. We infer that Chan's observation is valid in other dimensions too.

That in our opinion, could also be their Achilles heel!

Postscript

While it is unusual for essays and research chapters to carry a postscript, we feel it necessary to append one owing to the peculiar methodology that was adopted to write this chapter. It was stated in the beginning that a postcolonial approach would be adopted for this chapter. To phrase it correctly, the chapter is an attempt at adopting a postcolonial approach to history in order to draw lessons in geopolitics.

Having taken this approach, it is necessary to define 'postcolonial' approach. John McLeod in his *Beginning: Postcolonialism* makes the distinction between post-colonialism and Postcolonialism as the previous marking a study pertaining to a subject in the era after colonialism ended, while in the latter case, as 'postcolonialism recognizes both historical continuity and change' (McLeod, 2012)[208]. While colonial discourses 'explored the ways the representations and modes of perceptions are used as fundamental weapons of colonial power' (Ibid, p.17), postcolonial school led by Edward Said-Gayatri Spivak-Homi Bhabha explored the ways in which the colonized perceived their colonial masters.

Postcolonialism therefore, in our interpretation, is an approach that studies how the oppressed or beaten views and understands the oppressor. In the context of the Opium Wars, China was unequivocally beaten and subjugated by British and other western powers, so much so that the resultant environment eventually led to a political implosion in China overthrowing the 'Heavenly Mandate' of dynastic rule, only to be replaced with communist rule.

We have also seen that the British and other foreign powers could not have subjugated China to unfair treaties, unless they had held themselves in the classical mold of racially and culturally superior nations. The Cambridge History cited in this chapter, in adequate terms, explains how sincerely the British led alliances believed in such constructs as evidenced from Palmerston's statements in the parliament exhorting the superiority of English race and English arms (P.195). The Cambridge History (P.185) also shows how the Chinese Emperor considered the foreigners, especially the British as nothing more than recalcitrant rebels who needed a bit of 'disciplining', if need be to bring them around to respect Chinese law. In fact, the mandate by the Emperor to Commissioner Lin in effect meant (Twitchett & Fairbank, 2008)[209]:

> They thought of the English more as recalcitrant rebels, whom Lin was going south to manage and pacify. If circumstances demanded it, he would resort to force, but this was not to be desired.
>
> Moral rectitude, decisive and unhesitating action, would awe the English as easily as it awed native opium dealers. 'War' was never the question.

An appropriate setting for postcolonial approach can be inferred from the above which facilitates reading the contemporary geopolitical developments from this perspective.

Chapter 12

Colombo Port City and its Implications on India's Maritime Security

Dr. R. Vignesh

Introduction

In the early years of the last decade, the news of two Chinese Submarines docking in Sri Lanka's Hambantota Port jittered the waves of anxiety among the Indian strategic community. Over the years the ever-growing Chinese presence in the Indian Ocean Region (IOR) has been the mainstay of discourse among India's strategic community. India over the last decade witnessed China's growing ingress into the geopolitics of the IOR through the building of strategic bases, lending loans and supporting pro governments across the Island nations of the Indian Ocean. As a response to this, India's policies towards the Indian Ocean in the last decade were centred on countering China's ingress and preventing its influence from further growth in the region which would ultimately threaten India's national security. However, in May 2021 the Parliament of Sri Lanka approved the Port City Commission Bill authorising the Colombo Port City Project which happens to be the most important component of China's Belt and Road Initiative (BRI). This development at the beginning of the decade signifies to India the fact that China's ever-growing presence in the Indian Ocean no longer remains a probability that needs to be countered but a reality that needs to be accepted and acted upon. This paper focuses on the road ahead for India's maritime security taking into account the inevitability of growing Chinese presence in the Indian Ocean.

Colombo Port City Project: The Consolidation of Chinese Footprint in the IOR

At a time when the World has been engulfed with the shadow of uncertainly cast by the ongoing COVID Pandemic, a major development that has unfolded in the Island State of Sri Lanka strategically located at the helm of the Indian Ocean Region (IOR) has not gone unnoticed by the Indian strategic community. In May 2021 as the Sri Lankan Parliament passed the Bill approving China backed Colombo Port City project, it marked a decisive development in the geopolitics of IOR.[210] For close to a decade the discourse in the Indian strategic community has been dominated by scepticism and suspicion towards the ever-growing strategic footprint of China through its the Maritime Silk Road (MSR) initiative which is the part of the greater One Belt One Road (OBOR) project. India had long perceived the MSR to be China's strategic encirclement of India in the IOR under the guise of an economic outreach programme. The American and Indian strategic community dubbed the MSR as the '*String of Pearls*' theory which envisioned China's insidious attempts to dominate critical sea lanes of communication which would eventually impede India's maritime security and also threaten its Freedom of Navigation (FON) which will threaten global maritime trade. As a result of this, over the past couple of years, there has been politics and the democratic transitions in the Island nations of the IOR have been centred around governments and leaders taking pro-China and anti-China stand.

Indian strategic thinkers have always viewed the pro-China leaders and political parties in these island nations as a threat to India's hegemonic influence in the IOR. Indian and Western observers have always viewed China's economic outreach to the island nations of the IOR as "*debt-trap diplomacy*" which has been interpreted as China's ploy to bring these nations to its control by extending to them huge amounts of financial loans and thereby acquiring greater military advantages from its shores. However, it has to be agreed that there is a great degree of ambiguity over China's economic outreach programme and this may indeed be purely economic, but what is undeniable is that these projects offer China a great degree of strategic influence and eventually enabling them to utilise it to enhance their military presence in the IOR.[211] As a result of this the Indian foreign policy efforts towards these island nations have centered on retaining them in India's sphere of influence. However, the approval by the Sri Lankan Government for the construction of the Colombo Port City Project settles the fact that the growing Chinese presence in the IOR is no more mere speculation but a reality that India must accept and act on. What this development further indicates is that this could eventually be the beginning of the consolidation of Chinese power projection in the IOR.

Implications to India's Security

Accepting the inevitability of Chinese presence in the IOR, it is important for India's strategic community to articulate exactly how it impacts India's national security and to what degree. It would be interesting to examine the statements made by the Sri Lankan President Gotabaya Rajapaksa since he assumed power in the Island Nation regarding his nation's non-partisan role in the power struggles of the IOR. Firstly, in July 2020, the Sri Lankan President categorically made the statement as:

> *"We genuinely want to strengthen our relationship. I have always said that we don't want to do anything which will jeopardise the security of India or act against the concern of India in any way. This is genuine."*[212]

This statement was viewed by many Indian observers as an assurance of the newly elected Sri Lankan President towards India's concerns about the growing footprint of China which directly threaten India maritime security. Again on March 2021 Rajapaksa had categorically made a statement that:

> *"The Government does not wish to be associated with the power struggles in the Indian Ocean Region by the global giants."*[213]

This statement has remained in tune with the Island nation's geopolitical stance towards an IOR as a harbinger of peace. As Sri Lanka in 1971 made the resolution in the 26th United Nations General Assembly and declared the Indian Ocean as a '*Zone of Peace*'.[214] This declaration by Sri Lanka was extremely significant for the geopolitical environment of that era which was shaped by the bitter Cold War rivalry. However, in a pretty ironic turn of events, the Island Nation itself got itself embroiled in a protracted Civil War that lasted for nearly three decades. Post the Civil War as Sir Lanka entered the reconstruction era it confronted a myriad of socio-economic challenges like recovering from the war-ravaged economy and social reconciliation with the ethnic Sri Lankan Tamil Community, it became certain that the Island nation would not be able to alone face these challenges. This where China with its colossal political, economic and military clout made inroads into a socio-economic scene of the Island Nation and with that brought the threat of militarization of the IOR akin to the situation in the South China Sea (SCS). Although the Sri Lankan President's speech of March 2021 at hinted the Island Nation's non-partisan stance towards the geopolitical power play unfolding in the IOR. But in reality months of after the statement, the Sri Lankan Parliament approved the Colombo Port City project that allows China to further consolidate its strategic footprint in the IOR. Despite the assuring statements made by the Sri Lankan President the turn of events over the last months only indicates the fact that China's growing presence in the IOR is an inevitable reality which India must accept and confront. Henceforth it's important to analyse and comprehend as in what ways the Colombo Port City project leverages China's strategic position in the IOR and in what ways that have detrimental effect on India's maritime security and tranquillity of the IOR as a whole.

Like every other pet project of China across the Indian Ocean which China claims to be economically oriented and India perceives it to be military-oriented, The Colombo Port City Project too is shrouded with intricacies that need to be deciphered. Firstly, there is a Chinese perspective that legitimately seeks to consolidate its economic and strategic clout in the region using the Colombo Port City Project. The other perspective is India's which is concerned with its maritime security views the Colombo Port City project as yet another element in China's strategic encirclement of India. Hence both these perspectives must be analysed to acquire a clearer view of how the Colombo Port City project may manifest itself as a strategic trump card for China in the IOR.

Strategic Leverage for China through the Colombo Port City Project

The Colombo Port City project endows China with several strategic leverages which can be broadly classified into two distinct categories namely Military Leverages and Socio-Political Leverages.

Military Leverage

Under this the specific domains where China's military power gains leverage through the Colombo Port City project to demonstrate its Hard Power in the IOR to further its political and economic interests in the region. These factors pose a direct threat to India's national security as it enhances the Chinese military capability in close vicinity to Indian Territory.

1. **Enhancing the Operational Reach of Chinese Military Power**

    The cornerstone military leverage of the Colombo Port City Project is that it endows China with unprecedented access to the IOR. The U.S. - China Economic and Security Review Commission was established by the United States Congress in October 2000 with a mandate to monitor, investigate and inform the American Government of the security and economic implications of the bilateral trade between USA and China. In March 2014, this commission published a report making an analysis of the large scale of Naval Exercise carried out by People's Liberation Army Navy's (PLAN) surface action group. This extensive naval exercise which was conducted in a span of twenty three days had a core objective of extending the PLAN's operation reach across the SCS, the eastern Indian Ocean and the Philippine Sea. A plethora of PLAN's operational proficiencies in antisubmarine warfare, air defence, electronic warfare and expeditionary logistics was put to test, which the commission principally viewed as China attempting to enhance its operational capability to seize the disputed islands and reefs in the SCS that it claims.[215] The same report made a special observation on how by then China initiated in expanding its strategic footprint across the IOR through the financing and construction of civilian port facilities in Sri Lanka especially the Hambantota Port. The report made its concluding observations by stating that the Chinese initiative in the Hambantota Port will significantly improve the PLAN's ability to replenish and establish staging points for logistic networks across the Indian Ocean.[216] Seven years later in 2021 the Colombo Port City project only reaffirms the fact that China has immensely progressed in establishing facilities that significantly increase its operational reach across the Indian Ocean.

2. **Enhanced Combat Capabilities**

    Apart from endowing the Chinese Military with Operational reach across the Indian Ocean, the Colombo Port City Project has the potential of becoming a staging post projecting its combat capability across the region. This project would bestow China easy means to deploy the fleets of PLAN in close vicinity India's sphere of influence in the region posing a critical security threat to South and South-eastern parts of India.[217] This would enable the PLAN's capabilities to protect and disrupt the Sea Lanes of Communications

(SLOC) in the region thereby effectively expanding its Bluewater naval capabilities. PLAN's Carrier Battle Group (CBG), nuclear submarines and other naval vessels will find it very easy to transit and operate across the IOR. Overall this brings Beijing close to Kanyakumari thereby critically threatening India's Maritime security. The credibility of this threat was immediately affirmed by Vice Admiral G. Ashok Kumar quoted:

"To declare whether the Colombo Port City Project is a threat or not is a very difficult question. But when somebody external to the region starts showing so much interest even though they might have rational reasons to do so, it was necessary to keep a close watch on their activities. The Indian Navy is very well prepared to secure the maritime boundaries of the country."[218]

3. Enhancing Intelligence gathering Capabilities

The Colombo Port City Project has the potential of enhancing the intelligence-gathering Capability of the Chinese Military in the IOR by manifold. In May 2019 the Colombo Gazette reported that Chinese intelligence agencies are believed to be operating in Sri Lanka. The report further stated that the increasing presence of Chinese intelligence agencies in Sri Lanka was enabled by the projects in Sri Lanka which were undertaken by Chinese companies.[219] Around two years later in January 2021 the Indian External Affairs S. Jaishankar expressed concerns that the protests against the East Container Terminal (ECT) was perpetrated by the Chinese Intelligence Agency to have it blocked. The ECT project was cooperation between the Governments of Sri Lanka, Japan and India to develop the facility and it was agreed that the Sri Lankan Government will retain complete ownership of the project while the operation to be carried out in a joint venture model. The project was envisaged with the arrangement Japan will finance the project by lending 500 million dollars to the Sri Lankan Government. The Sri Lanka Ports Authority (SLPA) will have a fifty one percent stake with the Indian firm Adani Group in developing the project. Many observers viewed ECT project as India's initiatives counterbalance the ever-growing Chinese infrastructure project in Sri Lanka. The Sunday Times reported that the Indian government viewed that the rhetoric and the narrative around the project was orchestrated by Chinese Intelligence Agencies.[220] Mr. Jaishankar reiterated the ECT as the priority project for India in his visit to Sri Lanka on

January 2021. But the following month citing the widespread protest against the ECT the Sri Lankan Government decided to scrap the project. If India's allegation of the Chinese intelligence being the perpetrating force by stirring a narrative that ultimately led to the protest is true, then this is an example of the Chinese infrastructure projects that can be utilised as an ingress point for China's intelligence operatives. Taking this into account it must be noted that The Colombo Port City Project only further exacerbates the critical threat posed to India's national security as the project presents an opportunity to China to establish listening posts and other intelligence-gathering infrastructure.

4. **Enhancing the capability for Coercive Diplomacy**

The most significant strategic leverage that the Colombo port city project bestows China is it enhances the ability of the PLAN to carry out coercive naval diplomacy that could reinforce the aggressive Chinese foreign policy in the region. Joshua T White of the Brooking Institution brings out in his research paper that there is good probability that China would attempt to coerce smaller states or rival powers in the region through its navy. He substantiates this claim by taking into account its actions in SCS and East China Sea (ECS) to coerce the smaller states of those regions, sometimes by even employing non-military vessels like maritime militias and Chinese fishing vessels. He further states that the mere presence of a Chinese Naval vessel beyond the territorial waters of a Small Island State of the Indian Ocean like the Maldives, is enough to send a coercive message not only to the Maldivian Government but also to India which has long been the unchallenged regional power. [221] The World has witnessed China's aggressive political and military resolve through especially its actions of militarisation and territorial expansion in the SCS, which have been characterised by a complete disregard of the UNCLOS. Retired Commodore Lalit Kapur feels their success in asserting their territorial claims in the SCS may have emboldened the Chinese Government and they would attempt to repeat the same strategy in the IOR through coercion and economic domination.[222] There is enormous merit to this statement as the examination of the Chinese activities in the SCS and ECS over the past couple of years indeed cast a credible threat of the string of naval and commercial bases in the IOR including the Colombo Port City would facilitate the

Chinese military capability to conduct coercive diplomacy which is detrimental to the stability of the IOR.

Socio-Political Leverage

Apart from military leverages the Colombo Port City project also offers China considerable opportunity to enhance its soft power capabilities in Sri Lanka. These socio-political leverages may not pose a direct threat to India's national security as the military leverages, but have the capability to latently change India's perception among its neighbouring countries which have traditionally viewed India's influence in the region in a positive manner. These leverages include the following:

1. Economic Outreach

The subjugation of South Asia by the Europeans in the past was initiated through economic means. The South Asian colonial history is a testament to how the European colonial powers used economic outreach as a guise to subsequently achieve political domination of the region. By observing China's economic outreach to South Asian nations like Sri Lanka one can draw parallels to the colonial history of the region. The developments in Sri Lanka over the past decade is a quintessential illustration of China's Debt Trap Diplomacy. The term alleges China purposefully lending unsustainable debt for infrastructure projects with the developing nations along with its Belt and Road initiative. Already Sri Lanka's Hambantota project is viewed as the illustration of this strategy with a Chinese owned firm acquiring a ninety-nine year lease in 2017 after the failure of the Sri Lankan government to repay its debts to China. Some observers have also laid accusations on the political leaders of Sri Lanka who despite knowing the ulterior motives of China's debt-trap diplomacy have used the Chinese lending for fulfilling their own domestic political ends.[223] Strategic commentators were quick to point out that the Sri Lankan Government's approval of the Colombo Port City Project as a sign of Colombo deliberately falling again into the premeditated scheme of China's debt-trap diplomacy through leasing its strategic assets debt-equity swaps for creating extra-jurisdictional special economic zones. Sri Lankan geopolitical analyst Asanga Abeyagoonsekera has attributed the Sri Lankan Government's hurried to pass of the Port City Bill to the worsening economic situation in the Island nation as a fallout of the COVID Pandemic.[224] Sri Lanka's foreign capital inflow has been heavily impacted and this was acknowledged by Secretary to the Sri Lankan President, Mr. PB Jaya Sundara who remarked that:

"The Colombo Port City Legislation enables Sri Lanka to create a service centre with an incentive structure that will encourage the Foreign Direct Investments (FDIs) on a much stronger footing."[225]

These developments are indeed indicators of China has successfully consolidated its footing in Sri Lanka through its economic outreach programme. The fact that China has indeed successfully projected itself as a reliable economic partner to smaller economies like Sri Lanka. However, the concern is whether Chinese generosity has an ulterior motive to jeopardise the security of the IOR.

2. Political Outreach

The consolidation of the Chinese political influence over Sri Lanka is the driving force CCP behind extending the generous economic and infrastructure projects as part of its greater BRI strategy. The Colombo Port City project yet again can be viewed as another political avenue for China to influence the political discourse in Sri Lanka. A notable development illustrating this fact is the Sri Lankan Government's issuing of the special coin to commemorate the centenary event of the establishment of the Chinese Communist Party (CCP). Observers were quick to decipher that this was indeed a sign of the Rajapaksha regime's China dependency.[226] Now that over the past decade China has very successfully managed to consolidate its economic foothold in Sri Lanka through the slew of economic and infrastructure projects, it can be expected they may initiate efforts to secure the political alignment of democratic nations like Sri Lanka. For India, this would fundamentally be a setback for India's neighbourhood policy which it has long enjoyed a de-facto political influence over its smaller neighbours owing to geographic, cultural and economic factors. As a result of this traditionally India's neighbours excluding China and Pakistan had symbiotic bilateral relations with India. However, China's political ingress into Sri Lanka further consolidates that the fact that India's special relationship with its smaller neighbours may be under threat, thereby threatening regional security.

3. **Socio-Cultural Outreach**

The successful Economic and Political ingress that infrastructure projects like the Colombo Port City offers China the avenue influence the social and cultural, which are critical for any dominating nation to acquire control of the socio-political narrative of the nation. A retired Indian diplomat noted that the recent trend of the Chinese footprint in Sri Lanka expanding into the island's Tamil-dominated areas which were traditionally bastions of India's influence owing to the Tamil population's linguistic, cultural and kinship bonds with their ethnic kin in India. However, the growing Chinese influence in these areas raises reasonable concern of Beijing pressuring the Sri Lankan Government to open the Northern provinces to Chinese infrastructure projects. He expressed that the growing cultural footprint into these areas could grow at India's cost.[227] This has already raised several red flags among the Indian strategic community by viewing the ingress of Chinese influence into the Northern Provinces of Sri Lanka as attempts by Beijing to establish its presence as close to the Indian coasts as possible. The biggest fear for India is that the proliferation of Chinese economic activity in the Northern Provinces and its subsequent social and political influences in the area could be later exploited by Beijing for a strategic reason.[228] A massive infrastructure project as the Colombo Port City would certainly give China further accelerate its socio-cultural influence in the Island nation, thereby threatening the peaceful bilateral relations of the India and Sri Lanka which largely is a result of close socio-cultural linkages of the two nations.

Conclusion

Taking into the consideration the plethora of strategic and socio-political leverages that the Colombo Port City offers to China, it is imperative for India to acknowledge and accept the China's success in consolidating its economic and political influence in Sri Lanka. India must, by taking into consideration this factor, recalibrate its relations with Sri Lanka as with its other smaller neighbours. One of the biggest challenges that India must confront is the perceived 'Big Brother Attitude' of India towards its smaller neighbours that caused considerable resentment among their political leadership and population. Hence India must genuinely rethink its strategy in its bilateral relations with Sri Lanka in order to discreetly counter the growing Chinese footprint there, which will subsequently culminate into becoming serious security implications for India in the coming decade.

Chapter 13

India and The Indian Ocean: Reflections on The Security Dilemma

Dr. Suresh R

The significance of the Indian Ocean to India's security has long been recognized. However, commensurate with the significance of the Indian Ocean to its national security no major initiatives were taken during the Cold War period. India's policy was centered on the proposal to the eliminate the presence of external powers from the Indian Ocean by the creation of peace zones (a suggestion put forth in international forums including the UN). Thus India's policy during this period was solely based on the implementation of UN General Assembly declaration on Indian Ocean as a Zone of Peace (IOZP). A marked change in policy has been reflected in the post-Cold War period with the advent of engagement with regional countries and external powers in the Indian Ocean. Similarly, the imperatives of non-traditional threat to its national security also prompted India to collaborate with regional and extra regional countries in the Indian Ocean region to address the common threat emanating from international terrorism as it demands a multilateral approach. This chapter is an attempt to examine how the maritime security of India is linked to peace and security situation in the Indian Ocean region.

Indian Ocean - Geopolitical and Strategic Significance

The Indian Ocean, which is the third largest Ocean in the world, is surrounded by Asia, Africa, Antarctica and Australia; the northern limits of the Indian Ocean are well defined by the landmass. The dividing line between the Atlantic and the Indian Ocean is the meridian of Cape Agulhas (20 deg.0 min.E). The meridian of the South-East Cape of

Tasmania (147 deg.0 min.E),the western exit of the Bass Strait and the median line between North-West Australia and the Peninsula of Malay (the Cape of Talbot through Timor, Sumba, Flores and Sunda Island up to Sumatra) form the dividing line between the Pacific Ocean and the Indian Ocean. The dividing line between the Antartic Ocean and the Indian Ocean is the 60 deg. 0 min. South latitude[229]. The total area of the Indian Ocean is 74.92 million sq km[230], which is 20.7 percent of the world's sea area and 14 percent of the earth's surface. (Islands, 1980) The average depth of the Indian Oceanis 38.59 kilometres. (Islands, 1980) The main constituent parts of the Indian Ocean are the Red Sea, the Arabian Sea, the Bay of Bengal, the Andaman Sea, the Persian Gulf, the Mosambique Channel and the Great Australian Bight. The Indian Ocean differs from the Pacific and the Atlantic Ocean in two important aspects. First, it is land-locked in the north, does not extend into the cold climatic region of the Northern Hemisphere and consequently is asymmetrical with regard to its circulation. Second, the wind system over its equatorial and northern portionchanges twice each year causing an almost complete reversal of its circulation. (Islands, 1980)Of all the oceans, the Indian Ocean offers the most suitable navigational environment round the year. Its winds are often predictable and remain at below gale force. It is mostly free from fog, mist and treacherous currents.

Geopolitics

Indian Ocean is considered as the heart of global geopolitics, especially in the era of changing dimensions of security concerns and the accelerated pace of globalization. Five narrow stretches of water, the Bab-el-Mandeb, the Strait of Hormuz, the Strait of Malacca, the Cape of Good Hope and the Sunda Strait, guard the eastern and western entrance to the Indian Ocean.[231] The Bab-el-Mandeb is the southern tip of the Suez Canal; the strait of Hormoz stands sentinel overthe oil flow by sea from Persian Gulf; the Strait of Malacca and the Sundra Strait control the sea borne traffic from the western Pacific Ocean; and the Cape of Good Hope overlooks the shippingroute around Africa[232]. From Pacific Ocean the Indian Ocean can be approached through Torrs Strait, the Arafura Sea, Timor Sea, Lombak, Sunda Straits, Malacca Strait, Bass Strait and even from the South of Australia. It is approachable from the Atlantic Ocean either through the Cape of Good Hope route or through the Gibraltar Straits, Mediterranean sea, the Suez Canal, the Red Sea and then through the Strait of Bab-el-Mandeb. The major sea routes, from Europe to East Asia, the Indian sub-continent, Australia and from the USA to the Indian sub-continent pass through the Indian Ocean. The minor sea routes are from Europe to West Asia, the East Africa and Mauritius. [233]

Indian Ocean Choke Points

There are fine important passages provide access into the Indian Ocean, of which five are key energy Seas Lines of Communications (SLOC). Choking any one of them would cause disruptionof seaborne trade, and uncontrolled volatility in oil and commodity prices, leading to upheavals in the global economy.

The major choke points (Navy I. , 2007) are:

1 Strait of Hormuz

2 Suez Canal

3 Strait of Bab-el-Mandeb

4 Malacca Strait

5. Lombok Strait

6. Sunda Strait

7. Six Degree Channel

8. Nine Degree Channel

9. Cape of Good Hope

Indian Ocean - Strategic Significance

The strategic importance of the Indian Ocean lies in its geographic setting as it is a sea-line of communication between the East and West. Further since power can exercise by controlling islandic territories of the Indian Ocean they are strategically important. These include from the west to east, Mallagasy, Comoros, Seychelles, Chogos Archipelago, Socotra, Indian Coral Atoll, Laccadives, Sri Lanka, the chain of 219 islandic spots of Andaman and Nicobar stretching from the South-western tip of Myanmar to the northern end of Sumatra, Mrgui Archipelago and the Cocaoislands. These islands have served as the maritime station from the very beginning and were colonized in the 17th and 18th centuries to act as stepping stones to the "Eastern treasures". Besides the islands, the Indian Ocean cuts across the mainland at various places, thus forming a large number of gulfs, like the Persian Gulf, Gulf of Oman, Aden, Aquba, Suez and Cambay which are also strategically significant.

Geopolitical importance of Indian Ocean Region

The Indian Ocean region includes 36 littoral and 11 hinterland[234] states making a total of 47 independent states with 30 per cent of the world population. The vast majority of the Indian Ocean littoral and hinterland countries attained their independence from the European colonial powers only after the end of the Second World War. Most of these countries in the region were either colonies, trust territories or protectorates under the British Empire which controlled the political, military and economic activities of the region till recent times. The economy of the regional countries were almost ruined by the colonialism and artificial national boundaries were drawn without any geographic, linguistic or ethnic considerations leading to intra-regional conflicts once the colonial powers left the Indian Ocean region. Moreover, in the westerncountries, economic and industrial revolution preceded the political revolution, whereas countries in the Indian Ocean region the political revolution preceded the economic and industrial revolutions. This led to social and political tensions in these countries due to gross economic inequality in the society. It was further augmented by the social inequality due to ethnicity, religion and caste differences. Politically, the region has a strange admixture of democracy, military dictatorship, and totalitarianism; several regimes in the region are politicallyunstable and provide a fertile ground for external intervention. In 1960 the commercial activities in the region increased enormously and the presence of natural resources of oil aroused the interests of the great powers in the region. All the countries in the region, except Australia, South Africa and Israel are developing countries. The above-mentioned three countries and Thailand are not members of the Non-aligned Movement (NAM). [235] It is the memories ofcolonialism, the desire to avoid entanglement in great power rivalries and the need to devotetheir resources to development that have led the vast majority of the countries in the Indian Ocean region to adopt the Non-aligned policy.[236]

Economically, the region has a great many diversities and disparities. The African region with its 8.7 million square km is marked with uneven and underdeveloped resources and low technological development low standard of living with very high annual growth rate of population. The Asian region with its 12.5 million square km of area has an uneven distribution of population, high pressure of population on its resource base, high growth rate of population, underdevelopment nature of economy, low standard of living and low technology development.

The Australian region is fairly developed like the South African area. The economy in the Indian Ocean region is predominantly agricultural in nature and the industrial base is weak.

Considering the population, the food production is less than the requirement, which put definite limitation on the countries in the region. The region is estimated to include more than 60 per cent of the world crude oil reserves[237] and is an important source of raw material and strategic minerals such as chromium, bauxite, uranium and manganese. Most of these materials areexported to the industrialized countries. The local economics lack the infrastructure necessary for the processing and full industrial exploitation of these materials. The relative dependence of these countries on the great powers for capital, technological know-how and technology transfer and manufactured goods is a very important factor influencing their external behaviour. The vastmineral resources and commercial crops added to the Indian Ocean region's strategic importance in relation to the industrially advanced countries in Europe, USA, Japan, China and Russia.

The surveys conducted in the Indian Ocean sea-bed reveals rich stocks of nodules of manganese, nickel, cobalt, copper, molybdenum, etc. Calculations show that one square mile of the sea-bed, where nodules are located could produce about 70,000 tons of minerals which would yield in value about $ 4, 00,000. One square mile of such nodules will yield among other mineral 30,000tons of Iron ore, 3,600 tons of aluminium 2,300 tons of manganese, 400 tons of cobalt, 1,200 tons of nickel and 650 tons of copper.[238] The Indian Ocean has got extensive marine food potentiality. The estimates show that the sea-bed can provide more than 12 million tons of catch fish every year. Again one-fifth of the world's total arable land lies in this region producing crops like wheat, rice, tea, coffee and cotton. In the Indian Ocean littoral and hinterlandcountries huge deposits of gold and diamonds are concentrated.[239]

The Indian Ocean carries a substantial proportion of international trade, even though the industrial production in the Indian Ocean region is less in relation to the world production.[240] The natural resources of the region greatly contribute to this factor. Approximately one-fourth of the entire cargo carried in world marine trade and about two-third of oil are loaded or unloaded inthe ports of the Indian Ocean region. Most of the countries in the Indian Ocean were colonies till 1945 and are not as developed as the countries in the West. The region could not play an effective role in world affairs because of its under developed economies.

Again, unlike the developed world, the Indian Ocean region abounds with conflict situations and bilateral and multilateral negotiation as a means to settle disputes peacefully has been very rarelyemployed. This has provided ample opportunities for external powers to interfere in the affairs of the countries in the Indian Ocean region.

Indian Ocean Policy

In 1947, when India became independent the Cold War had already started and the world was divided into two antagonistic blocs, one led by the USA and the other by former USSR. India decided not to join any of the blocs but to pursue an independent foreign policy.[241] India played a major role in the Bandung Conference of Afro-Asian nations held in April 1955 which laid the foundation of the Non-aligned Movement. India was one of the founder members of the Non- aligned Movement.

In the immediate post-independence period India's interests in the Indian Ocean were largely commercial and defensive. Its economic interests in Indian Ocean were few; largely due to inadequate technological capabilities it did not investigate and exploit its oceanic resources, with the exception of fisheries. India's commercial interest stemmed from its dependence on the Indian Ocean sea lanes for sea borne trade. India's security interests and requirement centered mainly around its land frontiers particularly Pakistan in the North-West.

A study group of the Indian Council of World Affairs in 1957 rightly stated the importance of Indian Ocean to India:

> *To India the security of this region is of paramount importance as oceanic routes across this ocean carry the bulk of her overseas trade. If these routes come under the control of countries not friendly to India, this would threaten very seriously her economic and industrial development, in fact, her very independence. Three sides of India's frontier are bordered by water-a serious matter. This cannot be lightly dismissed ... India although committed to a policyof non-alignment cannot possibly neglect her seaward defence. She has unquestionably got to think of having adequate naval forces to protect the miles and miles of her coastline ....*[242]

Even though the importance of the Indian Ocean to India's security was repeatedly[243] stressed India was constrained to give less attention to navy than land forces. This was due to a number of factors; first, the threat posed by Pakistan in the North West, second the threat posed by Chinain the North, third, the fact that Britain was a dominant power in the Indian Ocean which provided India some comfort because its presence was without any adverse spin off and fourth,in the overall planning of immediate dangers the threat from the Indian Ocean appeared least alarming, and hence the continued neglect of the Indian Ocean as a security threat.

The then Prime Minister of India, Jawaharlal Nehru commenting upon the entry of the US Seventh Fleet into the Indian Ocean, said on 19 December 1963; "If anything is obviously to our detriment we protest if not we do not." He also stated; "Indian Ocean is a vast area, we cannot say anybody cannot go round the area." (Secretariate P. , 1979) India took such a stand becauseat that time India favoured the US presence as a counter measure to the threat posed by China.[244] This stand of India had undergone a minor change in mid-1960's and India expressed mild protest (LokSabha, 1963) on the British decision to develop defence facilities in British Indian Ocean Territory along with the US in the Indian Ocean. But by the late sixties India strongly opposed the presence of outside great powers from outside in the Indian Ocean.[245] Towards the end of 1969 India had also decided to increase its naval capability and sought the cooperation of the countries in the Indian Ocean region to take steps for making Indian Ocean an area of peace and opposed the induction of outside forces into the Indian Ocean.[246]

Peace and Security in the Indian Ocean during the Cold War Period

In the early 1970 most of the Non-aligned countries of the Indian Ocean region were apprehensive of the great power military presence and rivalry in the Indian Ocean, because they felt that it could threaten their security and reduce their independent action. The idea of a peace zone in the Indian Ocean was mooted in the 1964 Cairo Conference of the Non-aligned countriesand was given a concrete shape in the form of a resolution at the 1970 Lusaka Conference of the Non-aligned countries.

The Non-aligned countries in the Indian Ocean region were successful in getting the UN GeneralAssembly to pass a resolution in December 1971, which called upon the members of the UN to make the Indian Ocean a zone of peace (IOZP) through the elimination of great power military presence conceived in the context of great power rivalry and competition.

The 1971 UN General Assembly resolution on IOZP was mainly an approach towards peace in the region by insulating the area from the great power military presence, as majority of the littoral and hinterlandcountries of the region which were members of the Non-aligned Movement felt that peace could prevail in the region by the elimination of outside great power military presence in the Indian Ocean. (UN Resolution, 1972)

Towards the end of the 1960, India took the decision to seek the co-operation of the countries in the region to make the Indian Ocean a zone of peace by insulating the area from the presence of the outside great powers. At the same time, India had also strengthened its naval capability.India, a non-aligned country, supported the Lusaka Summit resolution on Indian Ocean peace zone as it was in tune with India's security perception. Pakistan, an ally of the US, was in favourof the US presence in the region. Ironically, when the IOZP resolution was adopted by the UN General Assembly in December 1971, India and Pakistan were involved in an armed conflict ending up with the Indian army occupying the whole of East Pakistan. The dismemberment of Pakistan as a result of the conflict enhanced the fear of Pakistan about India in the South Asian region of the Indian Ocean. India, on the contrary, felt that outside military presence in the region, especially the US presence posed a threat to its security as it distorted the natural power hierarchy in the region. India strongly supported the 1971 UN resolution on IOZP as it felt that if implemented it not only ensured India's security but also enhanced its power position in the region. India could effectively meet any threat from China, too, with the friendly help from former Soviet Union even if the Soviet forces withdrew from the Indian Ocean as the Soviet Union shares a border with China and the Sino-Soviet rift continues. Paradoxically, though Pakistan supported the IOZP resolution in principle, it desired the US military presence in the Indian Ocean as it felt that only the US presence would ensure its security. Though Pakistan was unhappy that the US did not prevent the dismemberment of Pakistan it felt that even the security of West Pakistan would have been endangered after the Indian forces had occupied East Pakistan but for the US clear warning to India not to proceed further in West Pakistan.

In 1971, when the UN General Assembly meetings discussed the IOZP proposal, Pakistan had raised the issue of the threat posed by India to its security. (UN, 1972) Pakistan desisted from raising the regional issues in 1972 General Assembly meeting as there were some improvements in the Indo-Pakistan relation with the signing of the Simla agreement.[247] However, the Simla spiritdid not last long and Pakistan once again reverted back to focusing on the threat from within the region in the 1973 Ad hoc Committee on Indian Ocean meeting and the First Committee meeting of the UN General Assembly. In the Ad hoc Committee meeting Pakistan enthusiastically raised the issue of the regional threat to peace as the Committee was mainly constituted to find ways and means to implement the IOZP resolution with due regard to the security considerations of the littoral and hinterland countries in the Indian Ocean. During the initial period, India's response towards the IOZP ranged from a strong support to the 1971 UN declaration as it envisaged the elimination of great power military presence in the Indian Ocean to a covert acquiescence to the Soviet thrust in the Indian Ocean in the absence of any progress towards the implementation of the declaration.

In 1974, the nuclear explosion conducted by India led Pakistan to introduce a parallel proposal tothe Indian Ocean zone of peace in the form of South Asia as a Nuclear Weapon Free Zone (SANWFZ). (Document, 1974) Pakistan maintained that the acceptance of its SANWFZ as the first step towards making Indian Ocean a zone of peace. Pakistan was successful for the first time in incorporating in the IOZP resolution of 1974 the necessity to look into the regional issuesof the littoral and hinterland countries of the Indian Ocean. It continued to focus on the threat emanating from regional dominant power, India, and proposed a code of conduct to ensure an effective system of security within the Indian Ocean region. The code of conduct among other things, envisaged that military balance between dominant regional powers and weaker regional states should be maintained at a reasonable level in order to create an atmosphere of mutual confidence. India opposed the code of conduct and made it clear that any addition to the 1971 UN resolution on IOZP was unacceptable to it. In 1976, Pakistan termed the 1971 UN resolutionon IOZP as impractical and undesirable and abstained from voting for the first time.[248] India while supporting the 1971 UN resolution on IOZP strongly opposed the continued US presencein the Indian Ocean. The divergent stand of India and Pakistan on IOZP reflected their contrary perception on security. India, as a dominant power in the Indian Ocean, considered the external power presence as a major threat to security of nations in the Indian Ocean region, contrary to this Pakistan, a relatively weaker country in the region, supported external power presence, especially the US presence in the region.

A minor change in India's response towards the great power military presence was discernible when the Janata government came to power in 1977. The Janata government while following a 'balanced approach' opposed equally both the US and the Soviet military presence in the region.When General Zia-ul-Haq assumed power in Pakistan in July 1977 he reverted back to Pakistan'searlier stand of voting in favour of the IOZP resolution though it continued to harp on regional threat to peace in South Asia. (SIPRI, 1989)

The 1979 Littoral and Hinterland States Meeting in its final document incorporated the major items in Pakistan's code of conduct proposal, namely, the denuclearization of the Indian Ocean littoral and hinterland states, non-use of force and peaceful settlement of disputes, and agreements on the balancing of the military strength between the major littoral powers and the weaker regional countries. While Pakistan was happy with the inclusion of these items n the final document of the Littoral and Hinterland States Meeting, India was not in favour of its inclusion. India was against extending the territorial limits of the peace zone to the national boundaries of the littoral and hinterland states.[249]

The 1977-78, US-USSR talks on arms limitation in the Indian Ocean and the response of India and Pakistan reflected once again the divergent approaches of India and Pakistan in making the Indian Ocean a zone of peace. (Record, 1978)India supported the super power talks on arms limitation and termed it as a step towards the eventual elimination of great power military presence from the Indian Ocean. Pakistan, contrary, to this, was opposed to the super power talkson arms limitation as it considered that mere elimination of great power military presence or the limitation of it did not ensure the security of the smaller countries in the region against the threat emanating from dominant regional powers. Pakistan demanded the reduction of the military forces of dominant powers within the region.

The Soviet intervention in Afghanistan in December 1979 and Pakistan becoming one of the frontline states in the US counter strategy to contain Soviet expansionism in the Indian Ocean region led to Pakistan's strong support to the US presence in the Indian Ocean. Pakistan felt that its security was threatened by the Soviet troops stationed in Afghanistan and the presence of dominant power India. India's silence on the Soviet action in Afghanistan intrigued Pakistan. (Khalizad, 1987) Hence Pakistan, in addition to the code of conduct demanded the Soviet troop withdrawal from Afghanistan as a precondition to any initiative to make Indian Ocean a zone of peace. Unlike India, Pakistan was opposed to the early convening of the conference on Indian Ocean. India was concerned about the security threat posed by the militarization of the Indian Ocean and the US supply of sophisticated arms to Pakistan. Hence, India pleaded for an early convening of the conference on the Indian Ocean in order to implement the 1971 UN resolution on IOZP. By 1981, as the security environment in South Asia aggravated with the increased super power involvement, India was even agreed to consider the security concerns of the smaller countries in the region, once the reduction of great power military presence in the Indian Ocean was achieved.

Despite change of government in India and Pakistan in 1985 and 1988 respectively, both governments continued to maintain their respective stands on IOZP without any change. India continued to maintain that the sole purpose of IOZP resolution was the elimination of great power military presence in the Indian Ocean. Pakistan, on the contrary, maintained that the SANWFZ and other items included in the code of conduct were the necessary preconditions to make Indian Ocean a zone of peace. These stands of India and Pakistan were also reflected in the 1989 NAM, Commonwealth and UN General Assembly meetings. (Document, 1979)

During the cold war period India's major contention was that the great power military presence was the cause of regional disharmony and tension, hence it wanted the great powers to withdraw from the Indian Ocean. Pakistani contention, on the contrary, was that the regional disharmony was the cause of great power military presence and hence it wanted the resolution of regional issues first, before considering the elimination of great power military presence.

Thus, it is clear that India tried to enhance its power position not only by supporting the elimination of great power military presence as envisaged in the 1971 UN resolution on IOZP but also by keeping its nuclear weapon option open. Pakistan supported the US presence as it perceived threat from India. Pakistan believed that a just solution to regional issues including the Kashmir problem based on the UN resolution can be possible only with the US support. The divergent stand taken by countries in the region also helped the super powers to continue and enhance their military presence in the region. Simultaneously the cold war situation as a result ofsuper power rivalry also augmented the regional disputes.

The security situation in the Indian Ocean region during the Cold War period was appeared to bebased on three inter-related factors; first the asymmetries in the military power between intra- regional powers especially in the context of unresolved regional issues; second the outside great power interest and activities in the region; and third the interaction between intra-regional asymmetries and outside great power interests. In such a situation of mutual distrust among countries in the region any efforts towards peace would be an exercise in futility.

Security in the Indian Ocean: The Post-Cold War Scenario

Peace and security efforts in the Indian Ocean underwent a major turn in the post-Cold War period. The context in which the countries in the region initiated the IOZP has considerably been changed. The super power rivalry has come to an end with the disintegration of Soviet Union. However, a change in the international power structure, from bipolar system to unipolar/multiploar system, does not necessarily ensure peace in the Indian Ocean.[250] The threat perceived by countries in the region in the context of great power rivalry has been ended. However, the presences of the external powers continue in the Indian Ocean region. With the change in the international power structure, the threat perceptions of the countries in the region have also underwent a marked change. The post-cold war blurred boundaries between national security and international security on the one hand, and national security and human security on the other demands better cooperation among nations.

Security in the Indian Ocean: US role in the Post-Cold War Period

The US policy immediately after the end of Cold War was to ensure that no rival super power is allowed to emerge in Western Europe, Asia or the territory of the former Soviet Union, the US isto maintain sufficient military might to deter any nation or group of nations from challenging the US supremacy and to prevent proliferation of nuclear weapons and other weapons of mass destruction and deter attack from regional forces. (Times, 1991) This general policy of the US was well reflected in the Indian Ocean region also.

The geo strategic environment in the Indian Ocean underwent a radical change in the early 90due to two factors. One was the disintegration of the former Soviet Union which resulted in the formal end of cold war. The other was the Gulf war. As a consequence, all the earlier propositions of security in the cold war period have become totally redundant. The end of cold war has removed the necessity to attempt to prevent the negative consequences of superpower rivalry. Simultaneously the Gulf war shattered the illusion of regional security.

The Gulf war has left the US with the problem of protecting its security interest in the Persian Gulf for a long term. These interests include the continued supply of oil at reasonable price, the security of the Gulf Cooperation Council (GCC) countries and the prevention of any single power from gaining control over the bulk of the Gulf oil resources and using the revenue to undermine the regional order.

In the Cold War period a variety of strategies had been used to protect these interests. This includes reliance on the British presence in the region until 1971, support for Iran under the Shahuntil 1979 and support for Iraq during its war with Iran. The regional power equilibrium in the Persian Gulf was collapsed when the balance of power shifted decisively in favour of Iraq andthe countries in the region were unable to pose a credible deterrent to Iraqi aggression. This necessitated the outside power intervention in the region to maintain status quo.

The US strategy after its punitive action against Iraq was to evolve a security system in the north western part of the Indian Ocean with all the six members of the GCC. The US also received cooperation from Egypt and Syria in maintaining a big force to ward off any threat from any quarters in the region. But they could not get much support from all the GCC member countries, as a few countries were reluctant to have foreign troops in the region. Finally the US signed a 10 year agreement with Kuwait on 19 September 1991. The then US Defence Secretary, Dick Cheney told the US Congressional Committee in February 1992 that the US was going to expandits presence in West Asia and also its Rapid Deployment Force for swift decisive victory if the US has to fight against any third world country in the regional wars. Elaborating on his statementhe further said "…in South West Asia we are striving with friends and allies to build a more stable security structure than the one that failed on 2 August 1990. But we have major interest in that part of the world and we must remain engaged to protect those interests. Therefore, we will increase our presence compared to the pre-crisis period. Hence we must be prepared to face adversaries on their term possibly involving the use of weapons of mass destruction and ballistic or cruise missiles". (News, 1992) This was the immediate strategy of the US to meet the post- Cold War situation.

This strategy of the US had practical application in the region within a short span of time. The 11September 2001 (9/11) terrorist attack on US world trade centre and the consequent Afghanistan war to do away with terrorism from there, and ensuing Iraq war to dethrone the dictatorial regime of Saddam Hussein, have demonstrated the US capability to intervene effectively in the region to protect its foreign policy objectives through coercive means. These developments marked the active and effective involvement of an external power in the region to maintain international peace and security in accordance with its own perception.

After the terrorist attack on the US there were two important questions, on the state sponsored terrorism and on the security threats to nation states from non-state actors. The international organizations are not well equipped in terms of military power and resources to effectively meet any challenges to international peace and security posed by non-state actors. In such a situation, US, the sole superpower in the post-Cold War period, had taken over the responsibility to maintain peace and security in the region. The 9/11 attacks on the US attracted the attention of international community to wipe out terrorism from the region. The US led 'war on terror' once again legitimized not only the US presence in the region but also its active interventions. In the post-Cold War period there was realignment and regrouping in the Indian Ocean region. The Indo-US relation improved further and India had entered into close collaboration with the US on defence and security issues.[251]

Importance of External Power Presence

The existence of international terrorism in the region in the post-Cold War period, the shift in theinternational power structure from bipolar to uniploar, had also influenced the perceptions of countries in the Indian Ocean region about the external power presence. The sponsor of the IOZP, Sri Lanka now perceives the external power presence inevitable in the region. Likewise one of the strong supporters of the 1971 UN resolution on IOZP, India has no hesitation to work in tandem with the US to monitor peace and security in the region. This change in the perception of countries in the region about the outside power presence made the 1971 UN declaration on IOZP a dead proposal. The emerging security situation appended with the accelerated pace of globalization demands better cooperation between regional and extra regional countries in the Indian Ocean region. It also demands ensuring national security by enhancing self-defence capability, especially in the context of failure of global collective security mechanism to address threat to international peace and security posed by state and non-state actors and the existence of unresolved border disputes.

Indian Ocean in India's National Security

Indian Ocean is very important to India's military, economic, energy, environment, and human security. India has a coast line of 7516 km and an exclusive economic zone (EEZ) of 2 million sqkm. The significance of Indian Ocean was predicted by Sir Alfred Mahan way back in 1890s he stated Indian Ocean as the Ocean which decides the destiny of the 21st century. (Suresh, Peace inIndian Ocean: A South Asian Perspective, 2011) The importance of Indian Ocean to India has long been recognized. India occupies a central position in the Indian Ocean region, a fact that exercises an increasingly profound influence on India's security environment. Writing in the 1940s, K. M. Panikkar, like Mahan, stated the importance of the Indian Ocean to India that;

> *While to other countries the Indian Ocean is only one of the important oceanic areas, to India it is a vital sea. Her lifelines are concentrated in that area, her freedom is dependent on the freedom of that water surface. No industrial development, no commercial growth, no stable political structure is possible for her unless her shores are protected. (Pannikar, 1945)*

In tune with the above observations the first Prime Minister of India Jawaharlal Nehru observed "History has shown that whatever power controls the Indian Ocean has, in the first instance, India's sea borne trade at her mercy and, in the second, India's very independence itself." [xxi] It was in pursuance of this idea India had supported the 1971 UN declaration on IOZP during the Cold War period. In the post-Cold War period also India had emphasized the strategic significance of Indian Ocean. This was reflected in the Annual Report (2004-2005) of India's Defence Ministry, which noted that, "India is strategically located vis-a-vis both continental Asia and the Indian Ocean Region." Again the Indian Maritime Doctrine asserts: "All major powers of this century will seek a toehold in the Indian Ocean Region. Thus, Japan, the EU, and China, and a reinvigorated Russia can be expected to show presence in these waters either independently or through politico-security arrangements." (Defence, Annual Report 2004-2005, 2005) There is, moreover, "an increasing tendency of extra regional powers of military intervention in [IO] littoral countries to contain what they see as a conflict situation." (Defence, Annual Report 2005 - 2006, 2006) Accordingly India framed its naval strategy in the Indian Ocean.

Maritime Security and India's Indian Ocean Policy

Maritime security has become an important dimension of India's bilateral interaction with all Indian Ocean countries and regional organizations. Maritime security has become a multifaceted issue especially in the realm of non-traditional threat to security. The challenges in the field of non-traditional threat to security include maritime terrorism, smuggling transnational crime, drugtrafficking and illegal immigration. In addition, the natural disasters oil spills and effect of climate change are threats and challenges that impinge on the national security of the Indian Ocean countries. The economic dimension of security challenges in the Indian Ocean region willbecome important in order to ensure security of vital trade routes particularly the choke points in the Indian Ocean.

In the post-Cold War period, nations are very careful in their interaction with one another as the bipolar system ended. During the Cold War period there was some kind of discipline among nation states imposed by the ideological confrontation. The international politics of the post-Cold War is not the same in the Cold War period. There is no ideological confrontation at the international level. Nations are more concerned about resolving their basic economic problem rather on pure military security. International cooperation is required for the protection and promotion of national interests, concerning peace, security and development. No nation whatsoever powerful can protect its national interest by pursuing an isolationist policy. This understanding among nations forced them to unite and work together to resolve domestic and external problems through international cooperation.

India's maritime policy also underwent a sea change in the post-Cold War period. The policy of exclusive engagement and elimination of outside powers has given place to overt engagement with extra regional powers. This has been well reflected in India's joint military exercises along with the US, Japan, France, and Australia. India no longer considers the external power presence as a threat to its security. Rather it considers that a joint effort is required to wipe out the major threat to India and international community posed by terrorism. It is not possible for any single nation whatsoever powerful to address the menace of international terrorism single-handedly. India began to realize the importance of a realist approach in framing its foreign policy objectives and pursuing it through increased naval power and active collaboration with extra regional and intra-regional powers. This policy shift in India's stand is visible in the maritime doctrine and in the Navy's vision document published by the Indian Navy.

It essentially encompasses:

(i) Shaping a favourable maritime environment in the IOR for operations in peace and during conflict.

(ii) Preventing incursions by powers inimical to India's national interests by actively engaging countries in the IOR littoral, and rendering speedy and quality assistance in fields of interest to them.

(iii) Engaging extra-regional powers and regional navies in mutually beneficial activities to ensure the security of India's maritime interests.

(iv) Projecting the Indian Navy as a professional, credible force and the primary tool for maritime cooperation. (Defence, Annual Report 2005 - 2006 , 2006)

India has also ear marked the area which falls within its immediate concern. "India's growing international stature gives it strategic relevance in the area ranging from the Persian Gulf to the Strait of Malacca...." While enumerating the basic features of India's post-Cold War Indian Ocean policy "India has exploited the fluidities of the emerging world order to forge new links through a combination of diplomatic repositioning, economic resurgence and military firmness." (Defence, Annual Report 2004-2005, 2005)

Maritime Security Interests

India maritime security interests embraces the protection of India„s vast coastline of 7,516 km. India„s maritime zones, over which it has certain rights and obligations, include a territorial sea up to 12 nm (22 kms) from the baseline, a contiguous zone from 12 to 24 nm (22-44 kms), an Exclusive Economic Zone (EEZ) from 12 to 200 nm (22-370 kms) and a continental shelf up to 200 nm. These zones currently comprise 2.013 million sq km area of sea which is the 12th largest in the world and equivalent to two-thirds of the total land area. India's has thousand-plus island territories and offshore installations. Again nearly 70 per cent of India's energy requirements of crude oil are currently shipped from abroad, increased focus would be required on the ability to maintain the safety and security of energy shipments and the prevention of any disruption of supply through multilateral cooperation. Another important maritime security interest of India is the prevention of maritime terrorism through multilateral efforts.

India's maritime interests are as follows: (Navy I. , 2015)

1. Protect India„s sovereignty and territorial integrity against threats in the maritime environment.
2. Promote safety and security of Indian citizens, shipping, fishing, trade, energy supply,assets and resources in the maritime domain.
3. Pursue peace, stability and security in India's maritime zones, maritime neighbourhoodand other areas of maritime interest.
4. Preserve and project other national interests in the maritime dimension.

Maritime Security Objectives

The major maritime security objective of India is to safeguard national maritime interests at alltimes.

This includes:-

1. To deter conflict and coercion against India.
2. To conduct maritime military operations in a manner that enables early termination of conflicton terms favourable to India.
3. To shape a favourable and positive maritime environment, for enhancing net security inIndia„s areas of maritime interest.
4. To protect Indian coastal and offshore assets against attacks and threats emanating from or atsea.
5. To develop requisite maritime force levels and maintain the capability for meeting India„s maritime security requirements. (Navy I. , 2015)

The task of providing security to the vast coastline, unlike the land borders, is a complex phenomenon involving multiple stake-holders, such as shipping, fisheries, offshore exploration and production, tourism, and the scientific community. It is not only important to protect and promotes the multifarious interests of different stake holders but also involve them in the maritime security programme. Again many external factors that condition the peace and security in the Indian Ocean region have an impact on the maritime security of India. Therefore, any policy initiative towards maritime security of India is interplay of domestic factors and external factors. As far as the external factors are concerned it has less control. The success of India's Indian Ocean policy depends on framing a dynamic policy in tune with the external factors manifested and also considering the domestic prerequisites.

It appears that India has adopted a three-pronged strategy to ensure maritime security through a more inclusive and pragmatic Indian Ocean policy. Firstly through diplomatic means, India has pursued a policy of cooperation with all major players in the Indian Ocean, including extra regional powers. This policy would help India to increase its international stature. The Indo - US strategic partnership in the Indo–Pacific region is an earnest attempt in this direction. The alliance of India, US, Japan and Australia, the democratic countries initiative towards rule-based ocean governance and free and uninterrupted SLOC and sea borne trade also attempted to deter any potential challenge to peace and security in the Indian Ocean from any corner that pays less heed to rule based Ocean governance. The process of globalization has also accelerated better and cordial interaction with outside powers as the movement of people and commodities would further cement relation between nations.

India has developed a friendly and cordial relation not only by bilateral exchange with nations but also strengthened the bilateral cooperation through interactions in regional organizations, such as ASEAN, EAS, SCO, BRICS, ASEM, IBSA, APTA, BIMSTEC and IOR ARC. India is vigorously pursuing the objective to become a developed nation by 2020. This requires theIndian economy to maintain an annual average growth rate of 8 percent per annum. India has framed the "Look East" policy and later the Act East policy in pursuance of this objective. Now the Act East Policy is a vital part of India's foreign policy. More than an external economic policy or a political slogan, the Act East Policy was a strategic shift in India's vision of the worldand its place in the evolving global economy. It was also a manifestation of India's belief that developments in East Asia are of direct consequence to its security and development. Therefore India actively engaged in creating a bond of friendship and cooperation with East Asia that has a strong economic foundation and a cooperative paradigm of positive inter-connectedness ofsecurity interests. India becomes a member of the ARF in 1996 and considers it as an experimentin fashioning a pluralistic, cooperative security order reflective of the diversity of the Asia Pacific region. India is also a member of the East Asia Summit (EAS) which includes the ASEAN members and India, China, Japan, Republic of Korea, Australia, and New Zealand. It focuses on energy, environment, climate change, and sustainable development. The

Act East Policy of India has included not only vigorous interaction with ASEAN but also improved relation with China. The ultimate objective was to evolve an Asian Economic Community on thelines of EU.

India has also pursued a policy of strengthening its economic and military power. It appears that in order to increase the national power India not only declared itself as a nuclear weapon power but also augmented its non-nuclear defence capabilities manifold. The maritime doctrine of India focuses mainly on building blue water navy. (R, 2017) India's role in ensuring the security of Indian Ocean region has been recognized by major players in the region mainly because of the major shift in its external policy through a pragmatic approach. As a result India was not hesitant to cooperate with any regional and extra regional powers. India has undertaken several innovative steps towards the economic resurgence of the country. India's initiative to interact with nations at the bilateral and multilateral levels through various regional groupings appears to be based on this policy.

India's foreign policy has been adapted to the demands of the rapidly changing global, regional and domestic environments. The main drivers for reshaping India's foreign policy appears to have been the sustained dynamism of the Indian economy, emergence as a responsible Nuclear Weapon State, global expectations of India's role on the international stage and the capability to shoulder both regional and global responsibilities. India's engagement with the world community has grown to ensure a peaceful and supportive international environment that contributes to India's development goals. India advocates the need to evolve a new paradigm of cooperation, relevant to the contemporary world, in which global threats are addressed by global responses, and multilateralism becomes the preferred norm for addressing global challenges including terrorism, environmental degradation and economic meltdown.

Though India had made several strides in improving its relation with regional and extra regional countries, the India-Pakistan relation still remains one of distrust and mutual suspicion as it was during the Cold War period. This shows the great power rivalry was not the sole cause for regional disputes though great power rivalry accentuated regional rivalry. Again the India–China border dispute also remains without a solution though China is India's largest trading partner. It shows that neither the unresolved bilateral political issues, nor the divergent political systems based on democratic and totalitarianism, are a hindrance to economic relations between India and China. It also shows the growing significance of economic security rather than pure military security.

It appears that in the post-Cold War period pure military security considerations has been replaced by economic security. The existence of a nontraditional threat to security demands better cooperation among nations. The blurred boundary between international security and national security on the one hand and the national security and human security also demand better interaction among nations. In order to address the basic problems related to human security the countries in the Indian Ocean region has to come out of their Cold War period mind set. Thus peace and security in the Indian Ocean region depends largely on better interaction among countries in the region and extra regional countries to ensure human security. In the post-Cold War period any initiatives towards peace and security in the Indian Ocean region are dependent more on collaborations in economic security than on pure military security. The Indian Ocean Rim Association for Regional Cooperation (IOR - ARC) though a feeble attempt to establish economic community in the Indian Ocean, it is a welcome step towards stronger regionaleconomic forum.

It appears that in the post-Cold War period the initiative towards peace and security in the IndianOcean is to be undertaken at three stages:-

1. At the initial stage greater transparency is required in the economic and security relations among Indian Ocean countries.
2. In the second stage confidence building measures is to be undertaken at the bilateral andmultilateral levels with the active involvement of extra regional countries.
3. Towards the final stage organizational set up to maintain peace and security through greater interaction among sub regional forums such as SAARC, ASEAN, GCC, and BIMSTEC.

Ultimately maritime security of India depends largely on the security situation prevalent in the Indian Ocean region. Though the role of India in influencing the security situation in the Indian Ocean region is limited, it can play a leading role through diplomatic manoeuvering. With the advent of accelerated pace of globalization, the emergence of nontraditional threat to the security of nations, the growing significance of human security concerns, it is imperative to address issues related to maritime security in a comprehensive manner. The blurred boundary between human security concerns and national security concerns once again necessitates such an approach. In short, maritime security of India is interplay of domestic and external policy preferences and responses. The national security predicament in the Indian Ocean region is very difficult to comprehend. It seems to be a clash of democratic values and totalitarian traditions and the divergent means adopted by them in addressing their respective national security concerns. Thus the security dilemma in the Indian Ocean region offers both a challenge and an opportunity to frame India's maritime security policy.

Chapter 14

Maritime Security Challenges for India in the backdrop of Act East Policy

Dr. Sudhir Singh

India is one of the first countries which understood the importance of maritime security and expanded it to cope up with the emerging security and economic challenges. In the post-cold war global system, India has already emerged as an Asian power and making its strong imprint at the global level. India has started now to use its good geo strategic location situated in the north of the Indian Ocean as its natural guardian. Long ago, Kautilya stressed that every country is compelled to formulate its security policy in the backdrop of its geographical location. Geo strategic location remains an important determinant for any country. Bay of Bengal in the east and Arabian Sea in the West enable India's maritime synergies with other regions. By virtue of its excellent geographical location, India is a natural guardian of northern reaches of the Indian Ocean. Over 60 percent global trade commutes through this ocean. It stretches from India to Africa on one side and the shores of Australia on the other. Major crude oil supply routes for Asian countries are also through Indian Ocean.

India is well settled in the midst of the Indian Ocean. It is the natural custodian of Indian Ocean. Indian Ocean has become extremely significant because more than half of the global trade commutes through it. It also connects South China Sea near Malacca Strait which is extended to Andaman Sea. South China Sea connects Indian Ocean to the Pacific Ocean. The growing economic activities have kept the entire sea route of communication extremely congested and it has given birth to new unwanted activities like piracy in the region.

Since last few years, Indian navy have been extremely active in ASEAN, East Asia and larger plank of the Indo-Pacific. It has been one of the hallmarks of Act East Policy. Port calls, joint naval exercises and maritime capacity building programmes with friendly navies has uplifted India's geopolitical status in ASEAN and East Asia. Regular warships deploy in Bay of Bengal and the South China Sea has underlined India's nautical dimensions of India's Act East Policy. Regular and intense joint bilateral and multilateral naval exercises have underlined India's maritime interests in the Asia Pacific region.[252] Former Prime Minister Shri Atal Bihari Vajpayee clearly stated India's strategic priorities in November 2003

> *"the strategic frontiers of today's India, grown in international stature, have expanded well beyond confines of South Asia. Our security environment, ranging from Persian Gulf to Straits of Malacca across the Indian Ocean, includes Central Asia and Afghanistan, China, and South- East Asia. Our strategic thinking has also to extend to these horizons."*

Hence, Andaman Sea has become a strategically important place to play a major role in maritime security for India. Human civilisations have used Seas extensively for trade and commerce. Geographical location of India with the presence of a long coast line provides a huge opportunity in trade and security for its main land. On the other hand presence of ANIs also provide a secured strategy to monitoring the world's most strategic and overcrowded trafficked Malacca Strait, through which approximately 95,000 merchants, oil and gas cargos, pass through.[253]

To promote maritime component of "Act East Policy" and strengthen India's strategic interests and regional cooperation with ASEAN, Malacca Strait has to play a dominant role. India has developed the tri-command in Andaman and Nicobar Islands to strengthen its surveillance and monitoring the Malacca Strait as it provides a gateway to the South China Sea and the Pacific Ocean. Majority of Chinese oil supply ships from the Middle East still passes through this narrow way, which is a nightmare for the Chinese due to its proximity with the Andaman. India has already upgraded maritime relations with the Indo-Pacific countries and pledged to further accelerate the process. Since last few years , United States of America has revisited its Asia policy and adopted Indo-Pacific terminology to ensure rule based international order. Maritime power is extremely important to sustain the dominance of a country. ASEAN countries wishes India to play a counter balancing role against China in the region.

Act East Policy has been launched by the Modi government with its arrival in power in 2014 and since then it is sustainable phenomenon. Maritime connectivity with the countries of Southeast and East Asia has remained an integral part and fulcrum of this policy. India share maritime border with many countries of ASEAN (Myanmar, Thailand and Indonesia) and with the cooperation of these countries, India has ensured piracy free sea lanes of communication within its geographical reaches. India has also contributed immensely to ensure piracy free international navigation in adjoin waters and even in African coast and that has been appreciated by the international community. Modi Government. has also taken many proactive steps regarding maritime policy dealing with the region. It has accelerated the pace of cooperation with these countries in this domain and also engaged in multi-lateral naval exercises under different nomenclatures since last many years. More than this it has asserted that South China Sea is a disputed territory and all disputants' countries must be adhered with the relevant international law and must respect freedom of navigation for all. It is significant in the context of prevailing trust deficit with the disputant countries over the territory of South China Sea. China has virtually refused to adhere with the 2016 international judication in favour of Philippines. China has also divided ASEAN countries over the matter through its coercive diplomacy and expanding its writ over the waters of South China Sea. This sea is geotropically as big as whole India. In addition, it connects Indian ocean to the Pacific Ocean therefore it is strategically important for justice based international maritime order.

US is already a formidable maritime power and China has reoriented its military power consistent with its needs at sea. It is in this context that we have to look at India. Speaking in a seminar at Pune in September 2019, the Navy chief bemoaned the fact that the share of his service in the defence budget had fallen to 13 per cent in 2019, from 18 per cent in 2013.[254] Chinese president Xi Jingping has launched many ambition infrastructure program in recent past. He has also launched 'Maritime Silk Route' in 2015 which is intended to invest $ 40 billion in the project. China has already sitting in Hambantota in Sri-Lanka, Sitwe in Myanmar Gwador in Pakistan and Maldives. It has also established huge navy port at Djibouti , Africa and it can shelter 10,000 sailors. China is adamant to adhere with the relevant international laws in the context of South and East China Seas but at the same time pledged to enhance its presence in the Indian ocean.

The Chinese have celebrated their 70th anniversary of their foundation on 1st October 2019 to mark their military strength in the backdrop of looming tension with the United States and other countries over South China Sea and other issues. The PLA had the world's second-highest military spending at an estimated $250 billion last year, according to the Stockholm International Peace Research Institute. The United States, with a force of 1.3 million people, led in spending at $650 billion last year, or more than 2 times China's level. According to SIPRI China has about 280 nuclear warheads, compared with 6,450 for the United States and 6,850 for Russia.[255]

In this backdrop, the share of expenditure of Indian navy must cope up with the emerging strategic architecture particularly in Indo-Pacific region. The term Indo-Pacific has now become a key strategic term in our part of the world, albeit with different interpretations by the players concerned. For former United States President Donald Trump, it is a geopolitical entity which extends from the east coast of India to the western Pacific. For Prime Minister Narendra Modi, it is a region stretching from the east coast of Africa to the US coast itself. For some, it is the erstwhile Asia-Pacific now extended westwards; for most ASEAN countries, it is essentially their area with the South China Sea thrown in. For China, it is something which does not exist and is only a creation of the US and its cheerleaders.

Under Modi government India has accelerated its cooperation in the realm of maritime security with the like-minded countries. India has participated in the 23rd edition of the Trilateral Maritime Exercise Malabar 2019 with the navies of Japan and USA from September 26 to October 4, 2019. The massive naval drill was taking place off the coast of Japan. According to India, Malabar 2019 exercise will strengthen India-Japan-US naval cooperation and ensure enhanced interoperability between the three forces based on shared values and principles. India's Defence Ministry comments on the exercise:

> *"The Exercise would encompass conduct of complex maritime operations in the surface, sub-surface and air domains, and focus on Anti-Submarine Warfare, Anti-Air and Anti-Surface Firings, Maritime Interdiction Operations (MIO) including Visit Board Search and Seizure (VBSS) and tactical scenario-based Exercise at Sea. In addition, the partner navies would conduct official protocol visits, professional interactions including Subject Matter Expert Exchanges (SMEE), reciprocal ship visits, sports fixtures and social events during the harbour phase,"*

"Participation of Indian Navy ships and aircraft in the Exercise would significantly bolster the strong maritime bonds of friendship between the three countries and contribute to security and stability in the region," added the ministry.[256] The basic purpose of these type of multilateral naval exercises from the Indian point of view has been to ensure justice based freedom of navigation particularly in South and East China Sea. These exercises have not only assured our allies in the Southeast and East Asia for their security and Indian commitment it but also fulfilling wider spectrums of the need of our national interests.

QUAD and Maritime Priorities

The idea of QUAD was conceived by former Japanese PM, Shinzo Abe back in 2007 when he was PM for the brief period of time. PM Abe was pragmatic enough to anticipate growing Chinese might and its negative implications on Asian security. QUAD is basically trilateral arrangement where the United States, Japan and India agreed to work and declared objectives of this group has been to ensure justice-based order in the Indo-Pacific in particular and in the rest part of the globe in general. Coincidently these three countries are democracies as well so it was also known as 'arc of democracy'. This group has been engaged to organise joint naval exercises since its inception. It was organised by these countries since 1992. What they did is they give it a new flavour. Australia also did participate in some of the joint naval exercises but have been reluctant partner of the group. India was also not an enthusiastic partner. Both India and Australia were reluctant mostly due to the Chinese apprehension that QUAD is a military alliance to contain China in the guise of democracy. China not only expressed this apprehension but also issued a demarche to these countries. India and Australia have had cordial relations with China since the end of the cold war.

In 2017, Indian and the Chinese military had 72 days eye to eye situation at Doklam and finally it was resolved through dialogue and disengagement took place. Since May 2020, Chinese army has been offensive in western Himalaya region of Ladakh and standoff is going on till date. It has become one of the longest standoffs between the Chinese and the Indian military. Foreign minister, Jaishankar stated that situation at the LAC is worse after 1962 war. During the prevalence of the pandemic in 2020, Chinese army is offensive at the LAC. There may be gamut of explanations but one thing is more than certain that Chinese are not willing to resolve border crisis and their perception has been that they can bend India due to their better military powers, economic standing etc. Modi government has arrived in power in May 2014 and returned again in May 2019 with enhanced majority.

Modi government has adopted proactive foreign policy. On China front Modi government has been very sensitive. PM Modi met 12 times with Chinese president Xingping since last six years. They also held summit dialogue in 2018 and 2019. Both countries have many established mechanisms to sustain peace and tranquillity in the border. In June 2003, PM, A.B. Vajpayee visited Beijing and it was agreed that both countries National Security Advisors (NSA's) will be leading their respective delegations to resolve thorny border crisis. Till date 22 round of this high voltage talks have been taken place and this problem has not been resolved. However, China keeps incursions across the LAC and taking the line that it did happen because there is no demarcated border between India and Tibet because it refused to accept 1914 Shimla agreement on which McMahon Line was demarcated finally. In this agreement Tibet was also an independent participant. Interestingly China has accepted the same McMahon Line, to resolve border dispute with Myanmar in 1960's.

In this backdrop, Modi government has shown new vigour in QUAD right from May 2014 and accelerated the pace in recent years particularly after Doklam standoff. Australia has become more than active now for the expansion of QUAD. The United States have always been proactive member of the QUAD and so is the case of Japan. In September 2020, foreign ministers of the QUAD met on virtual mode and discussed range of regional and global issues. They had a summit of top leadership in March 2021.

The United States as a Factor

China and the United States has a trust deficit and instead of narrowing down it has widened. The United States has also publicly stated that free international navigation within international waters is one of its policy priorities. United States has deployed its warships within the South China Sea, which has been disputed after Chinese claims over its entire blue water and contested by its ASEAN neighbours. The United States has also started 'Malabar Exercises' along with India, and Japan since 2007 to ensure a free flow of international navigation. Later on, Australia also joined it and it was one of the areas which were stressed by the Americans during President Trump Delhi February 2020 visit. In the backdrop of the eruption of the corona virus, the United States have deployed its fighter fleets in the South China Sea. India has also sent its fleet in these disputed waters. Japan and

Australia are also open supporters of the United States to ensure free flow of navigation in the Indo-Pacific region in general and in the South China Sea in particular.

New Biden administration in US has vowed to sustain Indo-Pacific policy. Washington's present perception of China is generally negative. This perception has developed sustainably since last two decades. The focal point of the Trump administration China's policy was that America must abandon its illusions, realistically face the challenges that now exist, and adopt practical measures to balance against China's rise. Under President Donald Trump administration it has further gone up. President Trump administration has launched a trade war against China. Such an aggressive US stance has highlighted the vulnerability associated with China's heavy reliance on US high-tech imports and has consequently sparked discussion among scholars about the gradual decoupling of the two economics.[257] Prevalence of corona and its devastating impact on United States led western world to further weaken United States-China relationship. India and United States relations have improved enormously in recent years due to growing convergences of interests. Trump administration gave 2+2 status to India, which means that US secretary of state and secretary of defence will have a summit level talk to their Indian counterparts back in 2018 and the Biden administration has vowed to sustain the process. In March 2021, US secretary of defence visited India. It was a maiden physical visit by any top officer of the new Biden administration. Defence secretary Austin reiterated the US government's continued commitment towards strengthening the bilateral defence relations between the two countries. He expressed America's strong desire to further enhance the strategic partnership for peace, stability and prosperity in the Indo-Pacific region and beyond,".[258] Austin called the India-US relationship a "stronghold of free and open Indo-Pacific region." This displays the great importance the Biden administration has attached to India and its intent to reinforce bilateral ties with it.

Balance of Power in Asia

The balance of power theory is a core tenet of both classical and neorealist theory and seeks to explain alliance formation. With no authority above the state to come to its rescue in the event of an attack by dominant states attempt to prevent a potential hegemon from arising by balancing against it. According to Kenneth Waltz, founder of neorealism, "balance-of-power politics prevail wherever two, and only two requirements are met: that the order be anarchic and that it be populated by units wishing to survive".[259]

It has been opined by harbingers of international relations since last few decades that 21st century will be an Asian century. It has ignited with new wave of the game of balance of power in Asia. Despite cooperation in many areas, India and China has unprecedented trust deficit. Ladakh standoff has further widened this gap. This prevailing trust deficit have been directly related to Asian balance of power. Chinese mouth piece *The Global Times* accept this candid reality:

The fundamental problem between China and India is the lack of basic mutual trust. The border issue has been fully activated, forming the two societies' confrontation of wills. Both believe they have the advantage, and China's advantage is based on strength. The gap between China and India in national strength is much wider than in 1962. India's sense of superiority comes from its geopolitical mobilization capabilities. The US, Japan and Australia are trying to win over India. New Delhi believes Beijing is afraid of this since China is being strategically blocked by the US. India believes China will yield at the border.[260]

In the prevailing security system, many aspiring global powers are more than willing to dominate Asia. They are tempted with the prediction that 21st century will be as Asian century. China wished that it will dominate Asia and act per their own whims and fancy. Chinese perceives that India is their worst competitor and obstruction to dominate Asia. According to K Subrahmanyam, an eminent strategic thinker and author[261] "A successful and democratic India, which rises fast and eliminates its poverty in a reasonable period, is the biggest challenge to the legitimacy of China... The competition between India and China is, therefore, an ideological one"

Chinese behaviour in the backdrop of their acquisition of newly earned economic power has become unruly which is bound to create new balance of power and its by product is conflicts. China wanted to dominate Asia as America is dominating the globe but wanted multiple power structures at the global level. For Mearsheimer, rising powers tend to seek regional hegemony and China is heading in this direction.[262]

Chinese have shown this mindset while consolidating its dominance over South China Sea despite ardent opposition by the disputants of ASEAN and other concerned global powers. As former US foreign officer senior Alice Wels have stated just days before her retirement that China is doing nasty activities to harass its neighbours right from South China Sea to Himalayan border of India. China keeps alleging that India is doing incursions in Chinese territory. After standoff erupted in May 2020, Global Times -mouth piece of China -commented:

> *"India in recent days has illegally constructed defence facilities across the border into Chinese territory in the Galwan Valley region, leaving Chinese border defence troops no other options but making necessary moves in response, and mounting the risk of escalating standoffs and conflicts between the two sides.*[263]

The Chinese economy is three times bigger and so is defence budget. Despite this asymmetrical strategic status, India has aligned well with the like-minded powers who are very much interested to keep Asia multipolar. Countries of ASEAN and East and North East Asia despite their high-profile trade relations with China have serious trust deficit with it and they wish that India and other like-minded countries must play strategic balancer role in the region and keep Asia multipolar. The United States was trying its level best to do it since last few years under different nomenclature but Asian powers like India, Japan and South Korea had an impression that they have a working relation with China and they should not disturb it by their own acts. Eruption of the corona virus in December 2019 from the historical Chinese city of Wuhan dismantled all existing illusions of these countries. Facts coming out from China vindicates that China has deliberately exploded this virus to reap lucrative strategic and economic dividends. China has also become assertive against India in Ladakh sector and against disputant countries of ASEAN in the South China Sea. This new situation has created a new ambience of animosity against China in those countries and now they are more dedicated to ensure multiplicity in Asia and more than willing to consolidate the support of all like minded countries in this project.

China has taken gamut of offensive posturing from western Himalayan region of Ladakh with India till disputants of ASEAN at South China Sea. It has also created new hostility against Taiwan. Many European countries are now openly challenging 'One China Policy' and their representatives are visiting Taipei frequently. American health minister also visited Taiwan in August 2020. Before corona it was almost impossible. According to prestigious American magazine, Newsweek, Chinese president, Xi Jinping is the "architect' of the PLA recent moves against India. According to the magazine, the Chinese president has risked his future with the high-profile incursions into Indian territory that 'unexpected flopped' in the face of ferocious fightback by the Indian army. President Xi as the custodian of the communist party will take rectification campaign and mass persecution of foes, and also launch 'another brutal purge' following the Chinese army's failures on the Indian border.[264]

India is trying its level best to sustain the delicate relationship with China and cooperating on many fronts despite prevailing trust deficit. In the backdrop of Ladakh standoff, no matter which way it is going to turn, India and China are not going to cooperate on any ground in immediate future. This prevailing quantum of trust deficit between two biggest countries of Asia, who are also aspirants of global status will further consolidate the strengthening of the QUAD. Biden administration has vowed to sustain the engagement process to the QUAD and maritime component has emerged as the united factor within the group as they keep doing series of joint maritime exercises. Biden administration sent its secretary of state and defence in Asia in March 2021 in the midst of the QUAD summit. Chinese mouthpiece, Global Times criticise this visit.

> *"Unlike India and South Korea, Japan has fallen for the US "lip service," and suddenly portrays itself as the "anti-China vanguard" in this region. At the end of Blinken and Austin's trip to Japan, Tokyo and Washington issued a joint statement saying that "The US and Japan acknowledged that China's behavior, where inconsistent with the existing international order, presents political, economic, military and technological challenges." Blinken told a press conference following the meeting that their meeting covered not only the Diaoyu Islands, where China and Japan have disputes, but also Hong Kong and Xinjiang, on which Japan rarely openly criticizes China."*[265]

Indo-Pacific Synergy among QUAD Members

The concept of the Indo-Pacific was launched by President Obama administration to ensure rule-based system in the region. Maritime cooperation remains an important hallmark of this policy. It has been challenged by the resurgent Chinese. China has manifested it in South and East China Sea's. US has invested huge energy and time to ensure rule-based Indo-Pacific. India has emerged as an important ally of the United States since last two decades. In post-cold war scenario, all American presidents have visited India. According to Mr. Wong "India as a nation has invested in a free and open order. It is a democracy. It is a nation that can anchor free and open order in the Indo-Pacific region. And it's our policy to ensure that India does play that role and that it becomes over time a more influential player in the region,"[266] China was never comfortable with this nomenclature which has been emphasised by the United States since last one decade. In June 2019, Chinese trawler sank a Philippines boat and over 20 of its fishermen in serious crisis who have been finally rescued by the Vietnamese boats.[267]

The United States had signed a framework for defence cooperation with Maldives to deepen engagement in support of maintaining peace and security in the strategic Indian Ocean, the Pentagon has announced as the Trump administration looks for strengthening alliances in the Indo-Pacific to counter China's growing presence in the region.[268] The United States has already inked such an alliance with Japan, India, Australia and many other countries. The deepening bonhomie among QUAD member countries will push balance of power in favour of India even in case of mini or full-scale war. Chinese forces have not fought any war after 1979 Vietnam war. Even in Vietnam war the PLA had been given adequate "bloody nose" by the comparative smaller Vietnamese army. Indian army in contrast is considered war hardened army and have been involved in many wars and sustainable low intensity conflicts. QUAD is a group of militarily developed countries and in case of conflict their support to India will make its position stronger despite many existing odds. This has been tacitly admitted by By Hu Xijin, editor in chief of the Global Times.

According to Hu Xijin;

> *The key is really morality. China is a rising power that has been ideologically rejected by the US and the West. The countries that have territorial disputes with China also sympathize with each other. If China does decide to go to war with a neighbouring force, the international community will tend to favor the weaker side. Whether or not our moves are justified, the moral risks are high. Besides, the US will fully turn its public opinion machine against China. Therefore, we should not underestimate the complexity of a war.*[269]

Indo-Pacific idea is now attracting many new powers particularly in post corona global order. In a major diplomatic jolt to China, Germany has decided to focus on maintaining stronger partnerships with democratic countries in September 2020. It is intended particularly to the Indo-Pacific region in order to promote the rule of law. Berlin's drift towards the Indo-Pacific strategy comes as Europe has expressed concerns over China's track record on human rights.[270] Australia has become new aspirant to be proactive in the QUAD and desired to participate in maritime exercises. Analysts believe that India's decision to allow Australia to participate at Malabar 2020 could lead to a re-activation of the QUAD. The last time

Australia participated in the naval drill was in 2007 along with Singapore. During a high-profile speech on July 24 , 2020 at the US-India Business Council's India Ideas Summit, Pompeo announced that the "Quad is revived" and that his country "desires a new age of ambition" in its blossoming partnership with India.

> "We don't just interact on a bilateral basis. We see each other for what we are: great democracies, global powers and really good friends. India is one of the few trusted, like-minded countries whose leaders I call on a regular basis for counsel and collaboration on issues that span continents," Pompeo said during the online event.[271]

Conclusion

Maritime component has become the fulcrum of Act East Policy for gamut of reasons. Deepening of maritime relations with ASEAN countries and Japan can be viewed in this context. United States-India relations have also improved in a transformative manner in recent years. New Biden administration has vowed to sustain this process. The strengthening of India's maritime proactiveness is not only positive for India but in addition it is bound to ensure justice-based freedom for international navigation in the disputed waters.

Chapter 15

Human Smuggling: Maritime Transnational Crime in Tamil Nadu

R. M. Arivazhagan

Introduction

India is among the largest countries in Asia and has both land and maritime neighbours. The borders both land and maritime pose huge challenges to India to guard, deter and destroy inimical elements with catastrophic interests. The maritime border is a conduit for multiple types of smuggling ranging from human, drugs, arms, wildlife and gold to mention a few. The responsibility of guarding these borders is a part of a three tier system involving the Indian Navy, Coast Guard, and the Coastal Police of the respective state governments. These borders nurture criminal syndicates on either side paving the way for a number of nefarious criminal activities.

India has acknowledged the importance of managing its marine resources and illegal migration through territorial waters and in the high seas, for economic and security reasons. The primary challenge posed for Indian maritime security agencies is migration management due to the rampancy of migrant smuggling by sea through Indian waters. The acts of migrant smuggling in and around the region appears to serve the interests of a mixture of asylum-seekers and illegal migrants. It is needless to say that death has been a proven risk for these persons. India's lack of operational capacity to monitor and act in the maritime domain, including minimal and weak presence and inadequate intelligence collection, leaves Indian waters vulnerable to pirates, smugglers and witness to drowning migrants. The aim of this chapter is to highlight the rampant human smuggling with specific emphasis on the coasts of Tamil Nadu.

Background

The internationally accepted definition of migrant smuggling stems from the Protocol against the Smuggling of Migrants by Land, Sea and Air, which supplements the United Nations Convention against Transnational Organized Crime (Smuggling of Migrants Protocol). The Protocol defines the crime of migrant smuggling as '*the procurement, in order to obtain, directly or indirectly, a financial or other material benefit, of the illegal entry of a person into a State Party of which the person is not a national or a permanent resident.*' No Member State can adhere to the Smuggling of Migrants Protocol without prior adherence to the Convention against Transnational Organized Crime.[272]

Contrary to popular misperceptions, the act of Human Smuggling has been prevalent for long and to put it simply is a trans-nationally planned, meticulously coordinated and executed crime that is more often than not perpetrated by organized criminal syndicates and networks. It is to be borne in mind that it is not merely the smugglers who are in search of the lucrative business, but also the smuggled migrants, who are willing participants, who collaborate and connive in the commission of the crime. These smuggled migrants are desperate to leave their country of origin to seek new economic opportunities and greener pastures, either for individual or familial betterment. There are also certain circumstances that force these smuggled migrants trying to make a getaway from conflict and persecution like the Tamils from Sri Lanka which becomes a determinant in providing consent to being smuggled.

Countries are in a quandary due to the unsavoury global attention human smuggling has been receiving due to a spate of human disasters at sea that continue to occur during the transportation of illegal migrants. The organized human smuggler syndicates operating through clandestine transnational networks target rich, developed, countries as their most preferred and sought-after destinations. They also examine coastal security in place to find loopholes for easy transit. The mode of transportation of the migrants is mostly via fishing vessels, which are incapable of accommodating large numbers of illegal migrants as they are either ill-equipped or are hesitant. The smugglers in order to make quick money and huge profits normally ignore safety and sanitary aspects of sea transportation. It is a confirmed fact that most of the vessels used in human smuggling are utterly unseaworthy, making travelling in them inherently dangerous and often fatal.

The International laws in place are powerful instruments in this battle against human smuggling but are without teeth in terms of penalties. The United Nations Convention against Transnational Organized Crime (UNTOC) is among the latest in a series of conventions of international law that have been implemented to counter and prosecute human smuggling and is supplemented by three protocols.

(a) To prevent, suppress and punish trafficking in persons, especially women and children (Trafficking Protocol);

(b) Against the smuggling of migrants by sea, land, and air (Smuggling Protocol);

(c) Against the illicit manufacturing of and trafficking in firearms, their parts and components and ammunition (Firearms Protocol).[273]

Difference between Human smuggling and human trafficking

The words human smuggling and human trafficking are being used interchangeably but have different connotations. The act of human smuggling involves the provision of a service by the smugglers or syndicates, involving facilitating transportation or provision of fraudulent documents to an individual or a group of individuals who voluntarily seeks to gain illegal entry into a foreign country. On the other hand, the act of human trafficking largely involves exploiting persons including women and children solely for the purposes of forced labour or commercial sexual exploitation. It is also highly possible that the crime may originate as human smuggling but quickly lead to human trafficking.

The act of human smuggling normally does not involve coercion and the smuggled migrants invariably collaborate financially with these syndicates to help them make the journey. Human trafficking, by sheer contrast, is definitely involuntary. Human Trafficking unlike human smuggling need not necessarily involve movement or transportation at all and can occur within the country's borders too. A person can be trafficked in their very own home.

Human smuggling often involves procurement of deceitful documents and illegal transportation across a country's border, and in some cases can also include transportation and harboring once in the destination country. The smuggled migrant gives his or her consent to being moved and the transaction between the migrant and the smuggler is typically over once he or she has crossed the border and the smuggler has been paid in full.

However, in the case of trafficking the unintended victim changes hands from one trafficker to other and are subjected to terrible acts of violence and exploitation. However, not all smuggling cases involve human trafficking, nor do all cases of human trafficking begin with migrant smuggling.[274]

There are three fundamental differences between smuggling and trafficking and it involves the three factors involving consent, exploitation, and transnationality.

a) **Consent**- The smuggled person voluntarily agrees to being moved from one place to another in any of the three mediums. But the trafficking victims, have either not given their consent to be moved or, if they have, have been defrauded into agreeing to false promises and go on to face exploitation.

b) **Exploitation**- The transaction ends at the chosen destination where the smuggler and the smuggled person part ways. To the contrary, traffickers continue to exploit their victims all through the journey and even at the offloaded places.

c) **Transnationality**- Human smuggling always involves crossing international borders whereas trafficking occurs regardless of whether victims are taken to another country or moved within a country's borders.[275]

The Smuggling of Migrants Protocol by the United Nations in 2000 aims to prevent and combat human smuggling by all mediums including sea and broadly covers offences committed and related to the facilitation of both illegal entry and illegal stay of smuggled persons who are not permanent residents and when the act is perpetrated to obtain financial or material benefits. However, the Smuggling of Migrants Protocol does not aim and intend to criminalize migrants and the stated intention of the Protocol is basically to criminalize and prosecute those who smuggle others for financial gain. The Indian Ministry of Women and Children Development clearly states the distinction between 'human trafficking and smuggling of migrants' in its anti-trafficking bill 2018.[276]

Determinants – Target Rich environment

Some of the key determinants in human smuggling involve abject poverty due to rampant unemployment, political suppression, and internal conflicts arising out of civil war, famine, ethnicity, culture or an unprecedented natural disaster. These factors set the benchmark to differentiate a migrant from a refugee. It is not mandatory for a migrant to be a refugee as a country can be used as transit to a third country as witnessed in Indian shores when fleeing Lankan Tamils used the Indian route to flee to Australia to seek safer pastures. But a refugee under the auspices of the UN High Commission of Refugee (UNHCR) needs to be protected mandatorily. It will then be determined if the smuggled entrant would fall under the category of a political refugee, or a migrant.

With continuous strife and civil wars in the Horn of Africa, Afghanistan, Myanmar and Sri Lanka there are no dearth of migrants willing to be smuggled out of the country voluntarily and the smuggling syndicates profit from such misfortunes.

Sri Lanka - India: Challenges at Sea

In formulating foreign policies pertaining to countries that have both geographical and cultural proximity like in the case of Sri Lanka and India, it is but expected that state governments would take advantage of their proximity and impose pressure on the Central Government to carve up foreign policies that are in line with the needs of the situation. It is often portrayed by the state that the centre remains insensitive to its demands and end up placing the national interest above states interest.

The migrants normally take this route to escape communal disharmony. It is a fact that the smugglers are connected ethnically or linked geographically to the smuggling territory to the migrants seeking to be smuggled out. Though there was an influx of refugees from Sri Lanka in the years 1983, 90 and 95 and the last wave of said influx was due to the extensive army operation carried out by the Sri Lankan forces against the Tamils. It is also the last wave that saw human smugglers attempting to smuggle these persons to Italy, Australia and New Zealand. Unofficial reports cite that more than 60 percent of these illegal trips ended in success for these persons.

The smugglers tend to form a criminal nexus with the local moneylenders to pawn their jewellery or land to sponsor the trip for a member of the family or to raise the required funds. Thus, the criminal nexus between smugglers, moneylenders, corrupt custom officials has grown into a major crime network.

One illustration of the exponential growth of this crime, involves Ukrainian ships using deep waters to dock beyond the EEZ of Sri Lanka to pick up gullible migrants. They sail under difficult conditions with rationed food and water and nil access to medicines.

Smuggling syndicates usually comprise of wealthy businessmen with political connections, known criminal gangsters, fishing boat owners, and experienced sea captains. The modus operandi of these operations is patterned. Usually conducted in restaurants by brokers posing as attendants who carry out the facilitation and the services of small time business staff, boat crew members, local fisherman, former security forces officers and drifting, unemployed youth are also utilized by the criminal syndicates. The operations of these criminal syndicates is structured and the hierarchy is well defined with a system of top-down control, and further broken up into separate individual operatives with tasks apportioned. There are certain areas such as Negombo in Sri Lanka, which witnesses rich businessmen using their own boats, crews and field people for the entire operation receiving complete benefits of the operation. However, in other regions the system is broken up into a financier cum boat owner, contracted ship captain, contracted crew and a set of field agents all coming together to execute the venture.

There are numerous incidents of attempted deterrence which have been documented. For instance, Malaysian authorities apprehended a group of 130 illegals and busted a racket of smuggling migrants to Australia and New Zealand who had deep connections with Malaysians and Indonesian authorities[277].

The coasts of Kodiyakarai to Rameswaram continue to remain the favoured landing spots for smugglers operating out of Tamil Nadu in connivance with their counterparts in Sri Lanka. Smuggling is facilitated by the presence of a large number of fishing villages, hamlets and soft-landing centres in the backwaters, forming part of the Gulf of Mannar. The landings are carried out when most fisher folk are out for work or in a few cases done with their tacit approval for monetary benefits. The conflicting geographical topography makes a 24x7 vigil almost impossible.

It must also be noted that the large coastline extending over 1076 kms with multiple porous areas facilitate smuggling. Rameshwaram's close proximity to Northern Sri Lanka with routes ranging from as low as 5 Nautical Miles also makes it easy for these smugglers. That is one of the main causes for the increasing human smuggling market in the area. Relevant data obtained in July 2021, reveals that a total of 58,668 persons from 18,937 families live inside camps and a total of 34,123 persons from 13,553 families of Sri Lankan origin outside the camps spread across Tamil Nadu.[278]

Despite the fact that the UNHCR has provided legal channels to seek refugee status, the persons concerned are reluctant to avail the facility due to inevitable delays and non-availability of an assured timeline. The Organization for Eelam Refugee Rehabilitation (OfERR), with offices in Chennai and Jaffna, organized a survey among 109 refugees who landed on Indian shores and it was ascertained that close to 30 percent of them had a proceeding pending against them or a family member, 16 percent of them had debts back home and they intended to flee without clearing the same and close to 20 percent of them did not have the documents required by UNHCR for repatriation, cumulatively making a potent recipe for the illegal travel. This fact was further corroborated by the Tamil Nadu Commissionerate of Rehabilitation and welfare of non-resident Tamils which virtually forces Tamils to resort to illegal means.[279] A domino effect is present in neighbouring states of Kerala[280] and Karnataka[281] where similar human smuggling racketing exists and the police force has apprehended many such syndicates.

Table 1: No. of incidence registered under The Passport Act 1967 in the Indian states and its Union Territories covers the large part of Southern peninsular

S.No	States/UT's	2017	2018	2019
1.	Tamil Nadu	134	149	185
2.	Kerala	74	48	54
3.	Karnataka	29	18	50
4.	Andhra Pradesh	04	04	05
5.	Telangana	13	21	18
6.	Maharashtra	40	97	98
7.	Odisha	0	0	0
8.	Puducherry	0	0	0
9.	Andaman &Nicobar	0	0	0
10.	Lakshadweep	0	0	0

Source: Data from NCRB Annual Report Volume I from 2017- 2019[282]

Table 2: No. of Overall incidence registered under the Foreigners and other Passport related Acts in the Indian states and its Union Territories covers the large part of Southern peninsular

S.No	States/UT's	2017	2018	2019
1.	Tamil Nadu	169	202	224
2.	Kerala	115	91	89
3.	Karnataka	72	108	105
4.	Andhra Pradesh	09	08	18
5.	Telangana	19	39	27
6.	Maharashtra	69	115	137
7.	Odisha	0	0	0
8.	Puducherry	0	1	1
9.	Andaman &Nicobar	1	9	4
10.	Lakshadweep	0	0	0

Source: Data from NCRB Annual Report Volume I from 2017- 2019[283]

Legal Provisions in India

India has a number of laws (enlisted below) in place which exist both in paper and spirit, although their implementation has been weak. The Registration of Foreigners Act 1939, The Foreigners Act 1946, The Foreigners (Entry into India) Rules 1950, The Foreigners Act 1964, The Citizenship Act 1955, The Passport Act 1967 and The Emigration Act 1983 are a few of them. The following are the security threats this crime poses – those which are not dealt with by the existing regime.

Strategic Threats to Maritime Security

(a) The huge influx of illegal migrants can upset the economic balance in the areas they reside in leading to unemployment issues.

(b) Lack of work to earn a proper livelihood can build frustration leading to conflicts with the local populace, creating a law-and-order problem for the recipient state.

(c) The common routes can be effectively used by the smugglers to resort to more serious crimes like narcotics, drugs and even transhipment of terrorists to cause disruptive activities.

(d) The neighboring countries can infiltrate their own agents to spy on or sabotage activities.

(e) Overpopulation in areas can lead to water shortages, pollution, breakdown of health infrastructure, shortage of public schools, inadequate transportation and insufficient entertainment facilities and hence would place a strain on public utilities.

(f) If the migrants work as cheap laborers out of financial desperation against the laid down local rates, it can cause disharmony with the locals considering they would be replaced by low-wage workers.

(g) The illegal use of these migrants by employing them would enable the employer to evade due and payable government taxes.

(h) There would be a burden on the government to provide proper health care facilities and if a pandemic strikes in a camp it would become extremely difficult to control.

Conclusion

Human smuggling should be viewed in the prism of serious transnational crimes which pose an imminent threat to human security. The smugglers use these gullible and desperate people who are eager to flee their homeland in fear of persecution or to escape abject poverty. They are invariably exploited and left at the mercy of the smugglers and the recipient countries. However, these migrants weigh the cost benefit ratio and resort to this desperate measure to secure a bright and a safer future for their kith and kin. There needs to be more teeth in the laws to strictly enforce action against the smugglers to deter this dangerous practice and the global community needs to work together to counter this menace.

Endnotes

Chapter 2

1 As cited in Nayef Al-Rodhan, Strategic Culture And Pragmatic National Interest, *Global Policy Journal*, 22 July 2015. https://www.gcsp.ch/News-Knowledge/Publications/Strategic-Culture-and-Pragmatic-National-Interest

2 Russell Moore, Strategic Culture--How It Affects Strategic "Outputs", CSC 1998, https://apps.dtic.mil/dtic/tr/fulltext/u2/a525913.pdf

3 Kerry Longhurst, On strategic culture, Research Gate https://www.researchgate.net/publication/327127183_On_strategic_culture

4 Alastair Johnston, Thinking about Strategic Culture, *International Security*, Volume 19, Number 4, Spring 1995, p 46 http://muse.jhu.edu/article/447377/pdf

5 Strategic culture: a reliable tool of analysis for EU security developments?, EFPU Conference Papers 2004 http://www.lse.ac.uk/internationalRelations/centresandunits/EFPU/EFPUconferencepapers2004/Margaras.doc

6 George K. Tanham, Indian Strategic Thought: An Interpretative Essay, RAND National Defence Research Institute, Santa Monica , California, USA, 1992, pp. 92 www.rand.org/pubs/reports/2007/R4207.pdf

7 As cited in Ali Ahmed, Strategic Culture and Indian Self-assurance, *Journal of Peace Studies*, Vol. 17, Issue 2&3, April-September, 2010. P.

8 'Note to K.N. Katju, 22 September 1955' in *Selected Works of Jawaharlal Nehru, Second Series* (*SWJN-SS*), Vol. 30, Delhi: Oxford University Press, 2001, pp. 346–48. as referred to in Zorawar Daulet Singh (2017): Foreign Policy and Sea Power: India's Maritime Role Flux, *Journal of Defence Studies*, Vol. 11, No. 4, October-December 2017, p.24 http://idsa.in/jds/jds_11_4_2017_foreign-policy-and-sea-power-india-maritime-role-flux

9 Ensuring secure seas : An Indian Maritime Security Strategy, Integrated Headquarters, Ministry of Defence(Navy), 2015, p.ii

10 Rodney Jones , India's Strategic Culture, 2006 https://fas.org/irp/agency/dod/dtra/india.pdf

11 Kanti Bajpai, "Indian Strategic Culture", in Michael R. Chambers ed., *South Asia in 2020: Future Strategic Balances and Alliances*, Strategic Studies Institute, U.S. Army War College, 2003, p.246

12 For a detailed discussion, refer R K Bhonsle, Jointness : An Indian Strategic Culture Perspective, *Journal of Defence Studies*, Vol. 1, No.1, August 2007 https://idsa.in/jds/1_1_2007_JointnessAnIndiaStrategicCulturePerspective_RKBhonsle

13 Leonid Savin, India and its strategic culture, Geoplotics.Ru, https://www.geopolitica.ru/en/article/india-and-its-strategic-culture

14 Sunil Khilnani, Rajiv Kumar, et al., Nonalignment 2.0: A Foreign and Strategic Policy for India in the Twenty First Century, 2012, p.iii https://www.kcl.ac.uk/sspp/departments/kii/documents/NonAlignment20.pdf

15 Tariq Fatemi, Indian Strategic Thinking, *The Tribune*, July 24, 2012 http://tribune.com.pk/story/412494/indianstrategicthinking/

16 Sunil Khilnani, Rajiv Kumar, et al., P.42

17 K.M. Panikkar, India and the Indian Ocean : An essay on the influence of Sea Power on Indian history, George&Allen Unwin, Bombay, 1971(Reprint) p.90

18 Arun Prakash, "A Vision of India's Maritime Power in the 21st Century", *Air Power Journal*, Vol 1 No 2 Winter 2006 (Oct – Dec), pp. 4

19 Indian Maritime Doctrine, Ministry of Defence (Navy), 2004

20 Refer Admiral Sureesh Mehta's Foreword, ibid., p.6

21 Ibid., P.64

22 http://aldeilis.net/mumbai/1686.pdf

23 Freedom to Use the Seas: India's Maritime Military Strategy, New Delhi: Integrated Headquarters, Ministry of Defence (Navy), 2007, p.96 http://aldeilis.net/mumbai/1686.pdf

24 Abhijit Singh, An Indian Maritime Strategy for an Era of Geopolitical Uncertainty, *Journal of Defence Studies*, Vol. 9, No. 4, October-December 2015, p.18 https://idsa.in/system/files/jds/jds_9_4_2015_maritimestrategy.pdf

25 Indian Maritime Doctrine 2009, Indian Navy Naval Strategic Publication 1.1, Ministry of Defence(Navy) 2009 https://www.indiannavy.nic.in/sites/default/files/Indian-Maritime-Doctrine-2009-Updated-12Feb16.pdf

26 Ensuring Secure Seas, Foreword by Admiral RK Dhowan

27 Balaji Chandramohan, India's Evolving Maritime Security Strategy and Force Posture, *Strategic Analysis Paper*, Future Directions International, March 3, 2016 http://www.futuredirections.org.au/wp-content/uploads/2016/03/India percentE2 percent80 percent99s-Evolving-Maritime-Security-Strategy-and-Force-Posture.pdf

28 India becomes sixth largest economy in the world, overtakes France, *The Indian Express*, July 12, 2018 https://indianexpress.com/article/business/economy/india-becomes-sixth-largest-economy-in-the-world-overtakes-france-5256279/

29 For a detailed examination of the Indian Naval Doctrine refer Iskander Rehman's "India's Aspirational Naval Doctrine" in Harsh Pant ed., The Rise of the Indian Navy: Internal Vulnerabilities, External challenges, Routledge, 2012 pp.55-79

30 K.M.Panikkar, ibid., p.99

31 Food, maritime and energy security to top I2U2 leaders meet next month, *Financial Express*, June 15, 2022 https://www.financialexpress.com/defence/food-maritime-and-energy-security-to-top-i2u2-leaders-meet-next-month/2561537/

Chapter 3

32 AIR State News, July 18, 2022. https://newsonair.gov.in/News?title=PM-Modi-addresses-Naval-Innovation-and-Indigenisation-Organisation-Seminar- percent26 percent2339 percent3BSwavlamban percent26 percent2339 percent3B-in-New-Delhi&id=444378

33 Navy chief calls for cooperative approach, *New Indian Express*, April 28, 2022 https://www.newindianexpress.com/nation/2022/apr/28/navy-chief-calls-for-cooperative-approach-2447376.html

34 Amit Thakker, A rising India in the Indian Ocean needs a strong navy, *New Perspectives of Foreign Policy*, Issue 16, October 2018 https://csis-website-prod.s3.amazonaws.com/s3fs-ublic/181017_RisingIndia.pdf? CNzNznkbk9I4zhq9ZCTrXKchnU3WU6r6

35 http://www.arabnews.com/?page=4&section=0&article=83442&d=8&m=6&y=2006

36 For a detailed report on the state of the ocean see http://www.nic.in:80/dod/ accessed Feb 21, 2005

37 The South Indian kings conquered parts of South East Asia and the influence is pronounced in the cultural realm to this day (as evident from the Indonesian traditional theatre form called *Gamelan* where the epic Ramayana is performed. See Peter Stack's East meets East in a Hindu Epic, *San Francisco Chronicle*, March 30, 1997), and also by the political and economic clout of the ethnic population settled there.

38 For detailed discussion refer my monograph, India's Maritime Power: Precedence and Prospect, Lecture Series 6, UGC Centre for Maritime Studies, Pondicherry University, February 2019 pp 18-22

39 http://www.indianexpress.com/news/govt-orders-coastal-security-restructuring/429319/0

40 Navy to helm centre on maritime security, *The Hindu*, December 17, 2018

41 Navy to shop for maritime patrol aircraft, spy drones, *The Times of India*, October 25, 2010 http://articles.timesofindia.indiatimes.com/2010-10-25/india/28271834_1_maritime-threats-spy-drones-p-8i-poseidon

42 T C Karthikeyan, India's Maritime security cooperation in the Indo-Pacific, Politico, Vol.4, No.1, 2015, p.118,

43 Note 16 cited in C.S.Anuradha's chapter, India's Blue Economy and Indo-Pacific, in Adluri Subramanyam Raju ed., *Indian Ocean & Indo-Pacific: India Betwixt*, Studera Press, New Delhi, 2020 p. 79

44 Malabar is the most complex naval exercise, *The Hindu*, January 2, 2022 https://www.thehindu.com/news/national/malabar-is-the-most-complex-naval-exercise/article38093935.ece

45 Sagar Kavach exercise to begin along Kerala coast today Times of India, May 10, 2022 https://timesofindia.indiatimes.com/city/kochi/sagar-kavach-exercise-to-begin-along-kerala-coast-today/articleshow/91454353.cms

46 Rajeshwari Pillai Rajagopalan, India Launches 3rd Arihant Submarine, *The Diplomat*, January 7, 2022. https://thediplomat.com/2022/01/reports-india-launches-3rd-arihant-submarine/

47 https://www.indiatoday.in/business/budget-2022/story/increase-indian-navy-budget-aims-enhancing-fleet-deter-chinese-navy-expansion-1907972-2022-02-02

48 Atul Chandra, Fighting Fleet, https://forceindia.net/cover-story/fighting-fleet/

49 Navy eyes govt route to buy carrier-based jets, *The Hindu*, July 6,2022

50 Navy accelerates indigenisation efforts, focus on weapons and aviation items, *The Hindu*, April 15, 2022. https://www.thehindu.com/news/national/navy-accelerates-indigenisation-efforts-focus-on-weapons-and-aviation-items/article65324255.ece

51 MSME to help in naval shipbuilding, *The Hindu*, July 16,2022

52 Defence exports touch 13,000 cr: official *The Hindu* July 9, 2022

53 The Hindu, March 19, 2022 https://www.thehindu.com/news/national/geography-in-indian-ocean-is-our-basic-advantage-and-we-are-utilising-it-navy/article65240475.ece

54 My article India's Asia Pacific rendezvous: A caveat, *Asia Pacific Journal of Social Sciences*, No.1, December 2010, p.18

55 My article Maritime Security in Indian Ocean, *South Asian Defence and Strategic Year Book 2007*, Pentagon Press, New Delhi, 2007.

56 Utham Kumar Jamadhagni, SLOCs and the imminent challenge for India, *Politico*, Vol2, No.1, 2014, p. 97

57 Ibid., p. 101

58 Refer my article on Maritime Transnational Crime in the Asia Pacific : Challenge and Response, *Area Studies*, Vol 1, No2, July-December 27, p. 92

59 https://www.newindianexpress.com/nation/2022/apr/25/gujarat-drug-haul-205-kg-of-heroinseized-from-container-near-kandla-port-dri-arrest-importer-2446282.html

60 Major drug haul: Heroin worth more than Rs 350 crore seized at Gujarat's Mundra port, *The Indian Express*, July 13, 2022. https://indianexpress.com/article/cities/ahmedabad/major-drug-haul-heroin-worth-more-than-rs-350-crore-seized-at-gujarats-mundra-port-8024350/

61 Indian Navy seizes Rs 3,000 crore drug from fishing vessel originating from Pakistan, *The Economic Times*, April 20, 2021 https://economictimes.indiatimes.com/news/defence/indian-navy-seizes-narcotics-worth-rs-3000-crore-from-fishing-vessel/articleshow/82144932.cms?from=mdr

62 3 foreign boats carrying arms, drugs intercepted off Lakshadweep, The Economic Times, March 19, 2021, https://economictimes.indiatimes.com/news/defence/3-foreign-

boats-carrying-arms-drugs-intercepted-off-lakshadweep/articleshow/81581029.cms?from=mdr

63 Munambam-human-trafficking-navy-coast-guard-vessels-to-conduct searches, *On Manorama*, January 15, 2019. https://www.onmanorama.com/news/kerala/2019/01/15/munambam-human-trafficking-navy-coast-guard-vessels-to-conduct-s.html

64 China's illegal, unregulated fishing in Indian ocean poses challenges, *WION*, February 11, 2022 https://www.wionews.com/india-news/chinas-illegal-unregulated-fishing-in-indian-ocean-poses-challenges-452343

65 Quad Summit: How Indian Navy could further Quad's agenda of checking China's illegal fishing, Times Now, May 23, 2022 https://www.timesnownews.com/exclusive/quad-summit-how-indian-navy-could-further-quads-agenda-of-checking-chinas-illegal-fishing-article-91737906

66 Sri Lankan Navy arrests 6 Indian fishermen, seizes boat for illegal fishing, India Today, July 21, 2022 https://www.indiatoday.in/india/story/sri-lankan-navy-arrests-indian-fishermen-seizes-boat-illegal-fishing-1978055-2022-07-21

67 Iran seizes 4 trespassing Indian fishing boats, arrests crew, February 4, 2018, https://stopillegalfishing.com/press-links/iran-seizes-4-trespassing-indian-fishing-boats-arrests-crew/

Chapter 4

68 Asian Oil and Gas Journal 2014

69 Tanaka 2015

70 Tanaka, 2015

71 Dr. P Paleri 2009

72 CG Archives

73 FICCI report, 2017

74 NFDB, Annual Report 2017-18

75 UN General Assembly, 2008

76 ICC-IMB Report, January 2019

77 ICC-IMB Report, January 2019

78 UNODC, Statistics and Data, 2018

79 Gemma Anderone, 2017

80 Pushpita Das, 2013

81 FICCI report 2017

82 FICCI report 2017

83 CG Archives 2019

84 CG Archives

85 Till Aug 2019, CG Archives

Chapter 5

86 Brooks, R. A. (2003). Making Military Might: Why Do States Fail and Succeed? A Review Essay. International Security, 28(2), 149-191.

87 Verma, A. (2019, September 14). Dragon on Doorstep: Chinese Assistance in Bangladeshi Submarine Base. The Kootneeti. https://thekootneeti.in/2019/09/14/chinese-assistance-in-bangladeshi-submarine-base/

88 Pant, Harsh. V. (2017, February 20). Why India's Military Needs to Move to Theatre Commands Now. The Quint. https://www.thequint.com/voices/opinion/why-india-military-needs-to-move-to-a-theatre-command-now-air-force-navy-army-reforms

89 1993 Mumbai serial blasts: Men on the ground from planning to execution. (2017, June 17). The Indian Express. https://indianexpress.com/article/india/1993-mumbai-serial-blasts-verdict-men-on-the-ground-from-planning-to-execution-mustafa-dossa-abu-salem-abdul-qayyum-riaz-siddiqui-tahir-merchant-firoz-khan-47

90 Kraska, J. (2010). Broken Taillight at Sea: The Peacetime International Law of Visit, Board, Search, and Seizure. Ocean & Coastal LJ, 16, 1.

91 Kuehn, J. T. Air Sea Battle and its Discontents. (2013, October 1). Proceedings Magazine, 139. U.S. Naval Institute. https://www.usni.org/magazines/proceedings/2013/october/air-sea-battle-and-its-discontents

92 Matsumura, M. (2014). The Limits and Implications of the Air-Sea Battle Concept: A Japanese Perspective. 15(3), 37.

93 The modernization of the Pakistani Navy is advancing at high speed. (2020, March 25). Meta-Defence.fr. https://www.meta-defence.fr/en/2020/03/25/Pakistan-Navy-Modernization-Goes-High-Speed/07820/

94 Kumar, Y., & Ghosh, P. K. (2020). The "Indo" in the "Indo-Pacific"—An Indian View. Naval War College Review, 73(2), 7.

95 Indian Navy: Terrorists being trained for attacks via sea: Sunil Lanba. (2019, March 6). The Economic Times. https://economictimes.indiatimes.com/news/defence/terrorists-being-trained-for-attacks-via-sea-sunil-lanba/articleshow/68279254.cms

96 Basu, J., & Kumar, N. (2019, August 31). Then Home Minister Mufti Sayeed protected terrorists in Kashmir. The Sunday Guardian Live. https: //www.sundayguardianlive.com /news /home-minister-mufti-sayeed-protected-terrorists-kashmir

97 Wilpon, A. (2016). Floating Armories: A Legal Grey Area in Arms Trade and the Law of the Sea. Geo. J. Int'l L., 48, 873.

98 Floating arsenals: The boats full of guns for hire against pirates. (2014, December 18). BBC News. https://www.bbc.com/news/world-africa-30512185

99 Exclusive: 'Will seek Pakistan help to trace terrorists if needed': Sri Lanka PM. (2019, April 26). Hindustan Times. https://www.hindustantimes.com/world-news/exclusive-will-seek-pakistan-help-to-trace-terrorists-if-needed-sri-lanka-pm/story-kIFvQtrgwOjRf12sSlzwpJ.html

100 Björnehed, E. (2004). Narco-Terrorism: The Merger of the War on Drugs and the War on Terror. Global Crime, 6(3–4), 305–324. https://doi.org/10.1080/17440570500273440

101 Cross border narco-terror becoming a major concern for India. (n.d.). The Week. Retrieved November 7, 2020, from https://www.theweek.in/news/india/2020/07/18/cross-border-narco-terror-becoming-a-major-concern-for-india.html

102 Energy Industry: The Sector Most Affected by Terrorism. (2020, February 19). Rise to Peace. https://www.risetopeace.org/2020/02/19/energy-sector-terrorism/vkioutsouki/

Chapter 6

103 First coordinator for national maritime security appointed, to report to NSA, *The Indian Express,* February 17, 2022 https://indianexpress.com/article/india/ashok-kumar-first-coordinator-for-national-maritime-security-appointed-7777016/

104 Abhijit Singh, ORF Expert Speak, February 21, 2022 https://www.orfonline.org/expert-speak/indias-maritime-security-coordinator-has-his-mission-cut-out/

105 https://www.southasiamonitor.org/open-forum/netaji-subhas-bose-nationalist-pragm atist-military-icon

106 Cited in Air Mshl BD Jayal, Gen VP Malik, Dr Anit Mukherjee and Adm Arun Prakash, A Call for Change: Higher Defence Management in India, *IDSA Monograph Series*, No. 6, July 2012, p. 23.

107 Nitin Gokhale, Higher Defence Management in India : Need for urgent Reappraisal, *CLAWS Journal*, Summer 2013, p.15

108 Lt Col B S Verma, Higher Defence Organisation, *Strategic Perspectives,* July-September 2013, p.3

109 For a detailed discussion on the scope and recommendations of the task force refer, Arun Prakash, India's Higher Defence Organisation: Implications for National Security and Jointness, *Journal of Defence Studies*, Vol.1, No.1 pp.13-31

110 New ias specialisation norm

111 As quoted in Nitin Gokhale's Higher Defence Management in India: Need for Urgent Reappraisal, *CLAWS Journal*, Summer 2013, pp.16

112 Anurag Bisen, India's Maritime Security: Five Concerns, *IDSA Issue Brief*, May 18, 2022. https://www.idsa.in/issuebrief/indias-maritime-security-five-concerns-abisen-180522

113 Cocaine worth over ₹500 crore seized near Mundra Port in Gujarat, *The Hindu*, May 26, 2022 https://www.thehindu.com/news/national/other-states/drug-seizure-near-mundra-port-in-gujarat/article65463978.ece

114 At 1st Maritime Security Group meet, NSA chief Doval stresses on coordination among stakeholders https://theprint.in/defence/at-1st-maritime-security-group-meet-nsa-chief-doval-stresses-on-coordination-among-stakeholders/1019264/

Chapter 7

115 International Chamber of Shipping, Shipping Facts, http://www.ics-shipping.org/shipping-facts/shipping-facts

116 International Chamber of Shipping, Shipping Facts, http://www.ics-shipping.org/shipping-facts/shipping-facts

117 : International maritime Organization. www.imo.org

118 http://www.ipa.nic.in/, Indian Ports Association.

119 SRI LANKA: THE NEIGHBOUR AT ADVANTAGE, https://www.maritimegateway.com/sri-lanka-the-neighbour-at-advantage/

120 V.O.Chidambaranar Port Trust, Preparation of Rapid Techno-Economic Feasibility Report for Development of Colachel Port in Tamilnadu, Report by Boston Consulting Group, Pg. 30

121 PM Modi inaugurates 'Maritime India Summit 2021', https://www.hindustantimes.com/india-news/pm-modi-inaugurates-maritime-india-summit-2021-101614669799677.html

122 Live Mint website, What is ideal distance between two ports - https://www.livemint.com/Opinion/vgefHtNgoR79iTJsSnzPKN/What-is-the-ideal-distance-between-two-ports.html.

123 Sri Lanka Ports Authority, https://www.slpa.lk/port-colombo/terminals

124 Sri Lanka Clears Adani Venture to Develop Colombo Port Terminal, Says India 'Approved' Firm, https://thewire.in/south-asia/sri-lanka-approves-public-private-venture-with-adani-to-develop-colombo-port-terminal

125 International Maritime Organisation, Revised MARPOL Annex VI. http://www.imo.org/en/OurWork/Environment/PollutionPrevention/AirPollution/Pages/Air-Pollution.aspx

Chapter 8

126 'Number of pirate attacks against ships worldwide from 2010 to 2021' Source: https://www.statista.com/statistics/266292/number-of-pirate-attacks-worldwide-since-2006/ (Accessed on 15 March 2022)

127 'Number of actual and attempted piracy attacks in India from 2015 to 2020'. Source: https://www.statista.com/statistics/1122257/india-number-of-actual-and-attempted-piracy-attacks/

128 'Maritime piracy major cause of concern for over two lakh Indian seafarers: MUI'. Source: https://economictimes.indiatimes.com/news/defence/maritime-piracy-major-cause-of-concern-for-over-two-lakh-indian-seafarers-mui/articleshow/79989175.cms?utm_source=contentofinterest&utm_medium=text&utm_campaign=cppst

129 'Global maritime piracy incidents rise in 2020; here's why India and its seafarers should be cautious' Source: https://www.moneycontrol.com/news/trends/current-affairs-trends/global-maritime-piracy-incidents-rise-in-2020-heres-why-india-and-its-seafarers-should-be-cautious-6759251.html

130 Ibid

131 The Anti-Maritime Piracy Bill, 2019. Source: https://prsindia.org/billtrack/the-anti-maritime-piracy-bill-2019#:~:text=The percent20Bill percent20enables percent20Indian percent20authorities,nautical percent20miles percent20from percent20India's percent20coastline.

132 The Rise of Private Maritime Security Companies. Source: https://www.cato.org/publications/commentary/rise-private-maritime-security-companies

133 The use of armed security personnel should not be considered as an alternative to Best Management Practices. Source: https://safety4sea.com/using-private-contracted-security-guards-onboard-pros-and-cons/

134 The Rise of Private Maritime Security Companies

135 IMO Secretary-General Addresses the Issue of Armed Merchant Vessels. Source: https://gcaptain.com/secretary-general-addresses-issue/

136 The Central Board of Excise and Customs in exercise of the powers conferred under Section 157 of the Customs Act 1962, vide the M.F. (D.R. & I) Notification No. 35-Cus., dated 17th April, 1971 as amended has framed the Import Manifest (Vessels) Regulations, 1971 covering the manner of delivery and contents of the Import manifest. Refer http://www.cbec.gov.in

137 New report reveals boom in private military security forces fighting Indian Ocean pirates. Source: https://www.prnewswire.com/news-releases/new-report-reveals-boom-in-private-military-security-forces-fighting-indian-ocean-pirates-169421346.html

138 Shooting to Kill Pirates Risks Blackwater Moment. Source: http://www.bloomberg.com/news/2012-05-08/shooting-to-kill-pirates-risks-blackwater-moment.html/

139 Fishermen killed: India summons Italian envoy. Source: http://ibnlive.in.com/news/indians-killed-italy-says-ship-was-attacked/230861-3.html

140 Trade Notice – Pre Arrival Notification of Security (PANS) published by Adani PortsSource: http://www.adaniports.com/pdfs/99.pdf?f=99.pdf

141 Enrica Lexie case. Source: https://en.wikipedia.org/wiki/Enrica_Lexie_case

142 India charges 33 aboard armed US anti-piracy ship. Source: http://www.reuters.com/article/2013/10/19/us-india-ship-arrestidUSBRE99I02Q20131019

143 Court sets free crew of armed US Ship, says they came for food, fuel. Source: http://timesofindia.indiatimes.com/city/chennai/Court-sets-free-crew-of-armed-US-ship-says-they-camefor-food-fuel/articleshow/38155179.cms

Chapter 9

144 Chapsos, I. (2014). The Privatisation Of International Security: The Regulatory Framework For Private Maritime Security Companies, Using Operations Off Somalia, 2005-13, As A Case Study. Unpublished Phd Thesis. Coventry: Coventry University

145 Ibid.

146 The Nexus of State Monopoly on Use of Force and Security in the Horn of Africa - Kidist Mulugeta https://library.fes.de/pdf-files/iez/12480.pdf - Friedrich-Ebert-Stiftung

147 Buzan 1991:378

148 (Krahmann 2010:36)

149 The Privatisation Of Security And State Control Of Force Changes, Challenges And The Case Of Iraq - Joakim Berndtsson – Pg 50 Of PDF – University Of Gothenburg 2009

150 DCAF HORIZON 2015 WORKING PAPER No. 3 Private Military & Security Companies: Future Challenges In Security Governance Anne-Marie Buzatu & Benjamin S. Buckland

151 Srilatha Vallabu. Privately Contracted Armed Security Personnel In Indian Ocean Region. Patrick Chaumette Espaces Marins : Surveillance Et Prévention Des Trafics Illicites En Mer, Gomylex, Pp.265-279, 2016, Espaces Marins : Surveillance Et Prévention Des Trafics Illicites En Mer, 978-84-15176-72-5

152 Revisiting The Legal Framework For Private Military And Security Contractors: Maritime Perspective Vijaya Singh Gautam* &Vijay Mishra** Https://Doi.Org/10.21827/Grojil.8.1.166-1

153 Chapsos - (Bellamy 1997:130-2)

154 ILC, 'Articles On Responsibility Of States For Internationally Wrongful Acts' (12 December 2001) UN Doc A/56/10 (ARSIWA), Art 4, 5 And 8.

155 Ibid.

156 Market For Force: The Emerging Role Of Private Military And Security Companies In Contemporary Conflicts – Matthew Sutherland March 31, 2021 Market For Force: The Emerging Role Of Private Military And Security Companies In Contemporary Conflicts — The Security Distillery

157 Https://Legal.Un.Org/Ilc/Texts/Instruments/English/Commentaries/9_6_2001.Pdf

158 4 Articles On Responsibility Of States For Internationally Wrongful Acts, ILC Yearbook 2001/II(2) (ARSIWA), Arts. 5–11; See White And Macleod (2008).

159 Private Security Companies And Shared Responsibility The Turn To Multistakeholder Standard-Setting And Monitoring Through Self-Regulation-'Plus' Sorcha Macleod Neth Int Law Rev (2015) 62:119–140 And SHARES Research Paper 58 (2014), ACIL 2014-30, Available At Www.Sharesproject.Nl And SSRN

160 Ibid.

161 UN Doc. A/63/467–S/2008/636 - Sixty-Third Sess. 2008: Letter Dated 2 October 2008 From The Permanent Representative Of Switzerland To The United Nations Addressed To The Secretary-General (The Montreux Document).

162 9 November 2010, Available At Http://Www.Icoc-Psp.Org.

163 7.3.2 Chapsos, I. (2014). The Privatisation Of International Security: The Regulatory Framework For Private Maritime Security Companies, Using Operations Off

Somalia, 2005-13, As A Case Study. Unpublished Phd Thesis. Coventry: Coventry University - Page 211

164 Private Maritime Security Contractors And Legal Framework Commander Gurudeep Bala - Naval War College Journal Pg 81 - 90

165 Srilatha Vallabu. Privately Contracted Armed Security Personnel In Indian Ocean Region. Patrick Chaumette Espaces Marins : Surveillance Et Prévention Des Trafics Illicites En Mer, Gomylex, Pp.265-279, 2016, Espaces Marins : Surveillance Et Prévention Des Trafics Illicites En Mer, 978-84-15176-72-5. Ffhal-01525277f

166 Guidelines On Deployment Of Armed Security Guards On Merchant Ships (India Ministry Of Shipping, 2011).

167 CISF can join hands with private security agencies: Amit Shah; Mar 07, 2022 https://economictimes.indiatimes.com/news/defence/cisf-can-join-hands-with-private-security-agencies-amit-shah/articleshow/90037986.cms?from=mdr

Chapter 10

168 Diamond, J. (1998). Guns, Germs and Steel: A Short History of Everybody for the Last 13000 Years. London: Vintage.

169 Zinsser, H. (1943). Rats, Lice and History. London: Routledge.

170 Eckert, E. (2000). The retreat of plague from central Europe, 1640–1720: a geomedical approach. Bulletin of Historical Medicine 74, 1–28.

171 Cash, R.A. and Narasimhan, V. (2000). Impediments to global surveillance of infectious diseases: consequences of open reporting in a global economy. Bulletin of the World Health Organization 78, 1358–1367.

172 Reidl, J. and Klose, K.E. (2002). Vibrio cholerae and cholera: out of the water and into the host. Federation of European Microbiological Societies Microbiology Reviews 26, 125–139.

173 Sack, D.A., Sack, R.B., Nair, G.B. and Siddique, A.K. (2004). Cholera. Lancet 363, 223–233.

174 McNeill, W.H. (1976). Plagues and People. New York: Anchor Press.

175 Karlen, A. (1995). Plague's Progress. London: Indigo.

176 ISPSW Strategy Series: Focus on Defence and International Security; Maritime Security – Perspectives for a Comprehensive Approach. Lutz Feldt, Dr. Peter Roell, Ralph D. Thiele. Issue No. 222, Apr 2013.

177 Lane, H.C., Montagne, J. and Fauci, A.S. (2001). Bioterrorism: a clear and present danger. Nature Medicine 7, 1271–1273.

178 Kumar, S. (1995). Bubonic plague in Surat. Lancet 345, 714.

179 Kortepeter, M.G. and Parker, G.W. (1999). Potential biological weapons threats. Emerging Infectious Diseases 5, 523–527.

Chapter 11

180 Turner, Jonathan H; Beeghly, Leonard & Powers, Charles H (2002). The Emergence of Sociological Theory (5th Ed), Belmont CA: Wadsworth Thomson Learning, Pp 54-89

181 https://www.britannica.com/science/survival-of-the-fittest

182 Twitchett, Denis and Fairbank, John K. (Eds.) (2008). The Cambridge History of China, Volume 10, Late Ch'ing 1800-1911, Part I. Cambridge University Press: Cambridge NY, Pp

183 Ching, Frank (2018). With Xi Jinping's lifetime presidency, China could become more powerful than ever, *Scroll*, 19 March 2018, https://scroll.in/article/872209/with-xi-jingpings-lifetime-presidency-china-could-become-more-powerful-than-ever, accessed 16 October 2018.

184 Jones Jr., Charles C. (1878). The Life and Services of Commodore Josiah Tattnall, Morning News SteamPrinting House, Savannah, Georgia, Pp 99-100.

185 For a detailed report covering how the burning and looting of the Yuan Ming Yuan has come to occupy a central theme being used by the Chinese Communist Party to impress upon its population the importance of strong government, see British Broadcasting Corporation's report: Chris Bowlby (February 02, 2015). The palace of shame that makes China angry, BBC News, Beijing (online) at https://www.bbc.com/news/magazine-30810596

186 From Yung Wing Biography. Retrieved from: https://www.liquisearch.com/yung_wing/biography#:~:text=In percent201863 percent2C percent20Yung percent20Wing percent20was percent20dispatched percent20to percent20the,western percent20powers. percent20The percent20arsenal percent20later percent20became percent20Jiangnan percent20Shipyard.

187 Yung Wing persuaded the Qing Dynasty government to send young Chinese to the United States to study Western science and engineering. With the government's eventual approval, he organized what came to be known as the Chinese Educational Mission, which included 120 young Chinese students, to study in the New England region of the United States beginning in 1872. The Educational Mission was disbanded in 1881, but many of the students later returned to China and made significant contributions to China's civil services, engineering, and the sciences.

188 Wang, H. (2009). Discovering Steam Power in China, 1840s–1860s. Technology and Culture, 51, 31 - 54.

189 Day, Jenny Huangfu (2015). From Fire-Wheel Boats to Cities on the Sea: Changing Perceptions of the Steamships in the Late Qing, 1830s-1900s, Australasian Journal of Victorian Studies 20.1. Retrieved from: https://openjournals.library.sydney.edu.au/index.php/AJVS/article/download/9407/9306

190 Lai, Benjamin (2019). Chinese Battleship vs Japanese Cruiser: Yalu River 1894, Bloomsbury Publishing

191 Jiayao, Li (Ed.) (2019). China's National Defence in the New Era, Ministry of National Defence. Source: Xinhuanet

192 The reason to say so comes from the age old cardinal belief in deception that Chinese appear to firmly rely on and practice.

193 Office of Naval Intelligence (ONI), United States of America (2009). The People's Liberation Army Navy: A Modern Navy with Chinese Characteristics. Retrieved from: https://fas.org/irp/agency/oni/pla-navy.pdf

194 Ibid. P.9.

195 Fanell, James E. (2019) "Asia Rising: China's Global Naval Strategy and Expanding Force Structure," Naval War College Review: Vol. 72: No. 1, Article 4. Available at: https://digital-commons.usnwc.edu/nwc-review/vol72/iss1/4

196 Yu, Miles Maochun (2018). Did China Have A Chance To Win The Opium War?, Hoover (online). Retrieved from: https://www.hoover.org/research/did-china-have-chance-win-opium-war

197 Twitchett, Denis and Fairbank, John K. (Eds.) (2008). The Cambridge History of China, Volume 10, Late Ch'ing 1800-1911, Part I. Cambridge University Press: Cambridge NY, P 191.

198 Twitchett, Denis and Fairbank, John K. (Eds.) (2008). The Cambridge History of China, Volume 10, Late Ch'ing 1800-1911, Part I. Cambridge University Press: Cambridge NY, P 195.

199 Srinivasan, Dr R (December 01, 2020). RCEP and Emerging Trends in the Indo-Pacific, Chennai Centre for China Studies (online). Retrieved from: https://www.c3sindia.org/business-economics/rcep-and-emerging-trends-in-the-indo-pacific-by-dr-r-srinivasan/

200 Fanell, James E. (2019) "Asia Rising: China's Global Naval Strategy and Expanding Force Structure," Naval War College Review: Vol. 72: No. 1 , Article 4. Available at: https://digital-commons.usnwc.edu/nwc-review/vol72/iss1/4

201 Srinivasan, Gp Capt (Dr) R (December 28, 2020). Chinese Aircraft Carrier – From Macau, with Love, Defence Research and Studies (online). Retrieved from: https://dras.in/chinese-aircraft-carrier-from-macau-with-love/

202 Vavasseur, X. (2019, January 24). Naval News. Retrieved December 04, 2020, from Liaoning Aircraft Carrier, Returns To Sea After Refit: https://www.navalnews.com/naval-news/2019/01/liaoning-aircraft-carrier-returns-to-sea-after-refit/

203 BBC. (2019, July 29). BBC. Retrieved November 15, 2020, from China profile – Timeline: https://www.bbc.com/news/world-asia-pacific-13017882

204 Dahl, R. A. (2007). The concept of power. *Behavioral Science*, *2*(3), 201–215. https://doi.org/10.1002/bs.3830020303

205 Sevastopulo, Demetri and Hille, Kathrin (February, 10 2021). US admiral says Chinese military activity is rising in S China Sea, Financial Times (online). Retrieved from: https://www.ft.com/content/93294101-be11-41ef-8b54-c4bd83d559e5

206 Li, Jiayao (Ed.) (2019). China's National Defence in the New Era, Ministry of National Defence. Source: Xinhuanet

207 Chan, P. (2014). China's Approaches to International Law since the Opium War. Leiden Journal of International Law, 27(4), 859-892. doi:10.1017/S0922156514000399

208 McLeod, John (2012). Beginning: Postcolonialism, Viva Books: New Delhi, P 33.

209 Twitchett, Denis and Fairbank, John K. (Eds.) (2008). The Cambridge History of China, Volume 10, Late Ch'ing 1800-1911, Part I. Cambridge University Press: Cambridge NY, P 185.

Chapter 12

210 Srinivasan, Meera. (2021). *Sri Lankan Parliament passes Controversial Bill on China-Backed Port City.* Retrieved August 8, 2021, from https:// www.thehindu.com / news /international/sri-lankan-parliament-passes-controversial-bill-on-china-backed-port-city/article34608185.ece

211 White, Joshua T. (2020*). China's Indian Ocean Ambitions: Investment, Influence and Military Advantage.* Maryland: Global China. p.1

212 Sundarji, Padma Rao. (2020*). We don't want to do anything to jeopardise the security of India: Sri Lankan President Gotabaya Rajapaksa.* Retrieved August 8, 2021, from https://www.hindustantimes.com/india-news/we-don-t-want-to-do-anything-to-jeopardise-the-security-of-india-gotabaya-rajapaksa/story-aSX4jtDMbXLqDW7WoPpeWN.html

213 Srinivasan, Meera. (2021). *Will not allow other countries to push for separatism in the guise of power devolution, say Gotabaya Rajpaksha.* Retrieved August 8, 2021, from https://www.thehindu.com/news/international/will-not-allow-other-countries-to-push-for-separatism-in-the-guise-of-power-devolution-says-gotabaya-rajapaksa/article34187707.ece

214 The United Nations. (1971). *1971 The Indian Ocean – Zone of Peace.* Retrieved August 8, 2021, from https://lk.one.un.org/7060/en/the-indian-ocean-zone-of-peace#:~:text= The percent20 Declaration percent 20of percent20the percent20Indian,floor percent20limits percent20to percent20be percent20determined

215 U.S.-China Economic and Security Commission. (2014). *China's Navy Extends its Combat Reach to the Indian Ocean.* Washington DC: U.S.-China Economic and Security Commission. p.2

216 U.S.-China Economic and Security Commission. (2014). *China's Navy Extends its Combat Reach to the Indian Ocean.* Washington DC: U.S.-China Economic and Security Commission. p.4

217 Balasubramaniam, Thangavel K. (2020). *China's Rising Missile and Naval Capabilities in the Indo-Pacific Region: Security Implications for India and its Allies.* Alabama: Journal of Indo-Pacific Affairs. p.105

218 Times of India. (2021) *Chinese presence in Sri Lanka could pose a threat keeping close watch: Indian Navy.* Retrieved September 3, 2021, from https: Chinese presence in Sri Lanka could pose a threat, keeping close watch: Indian Navy | India News - Times of India (indiatimes.com)

219 Colombo Gazette. (2019). *Chinese Intelligence Agencies Operating in Sri Lanka.* Retrieved September 3, 2021, from https: Chinese intelligence agencies operating in Sri Lanka | Colombo Gazette

220 The Sunday Times. (2021). *Jaishankar expressed concerns over China's influence in Indian Projects.* Retrieved September 3, 2021, from https: Jaishankar expressed concerns over China's 'influence' in Indian projects | Times Online - Daily Online Edition of The Sunday Times Sri Lanka

221 White, Joshua T. (2020*). China's Indian Ocean Ambitions: Investment, Influence and Military Advantage.* Maryland: Global China. p.10

222 Kapur, Lalit. (2021). *India, China and the Indian Ocean: Reading the Tea Leaves and Preventing Coercion.* Retrieved September 3, 2021, from https: https://www .sundaytimes .lk/210110/news/jaishankar-expressed-concerns-over-chinas-influence-in-indian-projects-427885.html

223 Ferchen, Matt and Perera, Anarkalee. (2019*). Belt and Road Initiative: Why Unsustainable Chinese Infrastructure deals are a Two-Way Street.* Washington DC: Carnegie-Tsinghua Center for Global Policy. p.1

224 Abeyagoonasekera, Asanga. (2021). *How China won over local agency to shackle Sri Lana using a Port City.* Retrieved September 14, 2021, from https://www.orfonline.org/expert-speak/how-china-won-over-local-agency-to-shackle-sri-lanka-using-a-port-city/

225 Newswire. (2021). *No More big foreign loan projects: PB.* Retrieved September 15, 2021, from No more big foreign loan projects : PB – NewsWire

226 Abeyagoonasekera, Asanga. (2021). *Sri Lanka has Rajapakshas all over. It may import autocratic values from CCP model.* Retrieved September 15, 2021, from Sri Lanka has Rajapaksas all over. It may import autocratic values from CCP model (theprint.in)

227 Ramachandran, Sudha. (2018). *China Expands its Footprint in Sri Lanka.* Retrieved September 15, 2021, from https://thediplomat.com/2018/09/china-expands-its-footprint-in-sri-lanka/.

228 Pandit, Rajat. (2021). *China expands its activities to Sri Lanka's north, India worried.* Retrieved September 15, 2021, from https://timesofindia.indiatimes.com/india/china-expands-its-activities-to-sri-lankas-north-india-worried/articleshow/85820642.cms

Chapter 13

229 UN Document. A/AC,159/1/Rev.

230 UN Document. A/AC,159/1/Rev.

231 A detailed list of Straits and Channel in and adjoining Indian Ocean. See, UN Doc.A/AC.159/1.

232 Bezboruah, 1977

233 Secretariate L. S., 1979

234 In UN terminology 'littoral' applies to those of the Indian Ocean states which have a direct access to the Ocean or the adjacent Red sea and Persian Gulf, and hinterland

to the states which have no such access but are separated from the ocean by not more than one littoral state. See Segei Vladimirov "Indian Ocean Zone of Peace Conference – A Step Forward" New Times (Moscow) Vol.34, 1979, p.4

235 Pakistan becomes a member of the NAM only in 1979

236 Suresh, Indian Ocean as a Zone of Peace, 1992

237 Two-third of the World oil reserves is in Persian Gulf and Red sea, North-East African and Indonesia also have oil resources. The Indian Ocean region has around three-fourth of the total oil reserves of the world. The rest of the world mainly the developed countries are greatly dependent on the Indian Ocean region for oil. Studies showed that in 1976 the US imported about 38 per cent, Japan 75 per cent, UK 71 per cent, West Germany 78.3 per cent, and Italy 82 per cent of crude oil from West Asia. See Lok Sabha Secretariat, n.8, p.3

238 Ibid P3

239 Ibid

240 The countries in the Indian Ocean region mostly trade with the industrially developed countries of Western Europe, Japan, USA and USSR. The Intra-regional trade among them is comparatively very less.

241 Jawaharlal Nehru, the founder of India's Foreign Policy stated in September 1946: "In the sphere of Foreign Affairs, India will follow an independent policy, keeping away from power politics of groups aligned one against the other ....", See The Indian Annual Register 1946, Vol.II, Calcutta, Annual Register Office 1947, pp.252-53.

242 Indian Council of World Affairs, report on Defence Security in the Indian Ocean. (New Delhi, 1957) p.iii. K.M.Panikkar in his seminal work India and the Indian Ocean: An Essay on the Influence of Sea Power in 1945 argued that "the Indian Ocean must remain truly Indian" On the same line K.B.Vidya in his book Naval Defence of India, in 1947, argued that Indian Ocean can be an Indian lake if India is the Supreme and undisputed power over the waters of the Indian Ocean.

243 The Interim government had also recognized the necessity for a sufficiently strong naval force to guard India's long coastline and its sea-borne trade.

244 At that point of time India wanted the US presence because in the Sino-Indian conflict US indirectly backed India. See. The Times (London) 10 November 1962, p.7.

245 The External Affairs Minister of India, Dinesh Singh stated: "We are against the setting up of any foreign bases in this area". Lok Sabha, Parliamentary Debates, 19 March 1969, Cols.3

246 The External Affairs Minister, Dinesh Singh stated on 19 March 1969: „Within the limitation of our resources we shall certainly take every possible step to safeguard our interest in the Indian Ocean". Lok Sabha, Parliamentary Debates 19 March 1969, Cols. 1-10; The Deputy Minister of External Affairs Surendra Palsingh on 18 December 1969 stated: "We want the Indian Ocean area to be made an area of peace and cooperation and any introduction of military forces from any side will be against our policy. We are also in touch with all the countries concerned about this matter

and there is a great deal of identityviews between us and the other countries" Rajya Sabha, Parliamentary Debates 18 December 1969, Cols. 4650-4653.

247 As per the Simla agreement both India and Pakistan agreed that they would strive to resolve their outstanding disputes bilaterally.

248 The abstention of Pakistan was mainly to attract the attention of international community towards the threat emanates from within the Indian Ocean region.

249 India had always refers to the 1971 UN Declaration on Indian Ocean as a Zone of Peace.

250 According to Richard N. Haass it is Non polar system. The principal characteristic of twenty-first- century international relations is turning out to be non-polarity: a world dominated not by one or two or even several states but rather by dozens of actors possessing and exercising various kinds of power. This represents a tectonic shift from the past.

251 For instance, the Indo-US Civilian Nuclear Deal; Joint Indo- US Naval Exercises in the Indian Ocean

Chapter 14

252 Scott Cheney Peters , India's Maritime Acts in the East, *Asia Maritime Transparency Initiative*, June 18, 2015.

253 Sudhir Devare, *India & Southeast Asia: Towards Security Convergence* (Singapore: Institute of Southeast Asian Studies, 2006).

254 Pramvir Das, Why India needs to enhance its sea power, Rediffmail.com, September 28, 2019.

255 China's show of military strength, *AP*, October 1, 2019.

256 Rediffmail.com, Malabar 2019: Indian Navy takes part in military drills with Japan and US forces, September 27, 2019.

257 Dingding Chen, "The case of ZTE and US-China Relations," *The Diplomat*, May 2,2018.

258 US Defence Secretary calls on PM Modi, conveys his country's strong desire to boost strategic ties, *PTI*, New Delhi, March 9, 2021.

259 Waltz, Kenneth N. (1979), *Theory of International Politics*, Reading, MA: Addison-Wesley, p- 121

260 India needs to show sincerity to implement 5-point consensus; Global Times editorial, *Global Times*, Beijing, September 11,2020.

261 General J.J. Singh (retd), India-Chna; *Lessons from History*, October 11,2019.

262 Mearsheimer, John J. "China's Unpeaceful Rise," *Current History*, 2006, 105 (690), P-161.

263 "Long Xingchun, India should Eschew Western Views of China for Border Peace," *Global Times*, Beijing, May 25, 2020.

264 Xi's aggressive moves against India 'unexpectedly flopped' Leading US mag, *The Times of India*, New Delhi, September 14, 2020.

265 Liu Caiyu and Zhao Yusha, US attempt to unite Asian allies against China fails to live up to expectations: observers, *Global Times*, Beijing, March 21, 2021.

266 India can play a weightier role in Indo-Pacific region: U.S., *PTI*, New Delhi, April 3, 2018.

267 Indrani Bagchi, ASEAN Links its Indo-Pacific Strategy to India's Outreach, *Times of India*, New Delhi, June 24, 2019.

268 US, Maldives sign defence deal amid China's growing presence in Indian Ocean , *The Times of India*, New Delhi, 13 September 13,2020, P- 17.

269 China must be militarily and morally ready for a potential war, Hu Xijin, Editor in Chief, *Global Times*, Beijing, September 11, 2020.

270 Germany breaks ranks with China, shifts to adopting Indo-Pacific strategy, *The Times of India*, New Delhi, September 14 2020.

271 Richard Javad Heydarian, Quad alliance 'arc of democracy' around China, *Asia Times Financial*, July 27, 2020

Chapter 15

272 UNDOC Research. (2018). *Global Study on the Smuggling of Migrants* (p. 19). New York: United Nations. Retrieved from - https://www.unodc.org/documents/data-and-analysis/glosom/GLOSOM_2018_web_small.pdf

273 Gallagher and F. David. (2014). *The International Law of Migrant Smuggling*, Cambridge: Cambridge University Press, 56.

274 Human Trafficking & Migrant Smuggling: Understanding the Difference. (2017). Retrieved 5 March 2019, from https://2009-2017.state.gov/documents/organization/245382.pdf

275 Smuggling and Trafficking Human Beings. (2015). Retrieved 11 March 2019, from https://www.hrw.org/news/2015/07/07/smuggling-and-trafficking-human-beings

276 The Times of India. (2018). Anti-trafficking bill maintains distinction between trafficking, smuggling of migrants: WCD. Retrieved from https://timesofindia.indiatimes.com/india/anti-trafficking-bill-maintains-distinction-between-trafficking-smuggling-of-migrants-wcd/articleshowprint/65201399.cms

277 Was people smuggling boat, intercepted with 130 Sri Lankan refugees, really heading to NZ?. *1 news* (2018). Retrieved 7 March 2019, from https://www.1news.co.nz/2018/05/06/was-people-smuggling-boat-intercepted-with-130-sri-lankan-refugees-really-heading-to-nz/

278 Jesudasan, D. S. (2022). Survey planned to ascertain how many Sri Lankan Tamils want Indian citizenship. *The Hindu*. Retrieved from https://www.thehindu.com/news/national/tamil-nadu/survey-planned-to-ascertain-how-many-sri-lankan-tamils-want-indian-citizenship/article38103387.ece

279 The Times of India. (2018). For some Sri Lankan refugees, illegal boats still only way home. Retrieved from https://timesofindia.indiatimes.com/city/chennai/for-some-sri-lankan-refugees-illegal-boats-still-only-way-home/articleshowprint/64360421.cms

280 Pal, A. (2019). Lack of jobs in India drove migrants on to boat for New Zealand, say relatives. *Reuters*. Retrieved from https://timesofindia.indiatimes.com/city/thiruvananthapuram/illegal-immigration-intel-agencies-to-pull-up-socks/articleshowprint/67579347.cms

281 Raghava, M. (2013). 88 Sri Lankan refugees stopped from migrating to Australia. *The Hindu*. Retrieved from https://www.thehindu.com/news/national/88-sri-lankan-refugees-stopped-from-migrating-to-australia/article4658397.ece

282 National Crime Records Bureau, Ministry of Home Affairs. (2017). *Crime in India, Volume -I* (p. 73). New Delhi. Retrieved from https://ncrb.gov.in/en

National Crime Records Bureau, Ministry of Home Affairs. (2018). *Crime in India, Volume -I* (p. 73). New Delhi. Retrieved from https://ncrb.gov.in/en

National Crime Records Bureau, Ministry of Home Affairs. (2019). *Crime in India, Volume -I* (p. 73). New Delhi. Retrieved from https://ncrb.gov.in/en

283 Ibid

Notes on Contributors

Dr. C. S. Anuradha is an Independent Researcher interested in Maritime and Strategic Affairs and a former Fulbright Fellow.

Dr. Utham Kumar Jamadhagni is Professor and Chair at the Department of Defence and Strategic Studies, University of Madras.

B. Ranjan is Deputy Inspector General of the Indian Coast Guard.

Group Captain A. V. Chandrasekaran is a veteran Indian Air Force officer and holds a doctorate in Defence and Strategic Studies.

Captain Swarup Bhangara is an Independent Maritime Consultant and a scholar in Maritime Affairs.

Dr. Ramakrishnan Ramani is Assistant Vice President at the School of Design Thinking and holds a doctorate in Defence and Strategic Studies.

Mahathi U is a final year LLB (Hons.) Student at the National University of Advanced Legal Studies.

Dr. Ashutosh Mukherji is Professor of Radiation Oncology at the Mahamana Pandit Madanmohan Malviya Cancer Centre.

Dr. R. Srinivasan is an independent researcher and Publisher cum Editor-in-Chief of Electronic Journal of Social and Strategic Studies.

Dr. R. Vignesh is a Research Analyst at the Military Affairs Centre, Manohar Parikar Institute for Defence Studies and Analysis (MP – IDSA).

Dr. Suresh R is Professor at the Department of International Relations and Politics at the Central University of Kerala.

Dr. Sudhir Singh is teaching at the Department of Political Science, Dyal Singh College, University of Delhi, New Delhi.

R. M. Arivazhagan is a URF Doctoral Research Fellow (Criminology and Criminal Justice Science – Defence and Strategic Studies) at the Department of Defence and Strategic Studies, University of Madras.

Index

CPSIA information can be obtained
at www.ICGtesting.com
Printed in the USA
LVHW101550090223
738797LV00035B/170

9 789395 675352